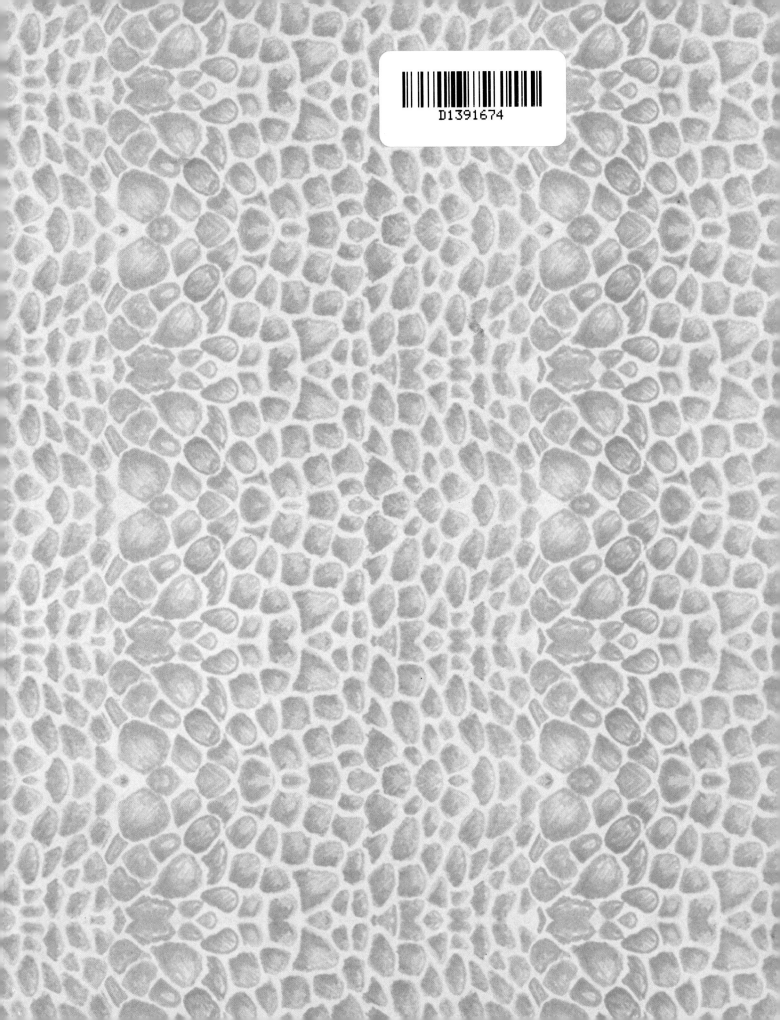

ENCYCLOPEDIA OF
DINOSAURS
AND OTHER PREHISTORIC CREATURES

Marks and Spencer p.l.c.
Baker Street, London W1U 8EP
www.marksandspencer.com

This book was created by

David West 👫 Children's Books

British Library Cataloguing-in-Publication Data

A catalogue record for this book is available from the British Library.

ISBN 1-84273-891-7

Printed in China

Designers
Julie Joubinaux, Rob Shone
Illustrators
Norma Burgin, Mark Dolby,
Graham Kennedy, Peter Komarnysky, Damian Quayle, Neil Reed, Pete Roberts
(Allied Artists)
James Field, Terry Riley
(SGA)
Mike Atkinson, Chris Forsey, Rob Shone
Editor
James Pickering

ENCYCLOPEDIA OF
DINOSAURS
AND OTHER PREHISTORIC CREATURES

JOHN MALAM & STEVE PARKER

MARKS &
SPENCER

CONTENTS

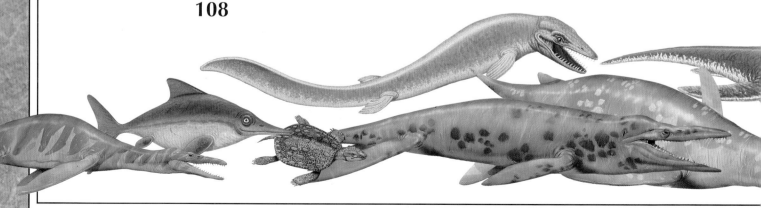

CHAPTER ONE

ANCESTORS OF THE DINOSAURS

Life first appeared on Earth about 3.8 billion years ago. From the first simple life-forms that lived in the sea, life gradually moved on to the land, and into the sky. Life learned how to survive in Earth's different habitats. Within each habitat were groups of animals specially adapted to live there. One group of animals that became very successful was the reptiles.

REPTILE CHARACTERISTICS

Reptiles are animals with backbones – they are vertebrates. They lay hard-shelled eggs, have scaly skin, and are cold-blooded (their bodies are the same temperature as their surroundings).

Dinosaurs were the largest reptiles on land.

When dinosaurs were alive, Earth was very different from the world we know today. This scene shows a landscape from about 100 million years ago. It was a time when the first flowering plants appeared, and when oak, maple, walnut and beech trees grew alongside conifers, cycads and ferns.

WHEN REPTILES RULED THE EARTH

At one time, long ago in the prehistoric past, reptiles were the most successful animals alive. The time in which they ruled the Earth is called the Mesozoic Era. It lasted for about 185 million years, starting 250 million years ago and ending 65 million years ago. Mesozoic means 'middle life'. It refers to an era mid-way between two other eras – the Palaeozoic ('ancient life') and our own Cenozoic ('recent life').

PREHISTORIC REPTILES

In the Mesozoic Era reptiles dominated the land, the sea, and the sky. Other groups of animals, such as mammals, fish and insects, lived alongside them. Because reptiles were so successful during the Mesozoic Era, this time of Earth's history is also known as the Age of Reptiles. Sea-living swimming reptiles belonged to a group known as the plesiosaurs. Sky-living flying reptiles belonged to a group known as the pterosaurs. And as for the reptiles that lived on the land, they are the best-known of all – the dinosaurs.

While dinosaurs roamed across the land, their reptile cousins commanded the sky and the sea. Fast-flying pterosaurs flew on leathery wings, and streamlined plesiosaurs, pliosaurs and fish-like ichthyosaurs ruled the sea.

MODERN REPTILES

After the Mesozoic Era ended, 65 million years ago, a new time in Earth's history began – our own era, in which mammals are the dominant animal group. Many reptile species, including dinosaurs, did not survive into this new age. However, some did, such as crocodiles, lizards, turtles and snakes.

There are nearly 6,000 different kinds of reptiles living on Earth today.

The world's first reptiles appeared about 300 million years ago. These new kinds of creatures evolved from an older group of animals, known as amphibians.

LIVING A DOUBLE LIFE

The word amphibian means 'double life', and describes a group of animals that can live both in water and on land. Amphibians were the first vertebrates to develop legs with feet, not fins. Their feet enabled them to move on the ground, and because their feet were webbed, they could also swim. Although they could survive on land, amphibians still had to spend some of their time in water. Like frogs and newts today, early amphibians laid their soft, jelly-covered eggs in water. But in order to live entirely on land, big changes had to happen in their bodies and their way of life.

LEAVING THE WATER

For ancient amphibians there were disadvantages to their watery way of life. Their young – tadpoles – were born in water, and many would have been eaten by predators, such as fish and water scorpions. Adult amphibians faced this danger, too. For more of them to survive, amphibians had to learn how to live entirely on dry land.

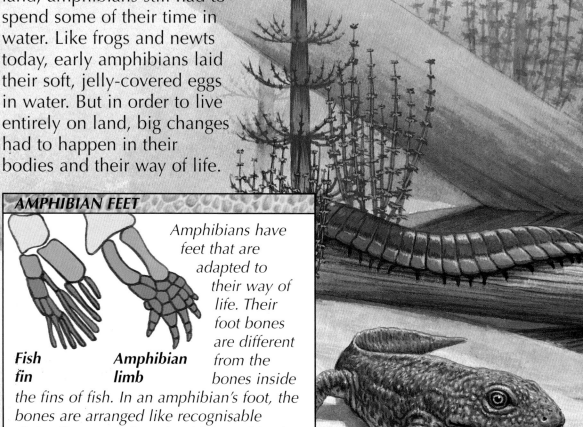

AMPHIBIAN FEET

Amphibians have feet that are adapted to their way of life. Their foot bones are different from the bones inside

Fish fin   **Amphibian limb**

the fins of fish. In an amphibian's foot, the bones are arranged like recognisable digits (fingers and toes), which enables it to walk, climb and dig burrows. Fish cannot use their fins in this way.

LIVING ON DRY LAND

Two big changes helped amphibians to live entirely on dry land. Over a long time, their thin, smooth skin thickened and became covered in scales. This new type of skin stopped their bodies from drying out. Also, they began to lay eggs with hard shells. Their young hatched on to land, not into water. These were the world's first reptiles.

MODERN AMPHIBIANS

There are more than 4,200 species of amphibian on Earth today. They are divided into three groups – frogs and toads, newts and salamanders, and worm-like caecilians (found in tropical regions). They range in size from tiny frogs just 1cm (one third of an inch) long, to salamanders that grow to 1.5m (5ft) in length.

Amphibians have lived on Earth for the last 350 million years. Like reptiles, mammals, fish and birds, they have backbones – but they can be separated from these other animal groups because they have moist, smooth skin without scales, hair or feathers. Amphibians were the world's first tetrapods – animals with four limbs. They evolved from fish that had fleshy, bony fins, known as lobes.

Eogyrinus

spent much of its time there. Instead, *Ichthyostega* may have developed its legs to help it clamber over plants which grew in the streams where it lived most of its life. Its short, stiff legs may only have had limited movement. To move on to land it may have hauled itself up by its forelegs while dragging its hindquarters.

EOGYRINUS
Carboniferous,
300 million years ago
Europe
4.6m (15ft) long

One of the largest amphibians ever to have lived, *Eogyrinus* was a powerful swimmer that moved quickly through the water by swishing its long tail from side to side. It may have been a predator, lying in wait in the shallows, in much the same way as a crocodile does today. Although probably better suited to hunting in the water, *Eogyrinus* could probably make a grab for prey passing close by on the land.

ICHTHYOSTEGA
Devonian, 370 mya
Greenland
1.5m (5ft) long
This creature is one of the world's first amphibians. Scientists describe it as a 'four-legged fish' because it has a fish-like head, body and tail. Its four legs with webbed toes show that it could walk, which means it had adapted to life on land, though it may not have

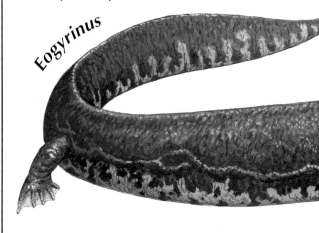

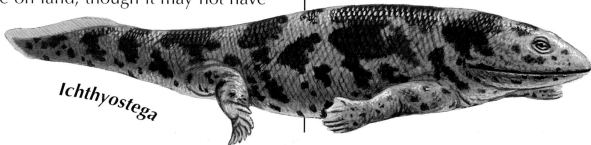

Ichthyostega

Eryops

ERYOPS

*Carboniferous,
290 million years ago
North America
1.5m (5ft) long*

Eryops was a large amphibian that lived in and near swamps. It was a meat-eater with a stout body and four short, sturdy legs. Its tail was short and its head was wide and long. Packed into its strong jaws were many sharp fang-like teeth, indicating that it was probably a predatory animal. *Eryops* may have hunted for fish, giant cockroaches, millipedes, dragonflies, and smaller amphibians and reptiles.

SEYMOURIA

*Permian, 280 mya
North America
60cm (2ft) long*

Seymouria was a small animal that spent most of its time on land, like a reptile, but which returned to the water to breed, like an amphibian. It walked by undulating its backbone from side to side. Its short forelimbs show it was a slow mover. *Seymouria* may have had a mixed meat and plant diet, which means it was an omnivore. It may also have been a carrion-eater, meaning it ate meat from animals killed by others, or which had died of natural causes.

Seymouria

ERYOPS – UNGAINLY ON LAND

Eryops *was one of the first true four-legged animals on Earth, able to walk on land. However, it was not a good walker. Its legs had to lift its heavy body clear of the ground, but because they were only short they could not raise it very high. When* Eryops *moved it probably dragged its belly on the ground. With this sprawling body posture,* Eryops *could only take short, broad strides. Its walk was slow and difficult, and it probably could not run.* Eryops *may have been a slow, ungainly mover on land, but when it returned to the water it might have been a good swimmer.*

A great variety of amphibians existed in the time before reptiles became the most dominant animals on Earth. Each species of amphibian evolved its own unique features, such as the gills of the adult *Gerrothorax*.

Diplocaulus

DIPLOCAULUS
Permian, 270 mya
North America
1m (3ft 3in) long
With a body shaped like that of a modern salamander, the amphibian *Diplocaulus* had an unusual triangular-shaped head. The 'wings' on either side of its head might have streamlined its shape, helping it to glide through the water. They might have been a safety feature, making it hard for predators to swallow *Diplocaulus*. Also, because they made the head seem large, they might have frightened some predators away.

MASTODONSAURUS
Triassic, 230 mya
Europe, Africa
4m (13ft) long
Mastodonsaurus was an enormous amphibian with a short body and tail, and a massive, flat skull. In a fully-grown adult the skull could be 1.5m (5ft) long. Its jaws were packed with many small, sharp teeth, and a pair of tusks pointed up from its lower jaw and through openings in the upper jaw. It is thought that *Mastodonsaurus* fed exclusively on fish, which it caught in the lakes, ponds and swamps where it lived.

Mastodonsaurus

PARACYCLOTOSAURUS

Triassic, 235 million years ago
Australia, India, South Africa
2.3m (7ft 5in) long
Paracyclotosaurus was a giant amphibian with a flat body, similar in looks to today's salamander – but much, much larger. Although it could live on dry land, *Paracyclotosaurus* probably spent most of its time in water. A fish-eater, it might have played a waiting game, lying just below the surface of the water. When an unsuspecting fish came within reach of its jaws, *Paracyclotosaurus* lifted its massive head, its mouth opened wide and the fish was sucked inside.

Modern predators, such as crocodiles, use this technique to catch some of their prey.

Paracyclotosaurus

GERROTHORAX

Triassic, 210 mya
Europe, Scandinavia
1m (3ft 3in) long
Gerrothorax was unusual among ancient amphibians because it retained its feathery gills throughout its adult life. In other amphibians the gills were lost as the animals matured from the larval stage (tadpoles) to their adult stage. *Gerrothorax*, which looked like a big tadpole with a flattened body, was able to breathe under water using its gills. It had a wide head, on the top of which were its eyes, set close together. It may have rested on the bed of a lake or a river, looking up through the water for a passing fish – and when one came close enough it ambushed it.

Gerrothorax

AMPHIBIAN LIFE CYCLE

Early amphibians, like today's toads and newts, began life in water. Larvae, called tadpoles, hatched from soft, jelly-covered eggs. They had gills. Front legs grew, then back legs. Adults lost their gills and breathed with lungs – on land and in water.

Acanthostega was an early tetrapod – an animal with four limbs which had fingers and toes. When the fossilised remains of this amphibian were first discovered it was thought to prove that animals had evolved legs in order to free them from a life in water – having legs meant they could move up on to the land. However, when the limbs of *Acanthostega* were looked at closely, it was realised that here was an animal that was much more at home in water than on the land.

FISH-LIKE TETRAPOD
Acanthostega had a mixture of fish-like and tetrapod features. It had the tail fin, nares (nostrils) and gills of a fish, and the legs and feet of a tetrapod.

HAPPIEST IN THE WATER
The limbs of *Acanthostega* are a clue to how it lived. Since its limbs lacked wrist and ankle joints, it is thought they would have been too weak to support its body weight out of water. So, perhaps *Acanthostega* spent most of its life in water, moving about by using its limbs as paddles. In shallow water it might also have been able to use its limbs to push its way through dense growths of plants. It had scales on its belly, but not on the rest of its body which, as in amphibians, was smooth. The scales suggest it needed to protect its soft underside, perhaps when it dragged itself on to dry land.

A group of Acanthostega *in the shallows of a lake. Some hunt for fish, others haul themselves on to land to grab at insects. A patch of spawn floats in the water. A predatory fish closes in on the group.*

ACANTHOSTEGA LIMBS

Acanthostega *had long limbs that ended in eight digits – its fingers and toes. Its feet were webbed, just like the feet of ducks and geese today. This would have helped Acanthostega to power through the water.*

ACANTHOSTEGA FACT FILE

Name: Acanthostega
Lived: 370 million years ago
Found: Greenland

Length: 60cm (2ft)
Diet: Fish, insects
Habitat: Lakes and ponds

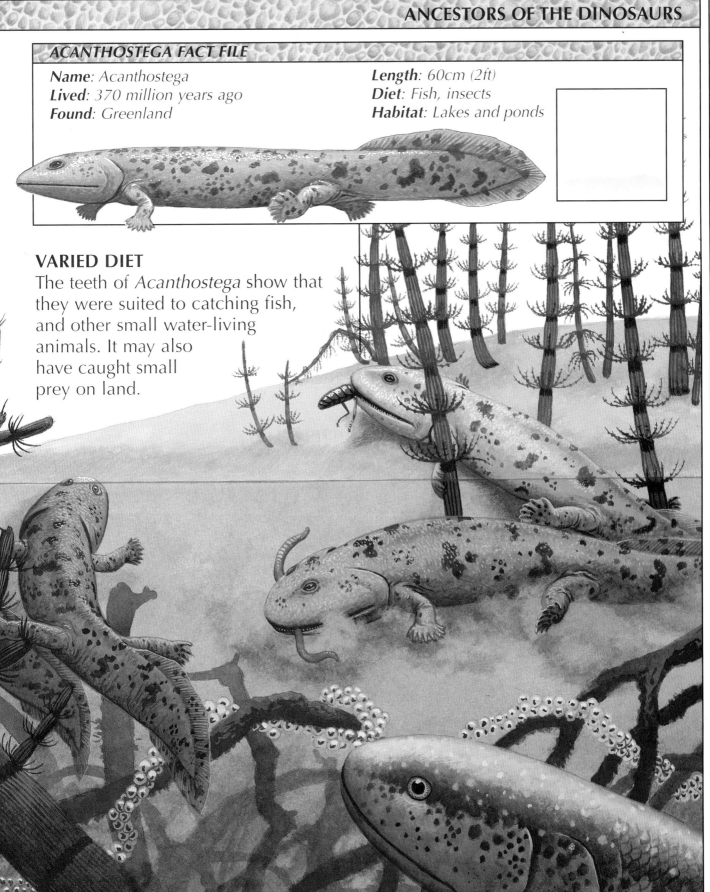

VARIED DIET

The teeth of *Acanthostega* show that they were suited to catching fish, and other small water-living animals. It may also have caught small prey on land.

The first reptiles appeared between 350 and 300 million years ago. While the paddle-like limbs of their amphibian ancestors had been steadily evolving into arms and feet with fingers and toes, an even greater change had been happening at the same time – the development of eggs with hard shells. It was this step forward that gave reptiles the final freedom from water – they no longer had to return there to lay their eggs. They were free to colonise dry land.

However, some experts think that *Westlothiana* is not a true reptile at all. They say it is still more like an amphibian. For this reason it is known as a 'reptiliomorph' – a form of reptile from which true reptiles evolved.

PETROLACOSAURUS

Carboniferous, 300 million years ago
North America
40cm (1ft 4in) long
An elegant, slender lizard, *Petrolacosaurus* is one of the oldest known diapsid reptiles. The diapsids were a group of reptiles characterised by two openings on the side of their skulls, to which groups of muscles were attached. The openings were located just behind the eyes. It was from early diapsids, such as *Petrolacosaurus*, that dinosaurs were later to evolve. Based on its resemblance to modern lizards, *Petrolacosaurus* was probably a fast-moving animal that chased after insects.

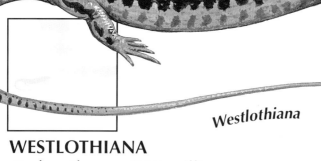

Westlothiana

WESTLOTHIANA

Carboniferous, 350 million years ago
Europe
30cm (1ft) long
Discovered in 1988, and named after the Westlothian district of Scotland where it was found, *Westlothiana lizziae* (or 'Lizzie' for short) had a mixture of early tetrapod and early reptile features. *Westlothiana* lived close to a large freshwater lake, probably hunting for millipedes, harvestman spiders, and insects. It could be one of the oldest reptiles found.

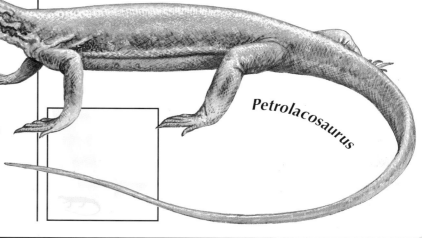

Petrolacosaurus

REPTILE EGGS

One of the most important characteristics of reptiles – ancient and modern – is that they lay hard-shelled eggs, known as amniotic eggs. Their hard shells mean that the contents of the egg do not dry out. For this reason they can be laid on dry land. The evolution of amniotic eggs made it possible for animals to live and breed on dry land, rather than having to return to water to lay their eggs, as amphibians do.

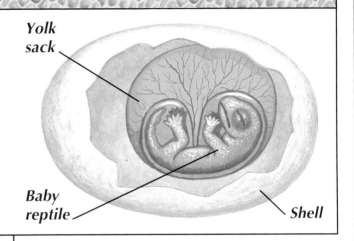

Yolk sack

Baby reptile

Shell

PALEOTHYRIS

Carboniferous, 300 mya
North America
30cm (1ft) long

A small, agile lizard-like creature, *Paleothyris* had sharp teeth and large eyes. It probably fed on insects and other small invertebrates (animals without backbones) which it chased after on the floor of its forest home. *Paleothyris* was an early reptile, yet it still had some features that were more amphibian-like than reptile-like, especially its skull. Dinosaurs were ultimately descended from creatures like *Paleothyris*, even though it was not yet a true reptile.

PAREIASAURUS

Permian, 250 million years ago
South Africa, Europe
2.5m (8ft) long

A heavily-built animal whose skin was covered with numerous interlocking bony scales, *Pareiasaurus* was a plant-eating reptile. The scales may have provided some protection against predators, as well as helping to stiffen its bulky body. Because *Pareiasaurus* was a relative of the turtles, it has been suggested that its scales might have evolved into their hard shells.

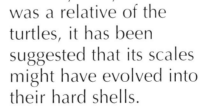

Pareiasaurus

In the long history of life on Earth, some kinds of animals failed to evolve beyond a certain stage – they were nature's dead ends. *Askeptosaurus* and the rest of its family of crocodile-like creatures fall into this category. Others, though, continued to develop, refining the features which made them successful. *Lagosuchus*, though not a dinosaur, had some features in common with them.

MILLERETTA

Permian, 250 million years ago
South Africa
60cm (2ft) long

Milleretta was a small, fast-moving early reptile that might have lived entirely on a diet of insects. Towards the back of its skull was a concave area which seems to suggest it had ear drums. If it did, then it probably had quite a good sense of hearing. Despite this advanced feature, *Milleretta* belongs to the anapsid group of reptiles, whose skulls are more like those of turtles, not lizards and snakes. This means that even though *Milleretta* was one of the first reptiles, it was not directly related to dinosaurs.

Scutosaurus

Milleretta

SCUTOSAURUS

Permian, 250 mya
Europe
2.5m (8ft) long

Similar in appearance to *Pareiasaurus*, to which it was related, *Scutosaurus* lived in small herds. It was a slow-moving bulky herbivore, feeding on vegetation that floated on the surfaces of freshwater lakes and pools. Its flat, leaf-shaped teeth had serrated edges which could easily cut through leaves and stems. There were gaps between its teeth, so water could freely drain from its mouth, leaving only the plants behind to be chewed. A fully-grown adult *Scutosaurus* grew a horn on its nose, and spikes pointed down from the jaw. Its skin was covered with bony projections – perhaps to protect it from meat-eating predators.

ASKEPTOSAURUS

Triassic, 220 mya
Europe
2m (6ft 6in) long
Askeptosaurus belonged to a family of early diapsid reptiles known as thalattosaurs. They were crocodile-like animals that seem to have spent most of their time in the water, only venturing on to land in order to lay their eggs. *Askeptosaurus* was a slender animal, with a long neck, body and tail. As a swimmer it probably moved like an eel, snaking its way quickly through the water. It was a fish-eater and might have been able to dive quite deep in search of its prey, which it snapped up with its long, toothy jaws.

Lagosuchus

LAGOSUCHUS

Triassic, 230 mya
South America
40cm (1ft 4in) long
A lightly-built early reptile, *Lagosuchus* is notable for its long, slender legs and well-developed feet – features it shares with many kinds of dinosaurs. With a body like this, *Lagosuchus* was made for running. Perhaps it used its ability to run fast to chase after insects which it caught and ate. It would also have put its speed to use when escaping from a predator who might have been out to catch it.

Askeptosaurus

REPTILE HANDS

The shape of an animal's hands reveals a lot about its lifestyle. Amphibians' hands are not good for grasping. Instead, with their webbed fingers and toes they are better suited to paddling through water. A reptile's hand is much more advanced, with long slender fingers that can grasp and pull at things, and dig into the ground.

Amphibian hand

Reptile hand

The story of life on Earth is the story of evolution – how living things have learned to adapt to changes over time. Some of the adaptations evolved by the early reptiles became important features of dinosaurs, pterosaurs and plesiosaurs. The diapsid skull, present in some early reptiles, is one such example, as is the ability to stand on two legs – a feature seen in *Euparkeria* and which became fully evolved in the meat-eating dinosaurs that came later. Other features, such as the strange scales of *Longisquama*, were not passed on to the dinosaurs.

LONGISQUAMA

Triassic, 230 million years ago
Asia
15cm (6in) long

This strange-looking creature is named after the unusual scales which grew in two rows along its back. These long, curved, bony projections have puzzled scientists since the reptile was first discovered in 1969. If these scales were held straight out on either side of its body, then perhaps *Longisquama* could have used them as an airfoil, giving it a 'wingspan' of about 30cm (1ft). If this is so, then it might have been able to glide through forests.

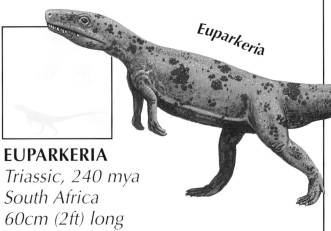

Euparkeria

Not everyone agrees with this. Some scientists think the scales were brightly coloured, and were used in courtship displays.

EUPARKERIA

Triassic, 240 mya
South Africa
60cm (2ft) long

A lightly-built meat-eating animal, *Euparkeria* had longer hind limbs than forelimbs, making it unlike most other early reptiles of its time. This distinctive feature may well have meant that *Euparkeria* could rear up on its hind limbs and run on two legs over short distances – one of the first reptiles to have this ability. Being able to run on two legs would have given *Euparkeria* an advantage over slower four-footed reptiles. It was from reptiles such as *Euparkeria* that dinosaurs and pterosaurs evolved.

Longisquama

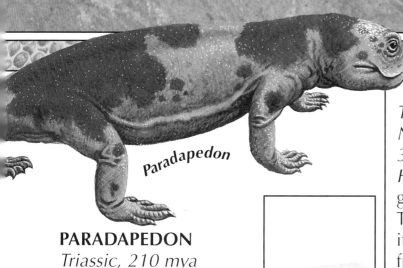

Paradapedon

HYPSOGNATHUS

Triassic, 210 million years ago
North America
33cm (1ft 1in) long
Hypsognathus had bony spikes growing from the sides of its head. They were probably used to defend it if it was attacked. By flicking its head from side to side the spikes would have forced a predator to keep its distance. It was a herbivore, and it chewed on plants with blunt, peg-like teeth which were at the back of its mouth. A small, squat animal, *Hypsognathus* was probably a slow-mover.

PARADAPEDON

Triassic, 210 mya
Asia
1.3m (4ft) long
Paradapedon was a rhynchosaur – a barrel-shaped, pig-like animal that walked on all-fours. Rhynchosaurs were the most abundant reptiles of the mid to late Triassic period (about 220–200 million years ago). Like other rhynchosaurs, *Paradapedon* was a plant-eater. It used its beak to bite through tough plants, such as seed ferns. When conifers replaced ferns in the Jurassic period, the rhynchosaurs died out.

Hypsognathus

HOLES IN THE HEAD

Reptiles are divided into groups based on the number of holes in their skulls, to which muscles are attached:
1. Anapsids: have no holes.
2. Synapsids: have one hole either side.

3. Diapsids: have two holes either side. Dinosaurs, pterosaurs, and plesiosaurs evolved from the diapsid reptiles. Diapsids alive today include crocodiles, lizards, snakes and birds.

1. Anapsid
2. Synapsid
3. Diapsid

Eye socket

Nostril

Skull openings

1   2   3

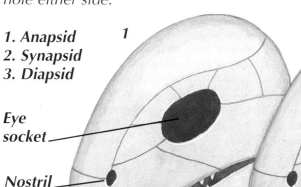

HYLONOMUS

One of the very first reptiles known to have lived on Earth was found at a famous fossil site at Joggins, in Nova Scotia, Canada. Here, sea action is constantly eroding the cliffs to reveal evidence of ancient animal and plant life. It was in 1851 that the fossilised remains of a new kind of prehistoric animal were discovered at the Joggins fossil site. It was given the name *Hylonomus*, which means 'forest mouse'. A small reptile, it lived about 310 million years ago.

LIZARD-LIKE

Hylonomus was one of the anapsid reptiles – the first group of primitive reptiles to evolve. As an anapsid its skull was solid – it was still like that of an amphibian. The only holes in its skull were for its eyes and nostrils. It probably did not have an ear drum. *Hylonomus* looked like a small lizard, and it probably lived like one too. It had a long, slender body and tail, four well-developed limbs, and its jaws were packed with small, sharp teeth.

Hylonomus reptiles on the floor of their forest home, shortly after a flood has felled many of the trees. One Hylonomus is about to climb into a rotten tree stump, from which it will be unable to climb back out.

HYLONOMUS FACT FILE

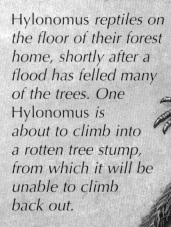

Name: Hylonomus
Lived: 310 million years ago
Found: Canada

Length: 20cm (8in)
Diet: Spiders, millipedes, insects
Habitat: Forest floors

FOREST FLOOR

Hylonomus lived on the floor of a forest in which trees grew to 30m (100ft). Seed ferns grew on the ground. In this shaded habitat, *Hylonomus* hid from predators, searched for food, and raised its young.

SHARP TEETH

A meat-eater, *Hylonomus* probably lived on a diet of insects and other small invertebrates, such as millipedes, worms, and spiders. Its sharp, pointed teeth would have bitten through these soft-bodied animals with ease. Its teeth may also have been able to puncture the hard shells of land snails, before its jaws closed and crushed the snails to pieces.

TRAPPED INSIDE TREE STUMPS

We know about Hylonomus *because several complete fossils have been found, all in one place. Millions of years ago a forest of scaly barked trees was flooded. The trees fell. After the flood,* Hylonomus *reptiles crept into the rotting tree stumps in search of insects. They became trapped, and died.*

About 80 million years before the emergence of the first dinosaurs, two major groups of animals appeared on the land. First came the curious 'sail backs', from whom evolved the second group of animals – the mammal-like reptiles. In turn, these gave rise to mammals.

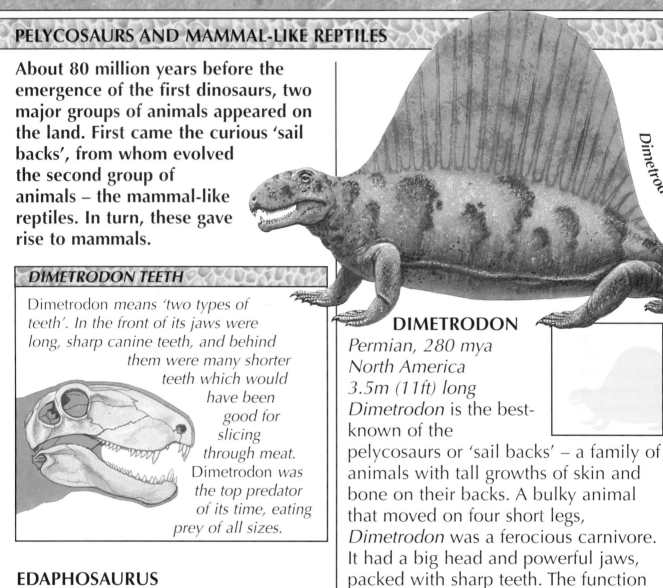

Dimetrodon

DIMETRODON TEETH

Dimetrodon *means 'two types of teeth'. In the front of its jaws were long, sharp canine teeth, and behind them were many shorter teeth which would have been good for slicing through meat.* Dimetrodon *was the top predator of its time, eating prey of all sizes.*

DIMETRODON
Permian, 280 mya
North America
3.5m (11ft) long
Dimetrodon *is the best-known of the pelycosaurs or 'sail backs' – a family of animals with tall growths of skin and bone on their backs. A bulky animal that moved on four short legs, *Dimetrodon* was a ferocious carnivore. It had a big head and powerful jaws, packed with sharp teeth. The function of the 'sail' is not clear. Most scientists think it controlled the animal's body heat, taking warmth in, and letting it out. Some say it was used in courtship and was brightly coloured.

EDAPHOSAURUS
Permian, 280 million years ago
North America and Europe
3.5m (11ft) long
With its distinctive row of skin-covered spines along its back, *Edaphosaurus* would have made a striking sight around the edges of the swamps and lakes where it lived. Unlike other pelycosaurs, such as *Dimetrodon*, *Edaphosaurus* was a herbivore. Its teeth were blunt and peg-like, which suggests they were used for chopping and chewing on plants, not on meat.

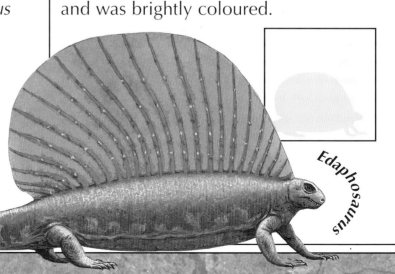

Edaphosaurus

TITANOSUCHUS

Permian, 270 mya
South Africa
2.5m (8ft) long
Titanosuchus belonged to a group of mammal-like reptiles (or reptile-like mammals) known as therapsids. These animals are the direct ancestors of the mammals, who began to appear around 200 million years ago. Therapsids had features which belonged to both reptiles and mammals. *Titanosuchus* was a predator. It had sharp incisor teeth and fang-like canines, perfect for biting and stabbing at prey, such as *Moschops*, a large, slow-moving plant-eater.

Titanosuchus

MOSCHOPS

Permian, 260 mya
South Africa
5m (16ft) long
The biggest of all the mammal-like reptiles was *Moschops*, a herbivore with a barrel-shaped body, short tail, and thick legs. Inside its bulky body was a massive gut – a typical feature of most plant-eating animals. *Moschops* needed a long gut to process the vegetation it ate, extracting the maximum amount of energy from its food. Like other herbivores it had blunt teeth. From the fossils found, it seems that *Moschops* lived in small herds, grazing on low-lying plants, just as cattle do today.

Moschops

The mammal-like reptiles – therapsids – were a major group of ancient animals. They appeared about 300 million years ago, and survived for 120 million years. Their skulls were like those of mammals, but most of them walked like reptiles.

TAPINOCEPHALUS

Permian, 270 million years ago
South Africa
4m (13ft) long

A large and strongly built mammal-like reptile, *Tapinocephalus* was a slow-moving herbivore, similar to *Moschops* which lived in the same region and at the same time. Like others in its family, *Tapinocephalus* had an unusually thick skull. No one knows for certain why this was – some scientists think it shows that *Tapinocephalus* was a head-butting animal. Perhaps adults clashed their heads together to decide who was the strongest member of a group.

Estemmenosuchus

ESTEMMENOSUCHUS

Permian, 255 mya
Europe
3m (10ft) long

A huge mammal-like reptile, *Estemmenosuchus* lived on the edges of pools and lakes, perhaps in herds. It might have had a diet of plants, such as horsetails, and small animals. A mixed diet like this would make it an omnivore. Its most striking feature was a 'crown' of bony horns. Their function is not known. They may have been used in courtship displays, when rival adults locked horns, as stags do today.

Tapinocephalus

ROBERTIA

Permian, 260 million years ago
South Africa
20cm (8in) long
Robertia belongs to a family of mammal-like reptiles known as the dicynodonts ('two dog teeth'). They are named after their two canine teeth which looked like small tusks – the only teeth they had. These long teeth grew down from the upper jaw. *Robertia*, like other dicynodonts, was a pig-like herbivore, able to tug at and bite through vegetation with its beak. One of the first dicynodonts to appear, it is thought that *Robertia* might have lived in a burrow – safely out of sight of any predators that might have hunted it.

PROCYNOSUCHUS

Permian, 260 million years ago
South Africa, Europe
60cm (2ft) long
Procynosuchus was a cynodont – a member of the 'dog-toothed' group of mammal-like reptiles. It was not a typical cynodont, since *Procynosuchus* had become adapted to life in water – cynodonts were more usually to be found living on the land. It swam by wiggling the front and rear ends of its stiff spine, like a crocodile, and paddled with its otter-like webbed hands and feet. *Procynosuchus* was a meat-eater.

Robertia

HORNED HEAD

Estemmenosuchus, *which means 'crowned crocodile', is named after the 'crown' of horns that grew on its skull. They could have been used in fights. They would also have shielded its eyes from harm. An adult's skull was 45cm (18in) wide – the size of a rhinoceros skull.*

Procynosuchus

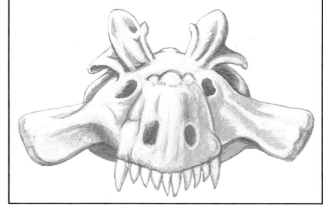

Among the later mammal-like reptiles were ones that had evolved true features of mammals. There was *Thrinaxodon*, which might have been hairy, and *Lycaenops*, a long-legged animal that walked with an upright posture, not a sprawling one like reptiles.

CISTECEPHALUS

Permian, 260 million years ago
South Africa
33cm (1ft 1in) long

Cistecephalus

Cistecephalus lived in underground tunnels, as moles and molerats do today. A small, strongly-built animal, *Cistecephalus* would have dug into the ground with its front paws, scratching away at the soil which it kicked out of the way with its back feet. In its dark, subterranean world, this mammal-like reptile would have eaten worms, beetles, snails and other small animals which fell into its tunnel network. *Cistecephalus* may also have eaten the soft underground stems of horsetails and ferns.

Lycaenops

LYCAENOPS

Permian, 260 mya
South Africa
1m (3ft 3in) long

Lycaenops – its name means 'wolf face' – was a lightly built meat-eater with long legs. Like the wolf of today, *Lycaenops* had a long and slender skull, with very long dog-like canine teeth set into both its upper and lower jaws. Pointed canine teeth were ideal for stabbing and tearing at the flesh of large prey, such as the herbivore *Moschops*, which it may have hunted. *Lycaenops* may have been a pack animal, living and hunting with others of its kind.

WALKING TALL

Lycaenops walked and ran with its long legs held close to its body. This is a feature found in mammals, but not in reptiles whose legs are positioned to the sides of their bodies. The ability to move like a mammal would have given *Lycaenops* an advantage over other four-legged animals, since it would have been able to out-run them.

THRINAXODON
Triassic, 250 mya
South Africa, Antarctica
50cm (1ft 8in) long

Thrinaxodon

LYSTROSAURUS
Triassic, 250 million years ago
South Africa, Asia, Antarctica
1m (3ft 3in) long

Lystrosaurus was a herbivore. It was a mammal-like reptile that belonged to the dicynodont group of animals – those with two canine teeth growing from their upper jaw. Its snout ended in a bony beak, like that of a tortoise, and would have been used to pull at and cut through vegetation. It is thought to have lived on the margins of lakes, and, like a modern hippopotamus, it might have spent time in the water feeding on aquatic plants.

Thrinaxodon was a small meat-eating cynodont – an animal characterised by having dog-like canine, molar and incisor teeth. *Thrinaxodon* was able to breathe while eating, an ability that mammals have but reptiles do not. It is suspected that *Thrinaxodon* was covered in hair – another important mammal-like feature not present in reptiles. Despite its looks, *Thrinaxodon*'s skeleton still had reptile-like features, which is why it is classed as a mammal-like reptile. It lived in burrows, coming out to hunt for its prey.

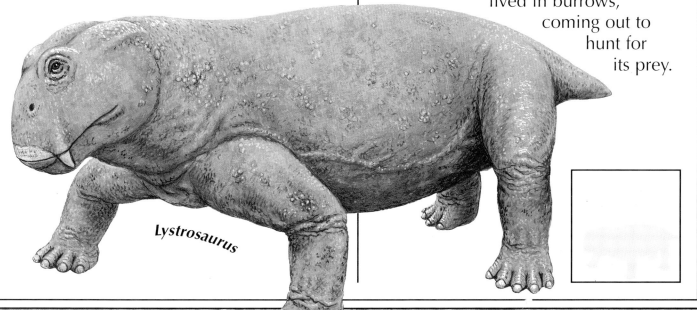

Lystrosaurus

THE PERMIAN MASS EXTINCTION

Towards the end of the Permian period of Earth's history, about 248 million years ago, something happened that led to the death of almost all life on the planet. It was the largest mass extinction of animal species ever to happen – greater even than that which wiped out the dinosaurs millions of years later.

The Permian mass extinction event killed off an estimated 70 per cent of all life on the land, and 90 per cent of all life in the sea. It might have taken as little as 100,000 years for Earth's animal life to die out – some scientists say it happened in only 10,000 years! The cause – or causes – are not certain: many theories exist to explain what happened so long ago.

DEATH FROM VOLCANOES

Massive volcanic eruptions in Siberia, Northern Eurasia, happened at the end of the Permian period. They would have sent huge amounts of carbon dioxide and other gases into the atmosphere, causing acid rain to fall. This would have killed plant life. Animals could have starved.

DEATH BY SUFFOCATION

An increase in carbon dioxide in the atmosphere, from volcanic eruptions, would reduce the amount of oxygen in air and water. For animals everywhere this would have been a death sentence, and they would have suffocated.

As vegetation died out, the plant-eaters would have died with it. Meat-eaters would have become more and more desperate to find dwindling supplies of food.

DEATH FROM SPACE

A theory gaining support from scientists is that Earth was hit by a meteorite – a space rock. There is good evidence that the dinosaurs were wiped out when a meteorite struck the Earth 65 million years ago, so maybe a space rock also destroyed life on Earth 248 million years ago. If the impact was big enough it could have set off volcanic eruptions, and filled the atmosphere with deadly gases.

DEATH BY FREEZING

Another idea is that the Earth's temperature dropped, which led to the expansion of polar ice from the North and South poles. Evidence has been found for a cooling of the climate towards the end of the Permian period, but whether it was cold enough – or the drop in temperature lasted long enough – to kill off the world's animal life is not at all clear.

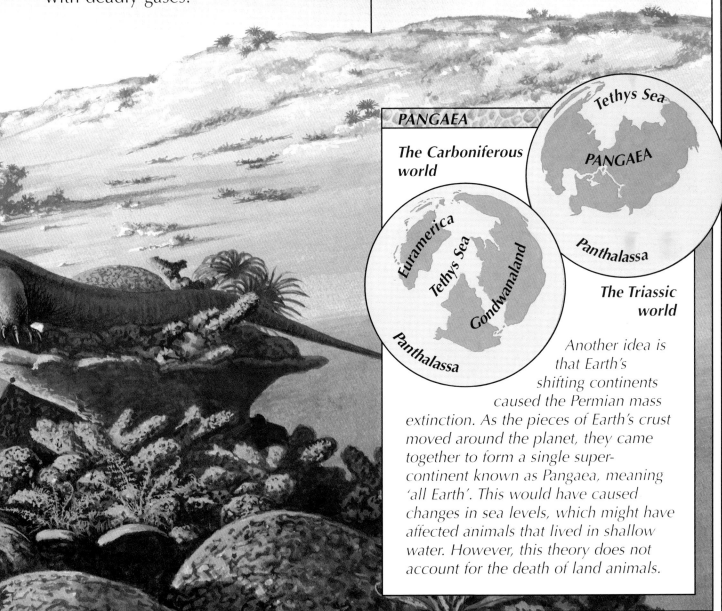

PANGAEA

The Carboniferous world

Euramerica

Tethys Sea

Gondwanaland

Panthalassa

Tethys Sea

PANGAEA

Panthalassa

The Triassic world

Another idea is that Earth's shifting continents caused the Permian mass extinction. As the pieces of Earth's crust moved around the planet, they came together to form a single super-continent known as Pangaea, meaning 'all Earth'. This would have caused changes in sea levels, which might have affected animals that lived in shallow water. However, this theory does not account for the death of land animals.

The catastrophe that wiped out most of Earth's animal life at the end of the Permian period, about 248 million years ago, changed the course of evolution. From the survivors came animals such as *Cynognathus* – still a mammal-like reptile, but with features more like those of mammals than reptiles. However, before mammals came to dominate the world, the dinosaurs ruled.

CYNOGNATHUS

Triassic, 230 million years ago
South Africa, South America, Antarctica
1m (3ft 3in) long
Cynognathus was a predator that hunted in packs for prey such as *Kannemeyeria.* Unlike other mammal-like reptiles, it had an upright posture, not a sprawling one. It might have been hair-covered, and its young might have been born live, not from eggs.

KANNEMEYERIA

Triassic, 230 mya
South Africa,
Asia,
South
America,
Antarctica
3m (10ft) long
A massive herbivore with sprawling legs, *Kannemeyeria* was a mammal-like reptile of the dicynodont family – animals with two canine teeth growing from their upper jaws. These were its only teeth, and its snout ended in a bony beak. *Kannemeyeria* lived in an open landscape, where it was hunted by predators such as *Cynognathus.*

Cynognathus

TEETH LIKE A MAMMAL'S

Cynognathus, *which means 'dog jaw', was a cynodont – an animal with dog-like teeth. It had powerful jaws packed with sharp incisors at the front, fang-like canines behind them, and cheek teeth edged with saw-like points – ideal for shearing through meat. Teeth like these show that* Cynognathus *was closely related to mammals.*

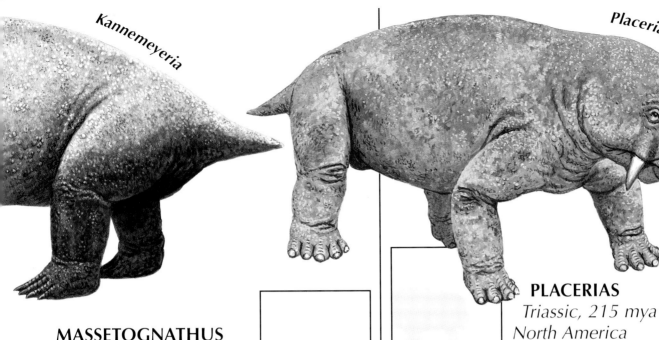

Kannemeyeria

Placerias

MASSETOGNATHUS

Triassic, 220 mya
South America
50cm (1ft 8in) long

Not all cynodonts were meat-eaters. The medium-sized *Massetognathus* was a plant-eater with cheek teeth specially adapted to chewing on vegetation. It still had the distinctive long snout of the cynodont family, with nipping incisors and fang-like canines, but its cheek teeth were not pointed. Instead they were flat-topped and were covered with a number of low ridges, which made them good for grinding away at stems, roots and other plant material. *Massetognathus* had clawed feet and a long dog-like tail. It may have been covered with hair.

PLACERIAS

Triassic, 215 mya
North America
3.5m (11ft) long

The two tusks in the upper jaw of *Placerias* show that it was a member of the dicynodont family of mammal-like reptiles. In front of its tusks was a large, bony beak. In a fully-grown adult the skull was about 60cm (2ft) long. *Placerias* was a herbivore. It probably used its tusks to dig into the ground, uprooting vegetation to eat. Its beak was used to shear through plant material – from tough roots to soft stems and leaves. *Placerias* looked a little like a hippopotamus – it was bulky, had short legs, and wide, spreading feet with blunt claws. It might have lived in a seasonal environment, in which there were two seasons each year, one dry, the other wet. *Placerias* probably lived in herds, close to water. It was one of the last of the dicynodonts, which, for some reason, became extinct about 210 million years ago.

Massetognathus

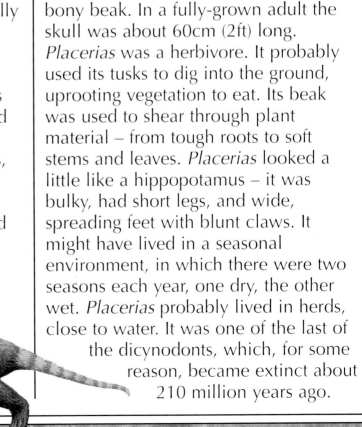

CHAPTER TWO

KILLERS
AND
SCAVENGERS

THEROPODS – THE MEAT-EATERS

In 1881, Othniel Charles Marsh (1831–99), a famous American fossil-hunter, said that all meat-eating dinosaurs (the carnivores) should be grouped together. Marsh suggested a name for this group. He said they should be called theropods, meaning 'beast feet'. The first theropods appeared about 225 million years ago, not long after the Mesozoic Era – the Age of Reptiles – had begun. Meat-eating dinosaurs survived for 160 million years, right until the time that dinosaurs died out, 65 million years ago.

CREATURE FEATURES

Most meat-eating dinosaurs walked on two slender legs that ended in three-toed, bird-like feet with sharp claws. They were able to move quite fast – certainly faster than the slower-moving plant-eating dinosaurs. Their arms were short, their chests were compact, their tails were long, their necks were curved and flexible, and their eyes were big.

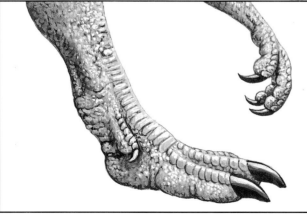

Hand and foot of a meat-eating dinosaur.

CHANGES OVER TIME

The meat-eaters evolved over the course of their 160-million-year existence. Their brains became larger, their limbs longer and more slender, and their eyesight improved.

Meat-eating dinosaurs lived on Earth for about 160 million years. There were many different species. They were the top predators of the Mesozoic Era.

TEETH AND BEAKS

Carnivorous dinosaurs either had teeth or beaks. Theropod teeth were thin and blade-like, with serrated ridges that ran along their front and back edges. When the carnivore bit into its prey, the serrations hooked themselves into the victim's flesh, cutting like the teeth on a saw blade deep into the meat. Small-sized meat-eaters generally had more teeth packed into their jaws than larger carnivores did. In toothed meat-eaters the longest teeth were to be found in the middle of their jaws, where more biting power could be applied by the jaw muscles. Some meat-eaters evolved jaws that had no teeth in them at all. Instead, these toothless theropods had bony beaks covered by a layer of horn. Unsuitable for biting into meat, their beaks might have been used for cracking open eggs.

Dromiceiomimus

Trodon

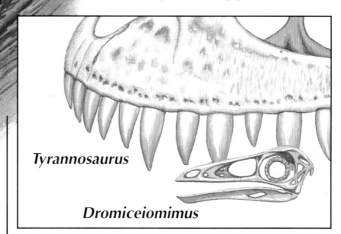

Tyrannosaurus

Dromiceiomimus

Some meat-eaters had teeth, some had beaks.

THE FIRST MEAT-EATERS

The first meat-eating dinosaurs appeared during the middle of the Triassic period, about 225 million years ago. They were quite a lot smaller, and not as highly evolved, as the better known larger carnivores that came later in the Mesozoic, such as **Tyrannosaurus rex**.

COELOPHYSIS

Triassic, 220 mya
North America
3m (10ft) long

Coelophysis

Coelophysis was built for pace and agility. To keep its weight down, its leg bones were almost hollow – a great help to an animal that relied on speed to catch its prey. Its front legs were small and were probably used for clawing and grasping at food. It might have been a pack animal, living and hunting in groups.

EORAPTOR

Triassic, 225 mya
South America
1m (3ft 3in) long

Eoraptor is an important animal because it is one of the world's oldest known dinosaurs – it lived near the very beginning of the Age of Reptiles. *Eoraptor* was a small dinosaur that moved around quickly on two long, slender legs. Its legs were twice as long as its arms. It was a meat-eater, and it may have been both a hunter and a scavenger. Inside its long jaws were many small, serrated teeth. *Eoraptor* fossils have been unearthed along the course of an ancient river in Argentina. This has led scientists to wonder if *Eoraptor* was a fish-eater.

Eoraptor

FAST MOVERS

Speed and agility were two crucially important abilities that meat-eating dinosaurs had to have. Without these skills, their chances of survival would have been reduced. Meat-eaters had to be capable of running as fast as the prey they lived off.

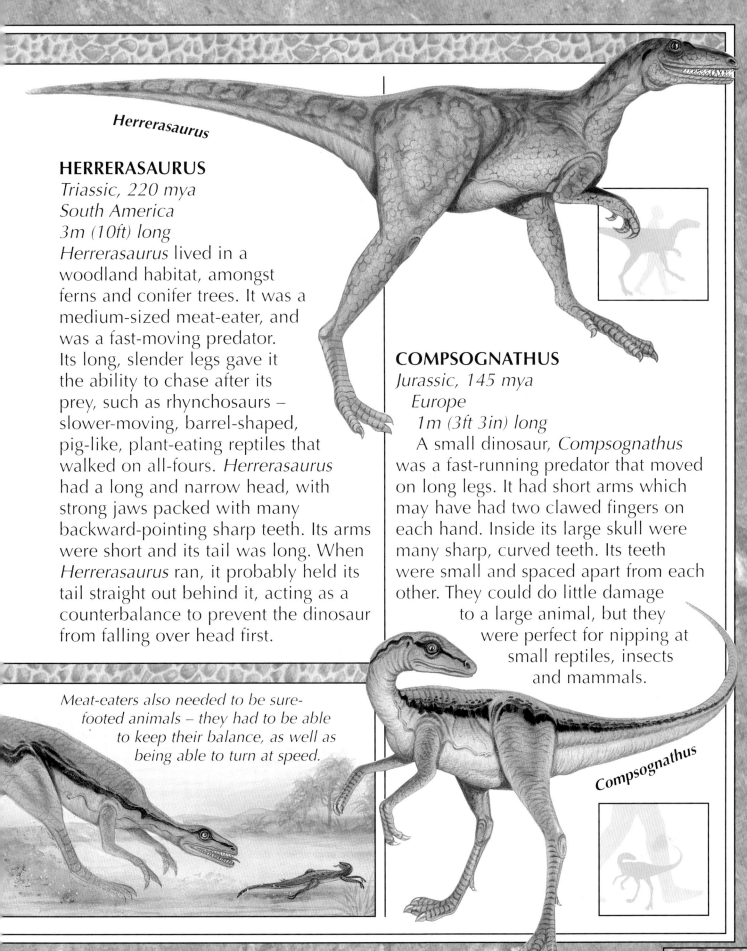

HERRERASAURUS

Herrerasaurus

Triassic, 220 mya
South America
3m (10ft) long
Herrerasaurus lived in a woodland habitat, amongst ferns and conifer trees. It was a medium-sized meat-eater, and was a fast-moving predator. Its long, slender legs gave it the ability to chase after its prey, such as rhynchosaurs – slower-moving, barrel-shaped, pig-like, plant-eating reptiles that walked on all-fours. *Herrerasaurus* had a long and narrow head, with strong jaws packed with many backward-pointing sharp teeth. Its arms were short and its tail was long. When *Herrerasaurus* ran, it probably held its tail straight out behind it, acting as a counterbalance to prevent the dinosaur from falling over head first.

Meat-eaters also needed to be sure-footed animals – they had to be able to keep their balance, as well as being able to turn at speed.

COMPSOGNATHUS

Jurassic, 145 mya
Europe
1m (3ft 3in) long
A small dinosaur, *Compsognathus* was a fast-running predator that moved on long legs. It had short arms which may have had two clawed fingers on each hand. Inside its large skull were many sharp, curved teeth. Its teeth were small and spaced apart from each other. They could do little damage to a large animal, but they were perfect for nipping at small reptiles, insects and mammals.

Compsognathus

Large-sized meat-eaters began to appear in the Jurassic period. They reached their greatest size in the following time zone, the Cretaceous. Powerfully-built, and equipped with sharp meat-slicing teeth and claws that could scratch and rip into the thickest skin, these theropods might have roamed the land in small groups, as well as in ones and twos.

DILOPHOSAURUS

Jurassic, 190 mya
North America
6m (20ft) long

One of the earliest large-sized meat-eaters, *Dilophosaurus* is notable because of the unusual double crests of bone that grew on top of its head. It is not clear what they were for, or whether they appeared on both males and females.

One idea is that the crests were brightly coloured, and could have been used as signalling devices, perhaps to attract a mate at breeding time, or to mark an individual out as the leader of a group. Long claws grew from the toes of *Dilophosaurus*. They might have been used as weapons when it attacked another animal, kicking at it while its hands grasped at it. Scientists think that *Dilophosaurus* was a group animal that lived in small herds.

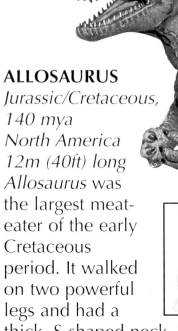

ALLOSAURUS

Jurassic/Cretaceous, 140 mya
North America
12m (40ft) long

Allosaurus was the largest meat-eater of the early Cretaceous period. It walked on two powerful legs and had a thick, S-shaped neck. Its arms were short, with hands that had three curved and pointed claws, each up to 15cm (6in) long. Inside its jaws were many backward-pointing teeth, serrated like steak knives so they could slice easily through meat. Each tooth was up to 10cm (4in) long. When attacking an animal larger than itself, *Allosaurus* may have hunted in packs. It probably hunted smaller prey on its own.

Allosaurus

Dilophosaurus

NEOVENATOR

Cretaceous, 125 mya
Europe
8m (26ft) long

Neovenator is related
to the *Allosaurus* of
North America, but it
was more lightly-built.
It was a fierce predator
whose large skull contained razor-
sharp teeth 5cm (2in) long. Claws up to
13cm (5in) long grew on its fingers.
This array of weaponry marked out
Neovenator as a formidable opponent
in a fight, and with its long legs it
would have been able to move about
swiftly, probably breaking into a run
over short distances. It has been found
on the Isle of Wight, off the south coast
of Britain, where it might have hunted
the plant-eating *Iguanodon*.

Neovenator

SCAVENGERS

*It is thought that meat-eating dinosaurs
were scavengers as well as predators.
While predators would have been active
hunters, stalking their prey then killing it,
scavengers ate meat from animals that
had been killed by others. Scavenging for
'free meals' saved energy, without the
danger of getting hurt in a fight.*

GIGANOTOSAURUS

Cretaceous, 90 mya
South America
15m (49ft) long

Giganotosaurus was a giant
carnivore, 2m (6ft) longer than
Tyrannosaurus rex. Because
several were found together, it is
thought it hunted in packs. It was
probably also a lone predator.
Its biggest teeth were 20cm (5in)
long. They would have sliced
deep into the flesh of a prey
animal, inflicting wounds from
which it died.

Giganotosaurus

These were some of the giants of the meat-eating dinosaurs – animals whose teeth, claws and muscular bodies were perfectly designed to attack their prey. Whether they acted alone or in packs, these theropods were among the most formidable of all hunters in the Age of Reptiles.

MEGALOSAURUS

Jurassic, 170 mya
Europe
9m (30ft) long
Megalosaurus was the very first dinosaur to be named, in 1822. Despite this, little is known about it. No complete fossil skeletons have been found, so scientists have tried to work out its lifestyle from that of other meat-eaters. They believe it was a predatory dinosaur that hunted herbivores, such as *Iguanodon*. *Megalosaurus* might also have been a scavenger, eating flesh from an animal that was already dead. Like a lion, it may have stayed in the vicinity of a kill for several days returning to feed on the carcass.

Ceratosaurus

CERATOSAURUS

Jurassic, 150 mya
North America, Africa
6m (20ft) long
Ceratosaurus had a short horn on the tip of its snout, and horny ridges grew near its eyes. It is not thought these bumps were used as weapons. Instead, they might have been used for display purposes. *Ceratosaurus* had a large head. When it ate, the bones of its skull moved from side to side, allowing it to gulp down big pieces of meat. When its teeth fell out, because of old age, disease or damage, new ones grew to replace them.

Megalosaurus

PACK HUNTERS

Hunting in packs gave meat-eaters the advantage over their prey. While one predator distracted the victim, forcing it to leave the safety of its herd, the pack closed in for the kill.

ALBERTOSAURUS
Cretaceous, 70 mya
North America
9m (30ft) long
Albertosaurus
was a fierce
predator and was a relative of
Tyrannosaurus. However, unlike
Tyrannosaurus, whose eyes looked
straight ahead, the eyes of
Albertosaurus were on the sides of its
head – so it might have had difficulty
seeing in front of it. To make up for its
poor eyesight it may have had a good
sense of smell. In front of its eyes were
two small horns which it may have
used for display purposes. It walked on
two strong muscular back legs, and
was probably a fast runner, with
a top speed over a short
distance of up to 30 kph (19 mph).

THERIZINOSAURUS
Cretaceous, 70 mya
Asia
12m (40ft) long
Not only was
Therizinosaurus
one of the last
dinosaurs on
Earth, it was one of
the strangest-looking ever to have
evolved. No complete skeletons have
been found. All that scientists have to
go on are parts of its arms and chest.
By comparing them with dinosaurs in
the same family, they think
Therizinosaurus might have looked like
the picture seen below, with a small
head at the end of a long neck. Its arms
were 2.45m (8ft) long, at the end of
which were three huge claws, the
longest of which grew to 70cm
(2ft 4in). Why it needed such long
claws puzzles scientists. Some believe
Therizinosaurus used its
giant claws to rip open
termite nests; others say
it used them to drag
plants towards its
mouth. Most agree it
was a meat-eater.

Perhaps the best-known of all the dinosaurs, *Tyrannosaurus rex* only appeared shortly before they died out.

Name: *Tyrannosaurus rex*
Lived: *70 mya*
Found: *North America*
Length: *12m (40ft)*
Diet: *Meat*
Habitat: *Open woodland*

POWERFUL KILLER

Tyrannosaurus rex was one of the largest of all meat-eating predatory dinosaurs (*Giganotosaurus* was bigger). It was a strongly-built theropod that stood on two powerful legs, holding its back level with the ground, its tail outstretched for balance. Its forward-facing eyes probably gave it good vision, to help it hunt for prey.

SURPRISE ATTACKER

Tyrannosaurus rex lived in open woodland. It was a habitat in which there were clearings, and stands of conifers, cycads, oak, maple and beech trees, while on the ground were ferns and flowering plants. Grazing on the lush vegetation were plant-eaters, which *Tyrannosaurus rex* stalked. If at first it couldn't see them, perhaps it caught their scent – it seems that this dinosaur had a keen sense of smell. With a victim in sight, *Tyrannosaurus rex* charged it down at speeds of up to 36 kph (23 mph), each of its giant strides covering 3.7–4.6m (12 to 15ft) of ground at a time.

BIG HEAD, BIG TEETH

Tyrannosaurus rex *had a massive head – about 1.5m (5ft) long. Its skull had large holes in it which helped to reduce its weight, making it light to carry around. Packed into its jaws were 50 to 60 blade-like teeth, some up to 23cm (9in) long.*

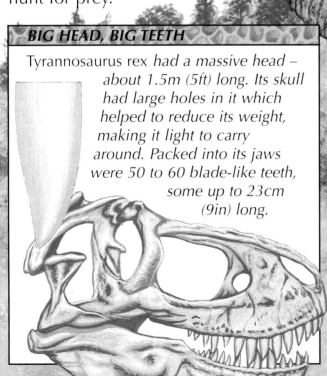

FULL TO BURSTING

Like a modern meat-eating animal such as a lion, *Tyrannosaurus rex* probably didn't eat every day. Instead, after it had killed its prey – a plant-eating animal – it gorged itself on the flesh, then ate nothing until it returned to the carcass for another meal a few days later. It may also have been a scavenger, feeding on animals killed by others.

An adult Tyrannosaurus rex *breaks cover and lunges at a plant-eating* Edmontosaurus *in a surprise attack.*

SMALL ARMS, HOOKED FINGERS

Tyrannosaurus rex *had short arms, with two clawed fingers on each hand. For such a strong animal its arms seem surprisingly feeble – but not if you imagine them used as hooks to hang on to its prey.*

Among the most recognisable of all the meat-eating dinosaurs were those with 'sails' of skin on their backs. These were the spinosaurs – large, fish-eating theropods who had long, crocodile-like jaws, and finger claws shaped like sickles.

SUCHOMIMUS

Cretaceous, 105 mya
North Africa
11m (36ft)
long

Suchomimus

ACROCANTHOSAURUS

Cretaceous, 110 mya
North America
13m (43ft) long

Acrocanthosaurus had 43cm- (1ft 5in-) long spines growing from its neck to its tail along its backbone. They may have had a skin 'sail' stretched between them. *Acrocanthosaurus* was a fierce meat-eater with a big head, 1.4m (4.5ft) long. Its jaws were filled with 68 serrated teeth, good for slicing through soft meat, but not for going through bone. Its arms ended in powerful hands which had three large, curved claws – well designed for capturing and holding on to its prey.

Closely related to *Spinosaurus*, and living at roughly the same time and in the same part of the world, was *Suchomimus*. It too had a 'sail' on its back, though not as high. Also a fish-eater, *Suchomimus* had a 1.2m- (4ft-) long snout, inside which were about 100 pointed teeth. The teeth were razor-sharp and angled slightly backwards, making it hard for a fish to slip from its mouth.

Acrocanthosaurus

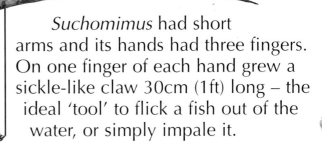

Suchomimus had short arms and its hands had three fingers. On one finger of each hand grew a sickle-like claw 30cm (1ft) long – the ideal 'tool' to flick a fish out of the water, or simply impale it.

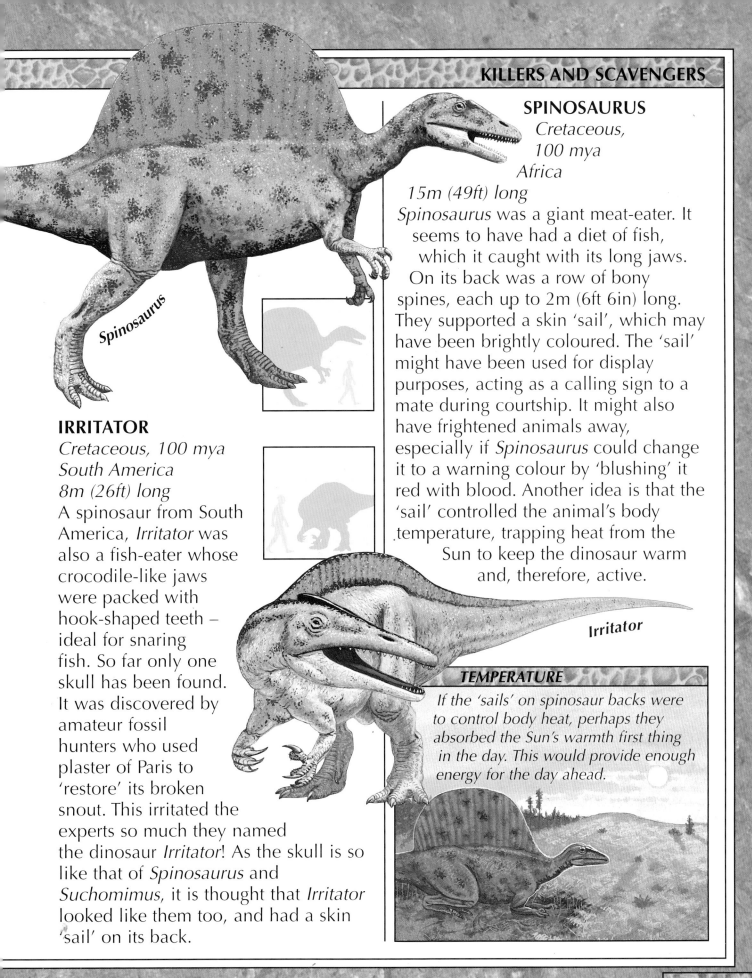

SPINOSAURUS

*Cretaceous,
100 mya
Africa*
15m (49ft) long

Spinosaurus was a giant meat-eater. It seems to have had a diet of fish, which it caught with its long jaws. On its back was a row of bony spines, each up to 2m (6ft 6in) long. They supported a skin 'sail', which may have been brightly coloured. The 'sail' might have been used for display purposes, acting as a calling sign to a mate during courtship. It might also have frightened animals away, especially if *Spinosaurus* could change it to a warning colour by 'blushing' it red with blood. Another idea is that the 'sail' controlled the animal's body temperature, trapping heat from the Sun to keep the dinosaur warm and, therefore, active.

IRRITATOR

*Cretaceous, 100 mya
South America
8m (26ft) long*

A spinosaur from South America, *Irritator* was also a fish-eater whose crocodile-like jaws were packed with hook-shaped teeth – ideal for snaring fish. So far only one skull has been found. It was discovered by amateur fossil hunters who used plaster of Paris to 'restore' its broken snout. This irritated the experts so much they named the dinosaur *Irritator*! As the skull is so like that of *Spinosaurus* and *Suchomimus*, it is thought that *Irritator* looked like them too, and had a skin 'sail' on its back.

TEMPERATURE

If the 'sails' on spinosaur backs were to control body heat, perhaps they absorbed the Sun's warmth first thing in the day. This would provide enough energy for the day ahead.

BARYONYX

The discovery of a new kind of meat-eating dinosaur is a major event, especially if its fossilised skeleton turns out to be almost complete. This is what happened in the case of *Baryonyx*, a previously unknown species of fish-eating dinosaur discovered in the south of England. Not only were almost all of its bones found, but even the remains of its final meal came to light.

GIANT THUMB CLAW

Baryonyx *had three fingers on each hand. There was a long curved claw on its inside fingers (its thumbs). In a fully grown adult, the claw was 35cm (1ft 2in) long, and it was probably covered with a horny sheath, just like the claw of a bird. The name* Baryonyx *means 'Heavy Claw'.*

Claw on left thumb

LONG-NECKED CARNIVORE

Baryonyx was a meat-eater that walked on two legs. It had a narrow head and a long snout, like a crocodile. Its arms were strong and its fingers had curved claws. It had a long, straight neck, which was unusual for big carnivores – most had necks shaped like a letter S. Its tail was long and straight.

LEAFY HABITAT

Baryonyx lived along the margins of rivers and pools, in a woodland flood plain where conifers, cycads, monkey puzzle trees, ferns and horsetails grew. *Baryonyx* shared this habitat with many other animals, such as the plant-eating *Iguanodon*, and the meat-eating *Megalosaurus*. Turtles and crocodiles lived in the water, and dragonflies flew in the air.

THE DISCOVERY

One of *Baryonyx*'s thumb claws was found in 1983 by an amateur fossil collector. He found it in a claypit in Surrey, England. That spring, scientists from London's Natural History Museum excavated the site, uncovering the fossilised bones of *Baryonyx*. Only its tail was missing.

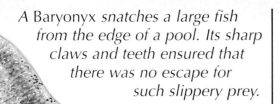

A Baryonyx snatches a large fish from the edge of a pool. Its sharp claws and teeth ensured that there was no escape for such slippery prey.

Name: *Baryonyx*
Lived: 125 million years ago
Found: Europe
Length: 10m (33ft)
Diet: Fish, and possibly carrion
Habitat: Marshy, open woodland

DIET OF FISH

When *Baryonyx* was excavated, the fossilised remains of its last meal were found within its stomach. Scientists identified teeth and scales from a species of fish called *Lepidotes*, a fish that grew to about 1m (3ft 3in) in length. Besides fish, *Baryonyx* might also have eaten carrion – meat from dead animals.

TOOTH-FILLED JAWS

Baryonyx *had a long, slender skull. It ended in a spoon-shaped tip, which would have been useful for scooping up fish. Seen from the side, its upper jaw was S-shaped – modern fish-eating crocodiles also have jaws this shape. Its jaws were packed with 96 small, sharp teeth.*

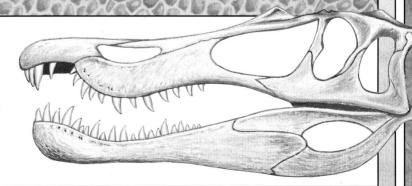

Meat-eating dinosaurs evolved many highly specialised features. Some, such as *Troodon*, became adapted to life in the far north of the world, where it was not only cold but where there were more hours of darkness than daylight. The ability to be able to see at night was a distinct advantage in the survival stakes. Other carnivores, such as *Avimimus*, grew into animals with many bird-like features – a sign that they were slowly evolving into a completely new kind of animal.

TROODON

Cretaceous, 70 mya
North America, Europe
2m (6ft 6in) long
A medium-sized carnivore, *Troodon* was a lightly-built dinosaur. With its long legs it was probably a fast runner, moving at speed after its prey, such as smaller reptiles and mammals. It may also have been an egg-eater, since its teeth have been found mixed up with shattered dinosaur eggs, suggesting they were part of its diet. Perhaps it also ate the defenceless hatchlings of other dinosaurs, raiding their nesting sites when the adults were not guarding their young.

SINORNITHOIDES

Cretaceous, 105 mya
Asia
1.1m (3ft 6in) long

Sinornithoides

Sinornithoides is one of the smallest meat-eating dinosaurs known – about the size of a turkey. Its long legs indicate it was a fast runner, and a large brain cavity inside its skull suggests it was an intelligent creature.

Sinornithoides had a compact body, and a long, whip-like tail that accounted for half its overall length. It probably ate small mammals and reptiles, as well as insects.

Troodon

ORNITHOLESTES

Jurassic, 150 mya
North America
2m (6ft 6in) long
Ornitholestes was an
agile carnivore that
lived in a forest habitat.
It ate lizards, small
mammals, and
possibly the first birds
which appeared in
the late Jurassic period.
It may also have been a
carrion feeder,
scavenging meat from
the bodies of dead
animals. *Ornitholestes* had a small
head and its jaws contained sharp
teeth. A bony crest grew on the top of
its snout. It had a long, thin tail. As it
ran, it held its tail straight behind it for
balance. To change direction,
Ornitholestes would have swung its tail
to one side.

Ornitholestes

AVIMIMUS

Cretaceous,
80 mya
Asia
1.5m (5ft) long
Avimimus was a long-
legged dinosaur that
resembled a bird – but it
was not a bird. Its head
was bird-like, with a large
brain, large eyes and a
toothless beak. Its arms
could be folded close to its
body, like a bird folds its
wings. Although no evidence
for feathers has been found on
Avimimus, some scientists believe it
may have grown them on its arms –
but it could not fly because its
arms were too short for flight.
Avimimus was probably an
omnivore, eating both plants
and meat, especially insects.

GOOD EYESIGHT

Troodon *had large eyes, about*
5cm (2in) across, which suggests it had
good vision. It may have been a night
hunter, able to detect its prey in the dark.
Given that it lived in the far north of
Canada and Russia,
close to the Arctic
Circle where
winter daylight
hours are short,
keen eyesight
would have been
essential for survival.

Avimimus

OVIRAPTOR

This dinosaur was found in the 1920s on top of a nest of eggs. They were thought to belong to *Protoceratops*, a medium-sized herbivore. It was decided the new dinosaur was stealing the *Protoceratops'* eggs, so it was named *Oviraptor*, meaning 'Egg Thief'. Then, in the 1990s, more eggs were found, similar to those discovered in the 1920s. Because one had a baby *Oviraptor* inside it, it was realised the dinosaur was not an egg-stealer after all. Instead, *Oviraptor* had been found sitting on a nest of its own eggs, incubating them until they hatched.

OVIRAPTOR SKULL

Oviraptor's skull was small and lightweight, with large holes for its eyes. The most striking feature of its skull was a tall, bony crest which grew above its nose. The crest was probably covered in a layer of horn. Its toothless beak was very much like that of a bird.

A group of Oviraptor dinosaurs at their breeding ground, tending to their nests of carefully arranged eggs.

BIRD-LIKE DINOSAUR

Oviraptor was a meat-eater with long legs, a long slender tail and large eyes. It had strong, clawed hands and a toothless beak. On top of its bird-like head grew a tall, bony crest, the function of which is uncertain. Scientists believe *Oviraptor* was covered in a layer of fluffy down, and it may have had feathers on some parts of its body, especially its arms. *Oviraptor* had long hands, which would have been good at grasping. Its three fingers ended in strong, curved claws, each about 8cm (3in) long.

VICIOUS KILLER

Oviraptor was a fast-running animal that may have chased after small prey which it killed with kicks, and pecks from its beak. Its beak shape suggests it may have eaten plants, in which case it was an omnivore – both a meat- and plant-eater.

Name: *Oviraptor*
Lived: *80 million years ago*
Found: *Asia*
Length: *1.8m (6ft)*
Diet: *Meat, insects, eggs, plants*
Habitat: *Semi-desert*

DOTING PARENT

Oviraptor lived in a dry, semi-desert habitat. It may have lived in groups. Its long legs indicate it was built for speed. If it was anything like a modern ostrich it might have reached speeds of up to 70 kph (43 mph) over short distances. The most remarkable aspect of its lifestyle is that it brooded over its eggs. This suggests that *Oviraptor* parents cared for their young.

NESTS AND HATCHLINGS

Oviraptor made its nest from sand scraped up to form a low mound. A clutch of long, oval eggs was laid in a hollow scooped into the top of the mound. About 15 to 20 eggs were laid in a circle. Like a bird, *Oviraptor* sat on the nest until the eggs hatched.

ORNITHOMIMIDS

One group of dinosaurs looked very much like the flightless birds of today – the ostriches, emus and chickens. These were the ornithomimids, meaning 'bird mimics'. They had long legs, clearly built for speed, toothless beaks, and slender arms with grasping hands. The dinosaurs of this group lived in many parts of the world.

ORNITHOMIMUS

Cretaceous, 70 mya
North America
3.5m (11ft 6in) long
A slender, long-legged dinosaur, *Ornithomimus* was a fast runner – though whether it ran to escape from danger, or to chase after prey is not known. It may have been an omnivore, like other members of its family that also had bony, toothless beaks. If this is true, then *Ornithomimus* may have had a mixed diet of insects, small reptiles and mammals, fruit, eggs, seeds and leaves. Its scissor-like beak would have cut through its food.

Ornithomimus

GALLIMIMUS

Cretaceous, 70 mya
Asia
6m (20ft) long
Gallimimus had a long, flat, toothless horny beak on a small head. It had large eyes, and its sight may have been good. Its neck was long and flexible, and its body was short and compact. When *Gallimimus* ran, it held its tail straight out behind it for balance. There were three fingers on each hand, tipped with pointed claws. It had long, slim legs, each with three clawed toes. *Gallimimus* was the largest of the ostrich-like dinosaurs.

Gallimimus

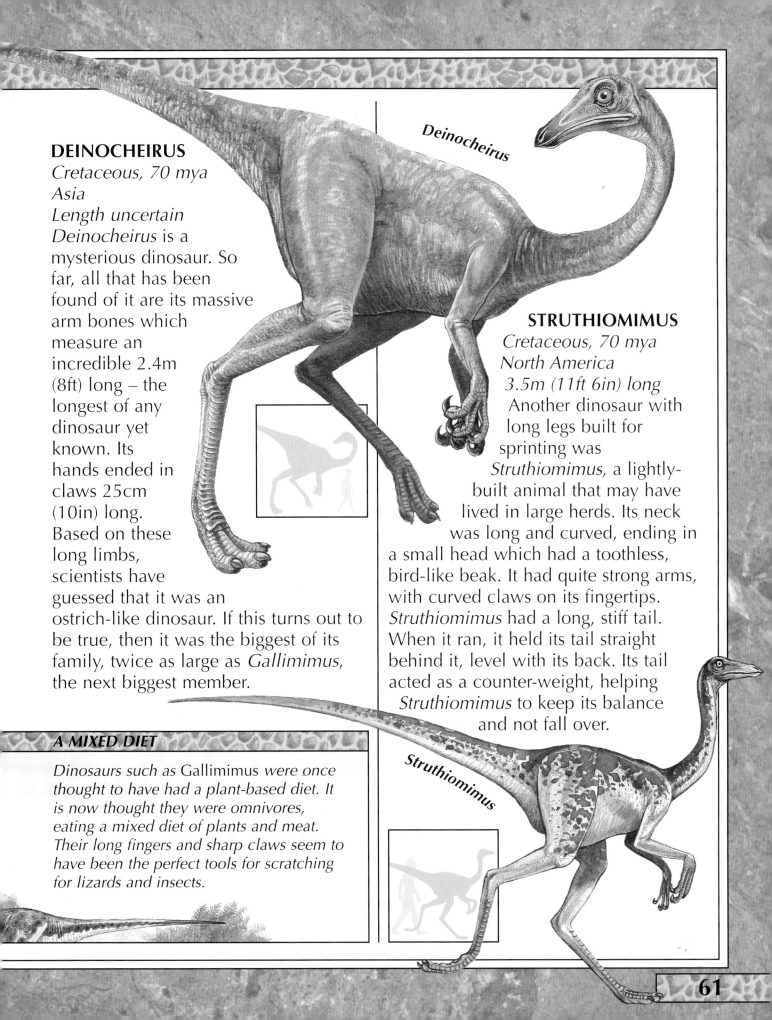

DEINOCHEIRUS

Cretaceous, 70 mya
Asia
Length uncertain
Deinocheirus is a mysterious dinosaur. So far, all that has been found of it are its massive arm bones which measure an incredible 2.4m (8ft) long – the longest of any dinosaur yet known. Its hands ended in claws 25cm (10in) long. Based on these long limbs, scientists have guessed that it was an ostrich-like dinosaur. If this turns out to be true, then it was the biggest of its family, twice as large as *Gallimimus*, the next biggest member.

Deinocheirus

STRUTHIOMIMUS

Cretaceous, 70 mya
North America
3.5m (11ft 6in) long
Another dinosaur with long legs built for sprinting was *Struthiomimus*, a lightly-built animal that may have lived in large herds. Its neck was long and curved, ending in a small head which had a toothless, bird-like beak. It had quite strong arms, with curved claws on its fingertips. *Struthiomimus* had a long, stiff tail. When it ran, it held its tail straight behind it, level with its back. Its tail acted as a counter-weight, helping *Struthiomimus* to keep its balance and not fall over.

A MIXED DIET

Dinosaurs such as Gallimimus were once thought to have had a plant-based diet. It is now thought they were omnivores, eating a mixed diet of plants and meat. Their long fingers and sharp claws seem to have been the perfect tools for scratching for lizards and insects.

Struthiomimus

Scientists call them the dromaeosaurs, meaning 'running lizards', but there's a more popular name for them – raptors. They were among the fiercest of all dinosaurs, equipped with long, slashing claws on their feet, and large, grasping hands. According to current thinking, these dinosaurs were the ancestors of birds. Some dromaeosaurs might have had feathers, and their arms could have developed into wings.

VELOCIRAPTOR

Cretaceous, 70 mya
Asia
1.8m (6ft) long
Velociraptor was a fierce predator, armed with sharp, serrated teeth and a large sickle-shaped claw on the second toe of each foot. When *Velociraptor* walked or ran, it held its savage claws off the ground, to prevent them from wearing down. In an attack on a prey animal, the claws were brought forward, and were used to slash at the soft parts of the victim, no doubt inflicting deep cuts. A *Velociraptor* fossil has been found locked in battle with a *Protoceratops*, a medium-sized plant-eater – evidence for one animal hunted by this carnivore. *Velociraptor* was probably a pack animal, preying on old and weak creatures.

PYRORAPTOR

Cretaceous, 70 mya
Europe
1.8m (6ft) long

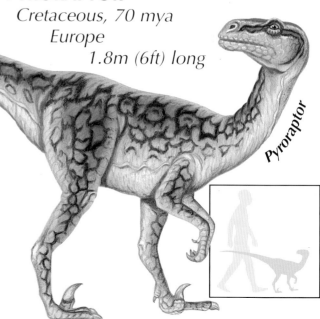

Pyroraptor

Pyroraptor was a small, two-legged theropod whose fossilised teeth, foot claws, arm and back bones were found in the south of France. Its curved, slashing claws, 6.5cm (2.5in) long, show that it was a dromaeosaur – one of the meat-eating, bird-like running lizards, very few of which have been found in Europe. *Pyroraptor* may be the same as *Variraptor*, also a dromaeosaur from the same area of France.

Velociraptor

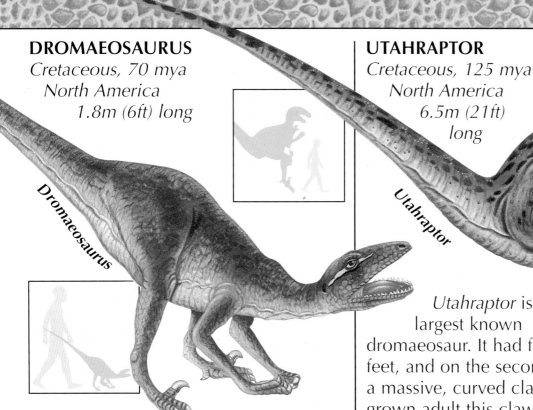

DROMAEOSAURUS
Cretaceous, 70 mya
North America
1.8m (6ft) long

Dromaeosaurus

UTAHRAPTOR
Cretaceous, 125 mya
North America
6.5m (21ft)
long

Utahraptor

Utahraptor is the largest known dromaeosaur. It had four-toed feet, and on the second toe was a massive, curved claw. In a fully-grown adult this claw was up to 38cm (1ft 3in) long. Its fingers were tipped with smaller claws. An agile predator, *Utahraptor* probably used a combination of speed and brute force to overcome a prey animal. It inflicted deep wounds by lashing out with its feet, using its killer claws to tear into an unprotected part of its victim's body, such as its belly, while holding on to it with its grasping hands and sharp, serrated flesh-cutting teeth.

Dromaeosaurus was the first of the dromaeosaurs to be found. Like the others of its family it was a fast-moving predator, and could probably race at up to 60 kph (37 mph) over short distances. It had powerful jaws packed with sharp teeth, and a large, curved claw on the inner toe of each foot. This could have been retracted when not in use – as a cat pulls in its claws. Big eyes reveal it had good eyesight.

INTELLIGENT HUNTERS

Dromaeosaurs were intelligent animals, able to communicate and work with one another. When hunting they worked in packs, following their plant-eating victims. Perhaps they were able *to separate an animal from the herd, especially if it was young, old or weak. Removed from the others, the pack of hunters closed in for the kill.*

DEINONYCHUS

Several fossilised skeletons of *Deinonychus* have been found, making it one of the most studied and best known of all dromaeosaurs. Built for speed and attack, *Deinonychus* was a formidable predator, able to wound an animal many times its own size. And because it hunted in packs, it was clearly an intelligent, calculating creature, able to outsmart its victims.

TERRIBLE CLAW

Deinonychus had a long, curved claw on the second toe of each foot. In an attack, the claw, which in an adult grew to 13cm (5in) long, was swung forwards and down. This powerful slashing action would have ripped open the flesh of a victim. It is from these claws that Deinonychus *is named, meaning 'Terrible Claw'.*

MAN-SIZED HUNTER

At 2m (6ft 6in) tall, *Deinonychus* was roughly the same height as a tall man. It moved swiftly along on two powerful hind legs. Each foot had three toes, and it was here that its most distinctive feature was to be found – a long and deadly claw. Its arms were long and its three-fingered hands were large with powerful, curved talons. Its neck was curved and flexible, allowing its head to move easily. There was little movement in its back and tail, which were held stiff and straight by powerful ligaments and bony rods. As it ran at speed, it held its tail straight out behind it, helping it to keep its balance. It had the large eyes of a hunter, suggesting that its eyesight was good.

TEARING TEETH

Deinonychus had a large head and jaws. Its skull was lightly built and its jaws were packed with many backward-curving teeth, 8cm (3in) long. They had serrated edges which helped Deinonychus *to rip into flesh, rather than slice through it. Powerful jaw muscles gave* Deinonychus *a fearsome, snapping bite.*

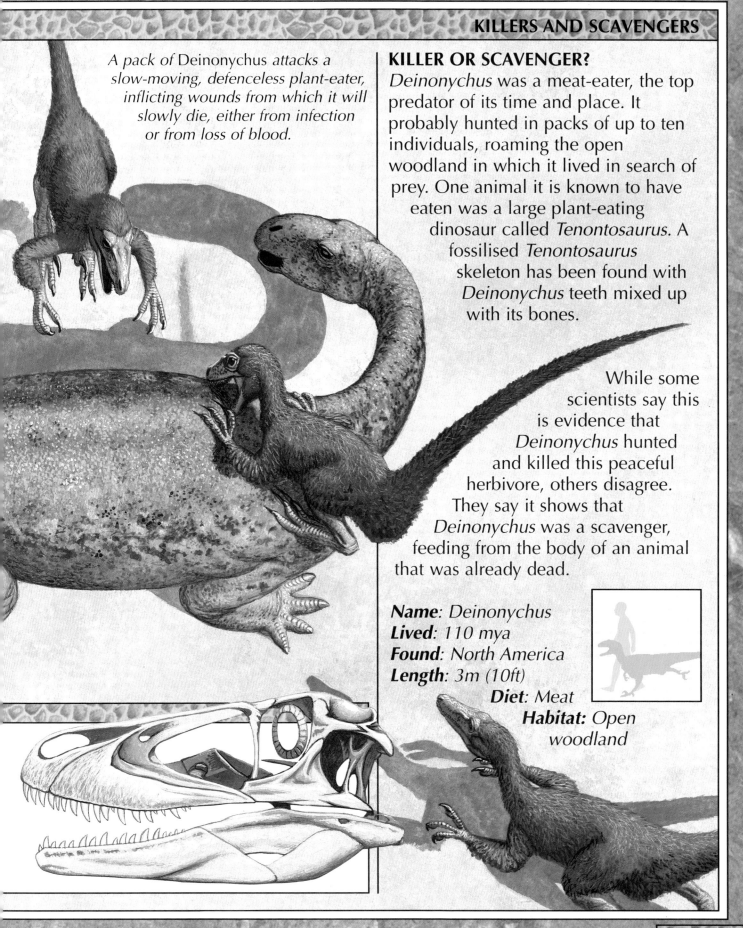

A pack of Deinonychus *attacks a slow-moving, defenceless plant-eater, inflicting wounds from which it will slowly die, either from infection or from loss of blood.*

KILLER OR SCAVENGER?

Deinonychus was a meat-eater, the top predator of its time and place. It probably hunted in packs of up to ten individuals, roaming the open woodland in which it lived in search of prey. One animal it is known to have eaten was a large plant-eating dinosaur called *Tenontosaurus*. A fossilised *Tenontosaurus* skeleton has been found with *Deinonychus* teeth mixed up with its bones.

While some scientists say this is evidence that *Deinonychus* hunted and killed this peaceful herbivore, others disagree. They say it shows that *Deinonychus* was a scavenger, feeding from the body of an animal that was already dead.

Name: *Deinonychus*
Lived: *110 mya*
Found: *North America*
Length: *3m (10ft)*
Diet: *Meat*
Habitat: *Open woodland*

Close relatives of the dromaeosaurs were small-sized, agile, meat-eating dinosaurs who looked a bit like birds. Their bodies were covered in fluffy down, their feathered arms seem like wings, and their clawed feet allowed them to climb into trees. These are the so-called 'dino-birds' – not quite birds as we know them today, but no longer dinosaurs either.

ARCHAEOPTERYX
Jurassic, 150 mya
Europe
60cm (2ft)
long

Archaeopteryx

Archaeopteryx had feathers and a wishbone, which are features of birds. Its wing feathers were asymmetrical (lopsided), which would have given it lift and allowed it to fly. However, it had teeth, a flexible neck, clawed fingers, long legs and a bony tail, all of which are features of reptiles. Despite looking like a bird, its wing muscles were weak, and it may have been unable to fly far. The claws on its wings might have helped it to grip and climb trees. Once it had clawed its way up a tree, it may have used its wings to glide from branch to branch.

PROTARCHAEOPTERYX
Jurassic, 150 mya
Asia
1m (3ft 3in) long

A feathered dinosaur from China, *Protarchaeopteryx* is notable for its long arms with their three-fingered clawed hands, and its fan-like tail. Its wing feathers were symmetrical in shape, like those of modern flightless birds. From this, it is thought that *Protarchaeopteryx* would not have been able to fly. However, because its arms and hands were so similar to those of small meat-eating dinosaurs, it is thought that the flight stroke of birds evolved from the up-and-down action of grasping for prey. But why did meat-eating dinosaurs grow feathers if they were not, at first, used for flight? The answer seems to be that feathers were grown for insulation – they were to keep the animals warm.

Protarchaeopteryx

MICRORAPTOR

Cretaceous, 125 mya
Asia
40cm (1ft 4in) long

A feathered dinosaur from China, *Microraptor* was an early member of the dromaeosaur family – the group of 'running lizards' that includes *Velociraptor*. Like other 'dino-birds', *Microraptor* did not have fully formed feathers, and it almost certainly could not fly. Instead, its body was covered with warm, fluffy down. Scientists who have studied its feet think that *Microraptor* used them to hold on to the branches of trees. This suggests that *Microraptor* may have spent some of its time off the ground, living partly in the trees. It had many small teeth, suitable for nipping at insects and other prey.

Microraptor

BAMBIRAPTOR

Cretaceous, 75 mya
North America
1m (3ft 3in) long

Bambiraptor

About the size of a modern-day chicken, *Bambiraptor* was a small meat-eating dinosaur whose body was covered in downy feathers to keep it warm. It probably could not fly – but it was a speedy runner, able to chase after prey such as small mammals and reptiles, which it killed using a combination of bites from its sharp teeth, kicks from its long toe-claws, and possibly even striking out with its whip-like tail.

TAKING TO THE TREES

A few years ago the idea of dinosaurs climbing trees would have seemed out of the question. Now though, as new species of feathered dinosaurs come to light, whose feet seem to have been made for grasping, it seems that these small creatures were tree climbers – like birds.

China has emerged as the place to find feathered dinosaurs, in an area of the country where the fine-grained rock has preserved the most delicate impressions of feathers. From these discoveries, the links between dinosaurs and birds are becoming ever clearer.

CAUDIPTERYX

Cretaceous, 130 mya
Asia
1m (3ft 3in) long
Caudipteryx, a feathered dinosaur from China, could not fly. Its arms were not long enough to work as wings, and its symmetrical 'flight' feathers, which were straight and even, were the wrong shape to get it airborne. To fly like a bird it would have needed asymmetrical flight feathers – ones that were curved and uneven. *Caudipteryx* had long legs and a short head with teeth at the front of the upper jaw. Its fan-like tail had feathers that grew to 20cm (8in) long. Like some modern birds, it swallowed small stones, which crushed its food to a digestible pulp.

Caudipteryx

SINORNITHOSAURUS

Cretaceous, 125 mya
Asia
1m (3ft 3in) long

Sinornithosaurus

The remarkable discovery about *Sinornithosaurus*, a turkey-sized carnivorous dinosaur from China, was not that it had feathers, but that it could 'flap' its arms. This was because its shoulder bones allowed it to move its arms up and down, raising them above its shoulders in a bird-like flapping motion. Scientists think that *Sinornithosaurus* used the up-and-down arm-flapping motion to keep balance while it ran at speed, chasing after small prey which it caught and ate.

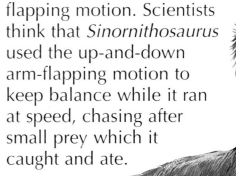

SINOSAUROPTERYX

Cretaceous, 130 mya
Asia
1m (3ft 3in) long

Sinosauropteryx

When scientists looked at the stomach area of *Sinosauropteryx*, a 'dino-bird' from China, they found traces of its last meal. This flightless bird-like creature was clearly a meat-eater, because inside its stomach were the jaw bones of a small mammal. *Sinosauropteryx*, like many other theropods, had sharp teeth with serrated edges – well suited to cutting into flesh. Unable to fly, its feathers were probably to insulate its body, keeping it warm.

FEATHERS FOR DISPLAY

Caudipteryx, meaning 'Tail Feather', was named after its eye-catching tail feathers. They may have been colourful and used in courtship displays, fanned out to attract a mate, just as birds do today. Perhaps it also spread its feathers so it seemed bigger than it really was – a trick to scare another animal away.

BEIPIAOSAURUS

Cretaceous, 125 mya
Asia
2.1m (7ft) long
Large and heavily-built, *Beipiaosaurus*, from China, is the biggest dinosaur so far known to have had feathers on some or all of its body, particularly its arms and legs. Its arms ended in scythe-like claws, like those of *Therizinosaurus*, to which it is related. Some scientists think it was a herbivore.

Beipiaosaurus

CHAPTER THREE

GIANT PLANT-EATING DINOSAURS

SAUROPODS – THE GIANT PLANT-EATERS

It was the famous American fossil-hunter Othniel Charles Marsh (1831–99) who gave a name to the biggest dinosaurs ever to live on land. In 1878, Marsh named them sauropods, meaning 'Lizard Feet'. These giants were plant-eaters (herbivores), and they first appeared about 220 million years ago. They were most abundant in the Jurassic period. The last of the sauropods died about 65 million years ago.

CREATURE FEATURES

Sauropods walked on all-fours, on thick, pillar-like legs. Adults ranged from 7m (23ft) to a massive 40m (130ft) long. They had long necks, long tails, and, for such big animals, their heads were surprisingly small.

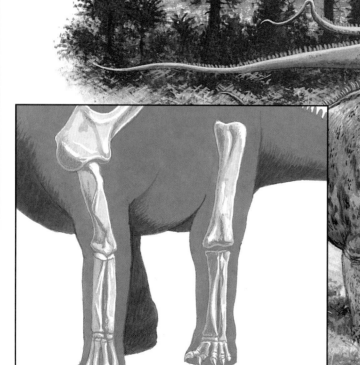

Brachiosaurus

Strong legs were essential to support the great weight of a sauropod's body. The leg bones of a sauropod were the longest and thickest bones in its skeleton.

FOOD FOR ALL THE FAMILY

Being tall had advantages. With such long necks, sauropods reached up to the tops of trees, where they ate foliage that smaller plant-eaters could not get to – including their own young. While adults browsed high up, their young ate leaves that grew lower down the trees. This way there was food for all, with the young not having to compete with their parents for food.

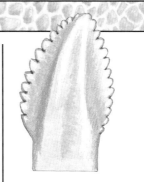
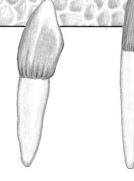

Plateosaurus tooth **Apatosaurus tooth** **Diplodocus tooth**

The teeth of herbivores were shaped to strip leaves from branches. Some had teeth shaped like spoons, others had peg-shaped teeth.

BIG FOR DEFENCE

Being big had advantages. The larger an animal is, the better it can defend itself, and this was probably true for sauropods. They could not outrun meat-eating dinosaurs, but their size meant that in an attack they could lash out with great power, using their feet and tails to inflict serious injuries.

WHERE IN THE WORLD?

Sauropods were a successful group of dinosaurs. They colonised wide areas of the world, and their fossils have been found on every continent – but not on Antarctica, yet.

Diplodocus

Camarasaurus

In a Jurassic landscape of about 150 million years ago, Brachiosaurus and other giant herbivores reach up to nip the leaves from the tops of trees.

Around 230 million years ago, a group of dinosaurs with long necks, small heads and large bodies appeared on Earth. They were plant-eaters and they flourished for some 50 million years, until they died out 180 million years ago. These were the prosauropods, which means 'before sauropods'. It is not known for certain whether they gave rise to the sauropods. Some scientists think they did, but there are some who think they are not related at all.

MELANOROSAURUS

Triassic, 220 mya
South Africa
12.2m (40ft) long

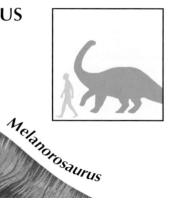

Melanorosaurus

Melanorosaurus, from South Africa, was a large, heavily built dinosaur with a long tail. It walked on all-fours, and its back legs were longer than its front legs. Its feet had five toes. Although no skull has yet been found for *Melanorosaurus*, it is thought that like other prosauropods it too had a small head, at the end of a long neck.

Melanorosaurus, and the other members of the prosauropod family, were the first dinosaurs to live entirely on a diet of plants.

PLATEOSAURUS

Triassic, 220 mya
Europe
7m (23ft) long
Plateosaurus is one of Europe's oldest giant dinosaurs. It had a small skull which was long and narrow, a long neck, and a pear-shaped body. Its weight was concentrated around its hips, and its back legs were longer than its front limbs. *Plateosaurus* may have been able to rear up on its back legs to reach the tops of tall trees, and it may also have been able to run upright on its hind legs to escape from danger. For most of the time it may have moved around on all-fours. It is thought that *Plateosaurus* was a herd animal.

Plateosaurus

MUSSAURUS

Triassic, 215 million years ago
South America
3m (10ft) long

Mussaurus was one of the earliest plant-eating dinosaurs of South America. It lived in a desert-like habitat, possibly in herds. Although no adults have yet been discovered, hatchlings have been found at a nest site. Baby *Mussaurus* hatched from eggs that were 2.5cm (1in) long – smaller than a hen's egg. An adult *Mussaurus* may have reached the size of a hippopotamus. It would have eaten tough cycad and conifer vegetation, whereas its young would have eaten the softer parts of plants.

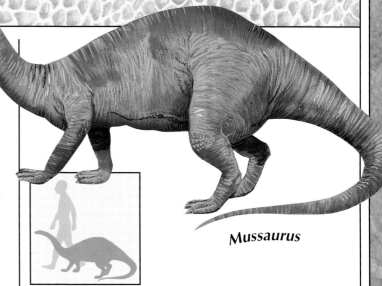

Mussaurus

WALKING WITH PLANT-EATERS

The prosauropods – and the sauropods who came after them – walked with their legs straight down beneath their bodies, as elephants do today. Fossilised footprints show that they walked this way.

RIOJASAURUS

Triassic, 220 mya
South America
11m (36ft) long

Riojasaurus

Riojasaurus was one of the largest, and also one of the earliest, of the prosauropod dinosaurs.

Unlike some of its relatives, such as *Plateosaurus*, this animal could not rear up on its back legs, even though they were slightly longer than its front legs. *Riojasaurus* kept all four feet on the ground when it walked, and when it browsed for food among high-growing vegetation. Despite its great size, *Riojasaurus* was not a particularly heavy dinosaur. Its backbones had hollow spaces inside them, helping to keep the animal's weight down. Because the sauropods, who appeared later, also had hollow backbones, some scientists believe this is evidence that they were descended from prosauropods, such as *Riojasaurus*.

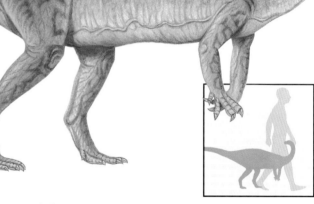

Thecodontosaurus

The world looked very different when the prosauropods were alive. The continents as we know them today did not exist. Instead, all Earth's land was joined together as one supercontinent, known as Pangaea. Dinosaurs wandered wherever they liked. However, when Pangaea split apart, today's continents began to form. The pieces of land moved around the globe, taking prosauropods and other animals with them. Fossils of prosauropod dinosaurs have been found on every continent – even Antarctica.

SELLOSAURUS

Triassic, 225 mya
Europe
2.4m (8ft) long
This small, lightly-built dinosaur was both bipedal and quadrupedal – it could walk on two legs and on four. It had five-fingered hands, with huge thumb claws. A plant-eater, it had a long tail, and its back legs were longer than those at the front. _Sellosaurus_ was similar to _Plateosaurus_, but it lived slightly before it, and it was also smaller. Its teeth were also different, which has led scientists to think it ate softer plants than _Plateosaurus_.

Sellosaurus

THECODONTOSAURUS

Triassic, 210 million years ago
Europe
2.1m (7ft) long
Thecodontosaurus had long legs and short arms. It is thought that it walked on all-fours when it was grazing at ground level, but when it spotted a meal growing high up it stretched up on its back legs. It may also have reared up on its hind legs in order to run or trot over short distances.

Thecodontosaurus had four toes on each foot and five fingers on each hand. Huge claws grew on its thumbs. They may have been used as hooks, to tug at and pull branches towards its mouth. It had spoon-shaped cheek teeth with serrated edges that pointed upwards.

LUFENGOSAURUS

Jurassic, 200 mya
Asia
6m (20ft) long

Lufengosaurus was a relative of *Plateosaurus*, whose fossils have been found in China. It was a long-necked animal with a small head, and its jaws held many widely spaced teeth.

Lufengosaurus was a plant-eater that walked on all-fours, though it may have been able to stand on its hind legs to reach high-growing leaves. It had long fingers, and big claws grew on its thumbs.

Lufengosaurus

Anchisaurus

GULPING THEIR FOOD DOWN

Plant-eating dinosaurs were leaf strippers and swallowers. Their teeth grew with spaces between them, so they could 'comb' soft leaves from the branches. Because they did not have chewing teeth, food that went into their mouths was gulped down, powerful muscles in their necks forcing it on its way to their stomachs.

ANCHISAURUS

Jurassic, 190 million years ago
North America, Africa
2.4m (8ft) long

A small plant-eating dinosaur, *Anchisaurus* walked on all-fours, with its body close to the ground.

However, when it was feeding, it might have been able to rear up on its back legs, resting its tail on the ground to support its body. By doing this it could reach vegetation that grew high up, biting off leaves with its ridged, spoon-shaped teeth, and holding them in its cheeks until ready to be swallowed. Once inside its stomach, the leaves were probably crushed to a digestible pulp by small stones, called gastroliths. *Anchisaurus* may have used its thumb claws to hook leafy branches, pulling them to its mouth.

MASSOSPONDYLUS

An example of a long-necked, long-tailed herbivore that lived in the early Jurassic period, *Massospondylus* was a prosauropod. It was a dinosaur that came before the truly giant plant-eaters of the later Jurassic, and it was a sign of what was to come.

LONG AND LOW

Massospondylus was long and low, measuring little more than 1m (3ft) tall at the hips. Like other prosauropods it had a bulky body, a long neck and tail, and its head was small. Its jaws had rounded peg-like front teeth, which were designed for stripping leaves from branches. *Massospondylus* had big hands with large thumb claws.

In a scene from the early Jurassic period of 200 million years ago, a group of Massospondylus *browse on low-growing vegetation, and on leaves at the top of tree ferns and ginkgoes.*

REACHING UP

It is thought that *Massospondylus*, like many other prosauropods, could raise its front legs off the ground, enabling it to walk on its hind legs over short distances and also to stretch up to reach high-growing vegetation. Like today's cattle, *Massospondylus* probably spent most of its time eating, and it may have travelled far in search of food. *Massospondylus* may have lived in herds, and it was a very common dinosaur in what is now South Africa, where many fossilised skeletons have been found.

STOMACH STONES

Herbivores swallowed stones which settled in their gizzards. Stomach stones, or gastroliths, crushed vegetation they ate into a digestible pulp. A Massospondylus from Zimbabwe, Southern Africa had gastroliths that came from 20km (12.5 miles) away from where its skeleton was found.

TREE-EATER

Massospondylus ate the vegetation of the Jurassic period – conifer needles, fronds from palms and tree ferns, leaves of the ginkgo tree, and horse-tails on the ground.

Name: *Massospondylus*
Lived: *200 mya*
Found: *Africa, North America*
Length: *5m (16ft)*
Diet: *Plants*
Habitat: *Open woodland*

MASSOSPONDYLUS THUMB CLAW

Massospondylus *had five fingers on its hands, and a large curved claw grew at the end of its thumbs. Perhaps these claws were used to scratch up vegetation, or to hook high branches and pull them towards its mouth.*

The sauropod family tree can be divided into several groups of giant plant-eating dinosaurs. Each group is different from the others. One group, known as the cetiosaurs, includes some of the first sauropods to have evolved. These animals had long necks, long tails and heavy bodies. Many of them had solid backbones, which was a feature of primitive, or early, sauropods.

Cetiosaurus

BARAPASAURUS

Jurassic, 200 mya
Asia
18m (60ft) long
One of the oldest of all sauropods, *Barapasaurus*, from India, had a big, heavy body, a long tail, and slender legs which were unusual in a giant plant-eater – other sauropods had thicker legs. Unfortunately its skull has not yet been found, but some of its teeth have. They were spoon-shaped and had serrated edges, and were clearly designed for combing leaves from branches. *Barapasaurus* may have lived in herds.

CETIOSAURUS

Jurassic, 175 mya
Europe, Africa
18m (60ft) long
Cetiosaurus is famous for being the first sauropod to be discovered, and also the first sauropod to be given a scientific name. Its giant bones were found in England in 1809, and in 1841 it was named *Cetiosaurus*, meaning 'Whale Lizard'. It was given this name, by the people who first studied it more than 150 years ago, because they thought it was some kind of sea creature, perhaps a giant whale or crocodile. Only later was it realised that it was a land-living animal. *Cetiosaurus* walked on four pillar-like legs. Because its neck was stiff, *Cetiosaurus* could not raise its head much higher than its shoulders.

Haplocanthosaurus

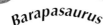
Barapasaurus

HAPLOCANTHOSAURUS

Jurassic, 150 million years ago
North America
22m (71ft) long

No complete fossils have yet been found of this sauropod – its skull is missing as are the last few bones from its tail. Despite the missing pieces, it is clear that *Haplocanthosaurus* was a large, four-legged plant-eater with a long neck and back, and long front legs. *Haplocanthosaurus* is the most primitive sauropod yet discovered in North America. Primitive, or early, sauropods had solid backbones – weight-saving hollow bones evolved amongst giant herbivores that lived later in the Jurassic period.

SHUNOSAURUS

Jurassic, 170 mya
China
10m (33ft) long

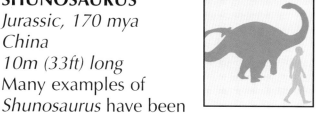

Many examples of *Shunosaurus* have been found in China, and it is one of the best-known sauropod dinosaurs. Its most striking feature was a spiky, bony club at the end of its long tail, formed from bones which had fused together. This heavy weight may have been lashed out at an attacker, forcing it to keep its distance. *Shunosaurus* is the only sauropod known to have had a tail club – a feature that is associated more with armoured dinosaurs such as *Ankylosaurus*.

Shunosaurus

HOLLOW BONES

As sauropods increased in size during the Jurassic period, their backbones changed. Instead of being formed from solid bone, they developed hollow spaces inside them. They were still strong enough to support the animal, but being hollow helped to reduce the animal's weight.

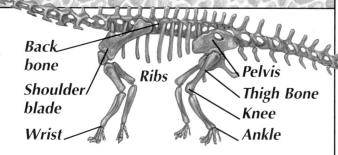

Back bone

Shoulder blade

Ribs

Wrist

Pelvis

Thigh Bone

Knee

Ankle

The camarasaurs were another group of sauropods. They emerged during the late Jurassic period, and seem to have survived until the end of the Age of Reptiles. Although they looked like other giant herbivores, camarasaurs had forward-pointing teeth, which in some species filled their jaws. It is these features that set them apart from other sauropod groups.

CAMARASAURUS

Jurassic, 150 million years ago
North America, Europe
18m (60ft) long
Camarasaurus had a small, long head with a blunt, round snout. Its strong jaws were packed with wide spoon-shaped teeth, designed to cut through tough, woody vegetation. While other plant-eaters grazed on the soft, juicy parts of plants, Camarasaurus ate the parts they didn't, such as twigs and branches. Only its young seem to have eaten softer vegetation. Its front legs were about the same length as its hind legs, and because of this Camarasaurus stood with its back level to the ground. It may have lived in herds, and bones found with grooves scratched on to them show that it was the victim of meat-eating dinosaurs, such as *Allosaurus*.

EUHELOPUS

Jurassic, 150 million years ago
Asia
15m (49ft) long
Unlike many other sauropods which had teeth only at the front of their jaws, *Euhelopus*, from China, had teeth all around its mouth – a feature it had in common with *Camarasaurus*. Even though their jaws and teeth were similar, *Euhelopus* had a much longer neck than *Camarasaurus*. Its neck contained 19 bones, which, in a fully-grown adult, reached about 5m (16.5ft) long, whereas *Camarasaurus* had a 12-bone neck, 3m (10ft) long. Its front and back legs were almost the same size as each other, which would have meant it walked with a level back, not a sloping one. *Euhelopus* had large nostrils on top of its head.

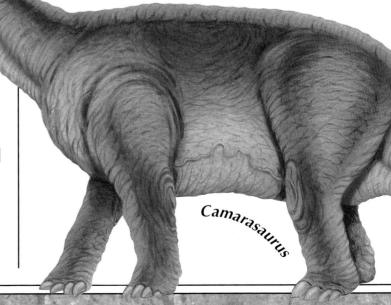

Euhelopus

Camarasaurus

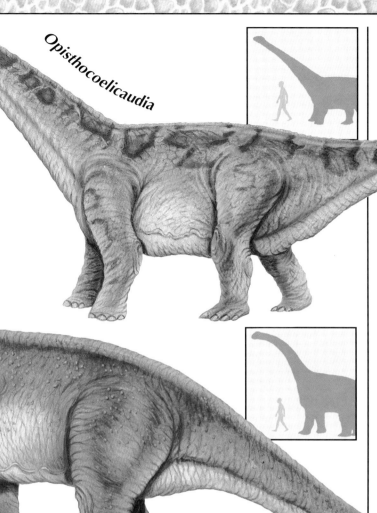

Opisthocoelicaudia

OPISTHOCOELICAUDIA
Cretaceous, 70 million years ago
Asia
12m (40ft) long

Opisthocoelicaudia lived
in Mongolia, in open forests,
where trees gave way to areas of
low-growing plants. It was one of the
last of the sauropods, and although
most scientists group it with the
camarasaurs, there are some who think
it belongs to another group – the
titanosaurs. Unfortunately, the skull and
neck of Opisthocoelicaudia have not
been found, so the mystery about
which group to put it in cannot be
easily solved. Its tail bones were found,
and because they were unusually
strong for a sauropod, scientists wonder
if it could have rested on its tail,
lifting its front legs off the
ground so it could reach
high-growing leaves.

CAMARASAURUS SKULL

The skull of Camarasaurus *shows that it had
big eyes and big nostrils. Its nose was on
top of its head. There were other holes in its
skull, helping to reduce its weight. This
sauropod probably had good eyesight and
smell, two important senses which would
have helped it find food and alert it
when dangerous meat-eaters came
near. Its teeth were up to 4cm
(1.5in) wide, each one
coated in a thick layer
of rough enamel.*

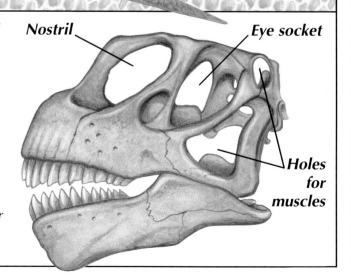

Nostril

Eye socket

Holes for muscles

BRACHIOSAURUS

Brachiosaurus was one of the 'giraffes' of the dinosaur world. It had an incredibly long neck and could reach high into the trees, as well as stretching out over a wide area of ground. After it had bitten off a mouthful of leaves, they were swallowed, unchewed. They went into its gizzard, where stomach stones, or gastroliths, crushed them into a pulp. To stay alive, it needed to eat 200 kg (440 lbs) of plants every day.

A forest of late Jurassic conifer trees is stripped of its leaves by a herd of hungry Brachiosaurus dinosaurs.

A GOOD SENSE OF SMELL

Brachiosaurus had nostrils on top of its head. The nasal openings were large and it is thought it had a good sense of smell. Perhaps its sense of smell was better than its sight, in which case it might have smelled food and other animals before seeing them.

— Nostril

Eye socket

MINIATURE BRAIN

The striking feature of *Brachiosaurus* was its very long, graceful neck. However, for such a huge creature, its head was small in proportion to the rest of its body, and its brain was tiny. It walked on four pillar-like legs and, unlike most other dinosaurs, its front legs were longer than its back legs. This meant that its body sloped down towards its short tail.

HERD DWELLER

Brachiosaurus is thought to have been a group animal, living in a herd. It probably spent most of its time either searching for food, or eating. When it came across a supply of food its long neck would have been put to good use. *Brachiosaurus* could stretch up to the tops of the tallest trees to graze foliage that grew 12–16m (40–52ft) above the ground. With its 52 chisel-like teeth it tugged and nipped away at leaves.

HIGH AND LOW

Brachiosaurus ate the main plants of the Jurassic period – leaves from ginkgo trees, conifer needles, palm fronds, and low-growing horsetails. Did *Brachiosaurus* rear up on its back legs, stretching its neck high into the air to reach leaves that grew at the top of tall trees? Or did it keep all four legs firmly on the ground, sweeping its neck from side to side as it grazed low-growing plants? Experts think that both these ideas could be correct.

BRACHIOSAURUS FACT FILE

Name: *Brachiosaurus*
Lived: *150 million years ago*
Found: *Africa, Europe, North America*
Length: *25m (82ft)*
Diet: *Plants*
Habitat: *Open woodland*

The group of sauropods known as diplodocids, meaning 'double beams' after beam-shaped bones in their tails, were the longest animals ever to live on Earth. They were like walking suspension bridges whose long necks were counterbalanced by even longer tails. Diplodocids were common dinosaurs in North America and East Africa in the late Jurassic period.

Apatosaurus

MAMENCHISAURUS

Jurassic, 160 mya
Asia
25m (82ft) long
Mamenchisaurus, from China, had one of the longest necks of all dinosaurs, measuring some 14m (46ft) long – more than half the animal's entire length! Its neck had 19 bones in it, each of which was supported by two overlapping rod-like ribs. This arrangement made its neck quite stiff, and it could only bend at the head and shoulders. *Mamenchisaurus* had a small box-shaped head, and its jaws held spoon-shaped teeth which were the ideal shape for combing through vegetation, stripping leaves from their branches. Stomach stones crushed the leaves to a digestible pulp.

Mamenchisaurus

APATOSAURUS

Jurassic, 150 million years ago
North America
21m (69ft) long
For a massive animal, *Apatosaurus* had a surprisingly small head, inside which was a tiny brain. A fully-grown adult *Apatosaurus* weighed up to 30 tonnes, its great weight supported by four thick legs. Its front legs were shorter than its back legs.

Each foot had short, stubby toes. On the front feet the toes were blunt, but the toes of the back feet ended in claws. As each foot pressed into soft ground, it made a footprint up to 1m (3ft 3in) wide. The nostrils of *Apatosaurus* were on top of its head. It was once thought it was a water-dweller, wading through deep water with its head held high like a snorkel. This idea is no longer thought likely.

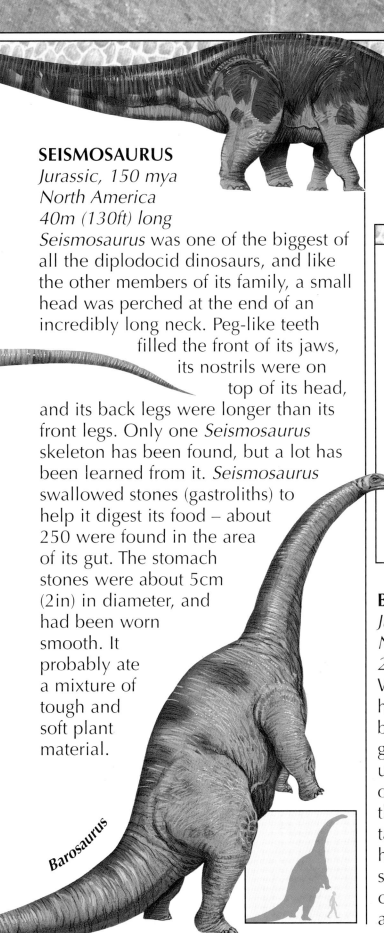

SEISMOSAURUS

Jurassic, 150 mya
North America
40m (130ft) long

Seismosaurus was one of the biggest of all the diplodocid dinosaurs, and like the other members of its family, a small head was perched at the end of an incredibly long neck. Peg-like teeth filled the front of its jaws, its nostrils were on top of its head, and its back legs were longer than its front legs. Only one *Seismosaurus* skeleton has been found, but a lot has been learned from it. *Seismosaurus* swallowed stones (gastroliths) to help it digest its food – about 250 were found in the area of its gut. The stomach stones were about 5cm (2in) in diameter, and had been worn smooth. It probably ate a mixture of tough and soft plant material.

Barosaurus

Seismosaurus

'WHIPLASH' TAILS

All diplodocids had long tails that tapered to thin whip-like ends. In an attack from a predatory meat-eating dinosaur, a diplodocid might have lashed out with its tail, using it like a whip to scare the attacker away.

BAROSAURUS

Jurassic, 150 million years ago
North America, Africa
27m (89ft) long

Why did diplodocids like *Barosaurus* have short front legs? It might have been a weight-saving feature, put to good use when these giants stretched up to feed. Perhaps *Barosaurus* and the others in its family were able to raise their chests and forelimbs, using their tails to support their weight. *Barosaurus* had an especially long neck, and at full stretch, with front legs raised high, it could reach plants growing 15m (49ft) above ground level.

Animals as big as diplodocids may have lived to be more than 100 years old. In its lifetime, an individual would have eaten tonnes of food, from soft leaves to woody stems. These dinosaurs were 'eating machines', whose small, pencil-like teeth nipped away day after day, while inside their bellies, stomach stones rolled around, mashing the plants to a juicy pulp.

SUPERSAURUS

Jurassic, 150 million years ago
North America
42m (138ft) long

Supersaurus lives up to its name – it was a super-sized dinosaur, one of the largest animals ever to have walked the Earth. Not only was it incredibly long (almost the length of two tennis courts), but from toe to head it was 16.5m (54ft) tall, its neck was 12m (39ft) long, and it weighed as much as 50 tonnes. *Supersaurus* supported its great weight on four pillar-like legs, and its feet spread out with wide, fleshy heel cushions, like those of an elephant. As it walked, its heel cushions acted as shock absorbers – its soles spread out to absorb the impact of each giant step. *Supersaurus* may have lived in herds that moved between feeding grounds. It is thought that it walked with its neck and tail more or less level with the ground.

DICRAEOSAURUS

Jurassic, 150 mya
Africa
14m (46ft) long

A smaller member of the diplodocid family, with a shorter neck and tail, but with a larger head, *Dicraeosaurus* is notable for its distinctive ridged back. This unusual feature, seen in only one other diplodocid, *Amargasaurus*, came from bone spines that projected upwards from its backbone, from its tail to its neck. Each spine opened out at the top to form a 'Y' shape, to which muscles were attached. *Dicraeosaurus* and *Amargasaurus* are thought to belong to an offshoot of the diplodocid family.

Dicraeosaurus

Supersaurus

AMARGASAURUS

Cretaceous, 130 mya
South America
10m (33ft) long
Amargasaurus was a medium-sized member of the diplodocid family, whose most notable feature was a double row of spines that extended 65cm (2ft 1in) out from its neck. Shorter spines also grew along its back. While some scientists think the spines supported a skin frill, others think they were covered in a hard, horn-like sheath – perhaps to be used as weapons of self-defence if *Amargasaurus* was attacked by a meat-eating predator. This dinosaur is known from a single set of fossils, found in Argentina. Its tail was not found, so its size is not known for certain.

A NECK FRILL ON AMARGASAURUS?

Amargasaurus had two rows of long, bony spines growing from its backbone, particularly along its neck. They may have had a covering of skin forming a frill, or a pair of frills. If so, this feature might have been a temperature regulator, used to absorb and release heat. Or perhaps it was used in courtship displays to attract a mate. Or maybe it was to scare predators away.

Amargasaurus

SMALL HEADS

Unlike carnivores such as Allosaurus, diplodocids had small heads which were long and sloping. Their eyes were set far back from the front of their snouts, and their nostrils were on top of their heads, usually above their eyes. Pencil-like teeth grew in the front of their jaws.

Diplodocus (10 tonnes)

Allosaurus (3 tonnes)

DIPLODOCUS

Diplodocus was one of the largest of the diplodocid dinosaurs. It is also one of the most studied. Over the years, ideas about it have changed. Once it was thought it dragged its tail on the ground when it moved. Now it is thought it held its tail aloft. Once it was thought it could reach up to the treetops. Now it seems it could hardly raise its head above its shoulders.

TAPERING TAIL

Diplodocus – 'Double Beam' – got its name from its long and flexible tail. There was an extra length of bone beneath each of its tail vertebrae, which protected the blood vessels inside its tail, and also strengthened it.

Their great necks stretched out in front, gently swaying as they walk, a Diplodocus herd moves on to the next feeding ground. If attacked, they might have lashed out with their tails, to scare away any predators.

10-TONNE BEAST

Diplodocus had a neck that was about 8m (26ft) long. Its tail was even longer, stretching out behind it for up to 14m (46ft) – about half of the dinosaur's total length. For such a giant-sized animal, *Diplodocus* had a tiny head, measuring only about 0.5m (2ft) long. Inside its mouth were many peg-like teeth that grew only in the front of its jaws. There were no teeth in the sides or back of its mouth. The back legs of *Diplodocus* were longer than its front legs, and there were five toes on each foot. *Diplodocus* weighed in at around 10 tonnes – about the same as two large elephants. For an animal as big and bulky as *Diplodocus*, it was lightweight because the bones of its spine had hollow spaces inside them.

HEAD HELD LOW

When it was on the move, *Diplodocus* held its neck and tail more or less level with the ground. Scientists believe that *Diplodocus* lived in herds, travelling from one feeding ground to the next. Recent studies suggest that it could not raise its neck much above its shoulder height. If so, then it could not have stretched up to reach leaves on trees, as many other sauropods did.

FERN-EATER

If *Diplodocus* could not raise its head higher than its shoulders, then it must have lived on a diet of low-growing plants, such as horsetails and ferns – not leaves from the tops of trees.

Name: *Diplodocus*
Lived: *150 million years ago*
Found: *North America*
Length: *27m (89ft)*
Diet: *Plants*
Habitat: *Open woodland*

DIPLODOCUS SKULL

The skull of Diplodocus *shows how its teeth were only in the front of its jaws. With a tug of its head, these forward-facing teeth combed their way through foliage, stripping off a mouthful of food.* Diplodocus *had between 50 and 60 weak peg-like teeth, and no chewing teeth.*

Nostril

Eye socket

Argentinosaurus

The last group of sauropods to appear were the titanosaurs, meaning 'gigantic lizards'. This group included animals that ranged from 7m (23ft) to giants of up to 30m (100ft) in length. Some, or perhaps all, had bony body armour – the only sauropods to have evolved this distinctive feature. The titanosaurs first appeared in the late Jurassic or early Cretaceous period, about 145 million years ago, and survived until the Age of Reptiles ended, 65 million years ago.

SALTASAURUS

Cretaceous, 80 mya
South America
12m (40ft) long
One of the smallest titanosaurs,

Saltasaurus, from Argentina, is also one of the most unusual. Until this dinosaur was discovered no one had suspected that sauropods had evolved 'armoured' skin, designed to withstand an attack from a predator. Apart from its skin, *Saltasaurus* had many features in common with other sauropods, such as a long, flexible neck, pillar-like legs, and a slender tail.

ARGENTINOSAURUS

Cretaceous, 90 mya
South America
30m (100ft) long
This is the heaviest of all known dinosaurs – the largest land animal ever to have lived. Only a few of its bones have been found, including backbones which are 1.5m (5ft) tall. From these it has been possible to work out the likely size of this giant dinosaur, which may have weighed 100 tonnes, or more. To reduce its weight, *Argentinosaurus* had hollow ribs – an unusual feature for a plant-eating dinosaur. It may have been hunted by the meat-eating *Giganotosaurus*.

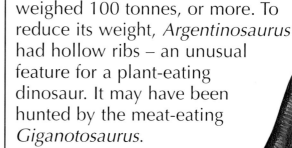

Saltasaurus

ALAMOSAURUS
Cretaceous, 70 mya
North America
21m (68ft) long

Alamosaurus is the only titanosaur from North America. It was one of the last of the giant plant-eaters, living right at the end of the Age of Reptiles. It would have made an unusual sight, since there had been no sauropods on the continent of North America for about 35 million years. Scientists think that *Alamosaurus* migrated into North America from South America – where most titanosaurs lived – after the Isthmus of Panama (a land bridge) joined the continents together.

MALAWISAURUS
Cretaceous, 100 mya
Africa
10m (33ft) long

Malawisaurus

Alamosaurus

Malawisaurus is one of the oldest titanosaurs to have been discovered, and also one of the smallest. It takes its name from the country where its fossils were discovered – Malawi in eastern Africa. Fortunately (and unusually), parts of its skull have been found, along with other fossilised bones. It is thought that *Malawisaurus* might have been armour-plated, but there is no evidence to prove this.

SALTASAURUS SKIN ARMOUR

Saltasaurus is notable for its unusual armour-plated skin. Oval, bony plates, about 10cm (4in) across, with pea-sized nodules between them, studded its back. A toughened skin like this was probably intended to protect Saltasaurus from the teeth and claws of meat-eating predators. In an attack, a carnivore would probably have looked for an unprotected part of the body to attack, such as the animal's soft belly.

As complete titanosaur skeletons are rarely found, it is hard to know what these big dinosaurs looked like. Because peg-like teeth found with their bones are like those from better-known dinosaurs, it used to be thought the titanosaurs belonged to the diplodocid family. Now, however, it seems this is just a coincidence, so titanosaurs are thought of as a separate group.

JANENSCHIA

Jurassic, 155 million years ago
Africa
24m (79ft) long

Janenschia is known from one incomplete specimen, from Tanzania. Its head was missing, as were many other important bones. For many years it has been thought of as one of the oldest of the titanosaurs, and one of the very few to have been found outside South America, where the group was most abundant. However, scientists are now beginning to think *Janenschia* was not a titanosaur after all. Some think it belongs to the camarasaur group of dinosaurs.

PARALITITAN

Cretaceous, 95 mya
Africa
25m (82ft) long

Paralititan

One of the heaviest dinosaurs known to have lived, *Paralititan* weighed an estimated 50 to 80 tonnes. Discovered in Egypt, *Paralititan* lived in a tropical tidal zone, where there were swamps, beaches, and mangroves – thickets of trees whose roots grew down from the branches. Only one incomplete *Paralititan* has so far been found, but the sixteen bones unearthed show that it belonged to the titanosaur family. Its head was about 9m (30ft) from the ground.

Janenschia

STRONG HEART

Sauropods had massive hearts that were strong enough to pump blood around their bodies. Every time a sauropod raised its head above its heart, its heart had to work extra hard. It would have had to pump blood against the force of gravity, moving it 'uphill' as it travelled along the animal's neck towards its brain.

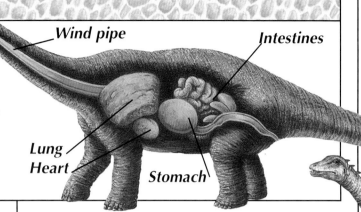

Wind pipe

Intestines

Lung

Heart

Stomach

AEGYPTOSAURUS

Cretaceous, 95 mya
Africa
15m (49ft) long

Named 'Egyptian Lizard' after the country where it was found, only a few backbones, leg bones, and part of a shoulder of *Aegyptosaurus* have ever been discovered. They were sent to Germany to be studied, but were destroyed in 1944, during the Second World War. Until new material is unearthed, *Aegyptosaurus* remains a mysterious dinosaur. It is considered to be a titanosaur because its leg bones are like those of *Saltasaurus*.

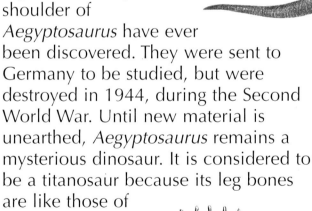

Antarctosaurus

ANTARCTOSAURUS

Cretaceous, 80 million years ago
South America, Asia
18m (60ft) long

Antarctosaurus, whose name means 'Southern Lizard' (a reference to it coming from the southern hemisphere), has been found in several countries of South America, and also in India.

At one time the continents of Asia and South America were joined, and *Antarctosaurus* would have been free to travel between them. Fragments of melon-sized round eggs have been found in South America, close to *Antarctosaurus* fossils. They could be *Antarctosaurus* eggs, or eggs of a titanosaur like it.

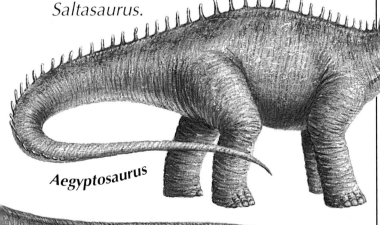

Aegyptosaurus

The titanosaurs were a widely distributed group of sauropods, whose fossilised remains have been found on all continents, except for Australia and Antarctica. Many specimens have been found in South America, where recent finds of eggs, thought to have been laid by titanosaurs, are revealing valuable information about the earliest stages in the life-cycle of these giant animals.

NEUQUENSAURUS
Cretaceous, 70 mya
South America
15m (49ft) long

Rapetosaurus

Neuquensaurus

Neuquensaurus, from Argentina, was a medium-sized titanosaur. It was a typical member of the group because its skin, particularly on its back, was covered in oval bony plates and bumps, known as osteoderms. These are bones that formed in the skin of dinosaurs, such as those found on the armoured dinosaur *Ankylosaurus*. Only parts of *Neuquensaurus* have so far been found, from which it seems it looked like *Saltasaurus*. It may turn out to be the same dinosaur, not a different one.

SAUROPOD EGGS

Eggs laid by sauropods were usually round, or almost round. They had a bumpy, textured surface. The eggshell of eggs thought to have been laid by titanosaurs was as thick as a pencil.

RAPETOSAURUS
Cretaceous, 70 mya
Africa
8m (26ft) long

A nearly complete skeleton of a young *Rapetosaurus* was found on the island of Madagascar, off the east coast of Africa. It is an important discovery because it is the first titanosaur found with its skull intact. Until it was unearthed in 1995, no one knew what the heads of these great animals looked like. *Rapetosaurus* had a small head with nostrils above its eyes, just like *Diplodocus*. However, the rest of its skull looks more like that of *Brachiosaurus*, to whom it seems to have been related. It had a long neck, and a long, slender tail.

HYPSELOSAURUS
Cretaceous, 70 mya
Europe
12m (40ft) long

Discovered in France and Spain, *Hypselosaurus* was an average-sized titanosaur, whose legs were thicker than other members of its family. It is notable for having been found close to a number of large eggs, almost round in shape, each about 30cm (1ft) long. It's difficult to prove the eggs were laid by *Hypselosaurus*, but if they were, this shows that sauropod dinosaurs were egg-layers (oviparous), and did not give birth to live young. A newly-hatched *Hypselosaurus* is thought to have weighed about 3kg (6.6lb), and an adult about 5 tonnes.

Hypselosaurus

A thick eggshell probably offered some protection to the embryo inside from predators. Pores on the eggshell allowed air to enter the egg for the embryo to breathe.

TITANOSAURUS

In 1871, part of a massive thighbone, 1.17m (3ft 10in) long was discovered near the town of Jabalpur, India. The bone was correctly identified as coming from a dinosaur, but it could not be matched to any dinosaur known at the time. When some large tail bones were unearthed in the same area of India, scientists realised they were dealing with a completely new dinosaur.

NAMING THE NEW DINOSAUR

The new dinosaur found in India was named *Titanosaurus indicus*, in 1877 by English geologist Richard Lydekker (1849–1915). The name meant 'Titanic Lizard from India', and, later, it was the first major dinosaur discovery in the southern hemisphere. It was the largest dinosaur then known, which was why Lydekker called it *Titanosaurus*, after the mighty Titans of Greek mythology – beings with great strength and power.

WHIP-LIKE TAIL

Titanosaurus looked similar to *Diplodocus*. It had a long neck and a whip-like, tapering tail. Like other titanosaurs, the skin on its back was studded with small armoured plates, or osteoderms.

TITANOSAURUS FACT FILE

Name: *Titanosaurus*
Lived: 70 mya
Found: *Africa, Asia, Europe, South America*
Length: 20m (66ft)

Diet: *Plants*
Habitat: *Open woodland*

In a late Cretaceous landscape, a group of Titanosaurus dinosaurs emerge from woodland to drink from a pool of fresh water.

OLD AND YOUNG TOGETHER

Titanosaurus may have been a herd dweller, constantly on the move with older and younger animals.

STONES IN THE STOMACH

As a herbivore, *Titanosaurus* probably ate the typical vegetation of the late Cretaceous period. Flowering plants, such as magnolia and viburnum, dominated the ground, replacing older species such as ferns and horsetails. There was no grass at this time. Oak, maple, walnut and beech trees grew alongside the still abundant conifers and cycads. Like other giant plant-eaters, *Titanosaurus* probably had stomach stones (gastroliths) in its gizzard, which crushed plants into a pulp that could be absorbed by the animal's digestive system.

DEATH OF A GIANT

Wherever Titanosaurus *went, its predators were not far behind. Its size was its best defence – the force carried by a flick of its tail, or a kick of a leg, would be enough to send an attacker reeling, in which case predators may have preyed on weaker animals – the young, the old, and the sick.*

CHAPTER FOUR

ARMOUR, HORNS AND PLATES

PLATED, ARMOURED, HORNED AND BONE-HEADED DINOSAURS

Not all plant-eating dinosaurs were massive, like the sauropods that thrived during the Jurassic period. They were just one of many groups of herbivores that evolved in the Age of Reptiles. Other groups of plant-eaters, smaller than the sauropods but every bit as interesting, included ones that evolved various forms of body ornaments – from bony plates that covered their backs, to spines and horns that grew from tails and faces. Scientists group these dinosaurs into several distinct families.

In a landscape of about 70 million years ago, a river provides drinking water for groups of armoured dinosaurs, horned dinosaurs, and bone-headed dinosaurs.

PLATED DINOSAURS

These were the stegosaurs – medium- to large-sized plant-eaters that walked on all-fours and which had several upright plates and spines growing from their backs and along their tails. The best known plated dinosaur is *Stegosaurus*.

Albertosaurus

Ankylosaurus

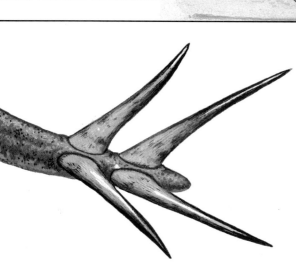

Some dinosaurs grew long, sharp spines at the end of their tails.

ARMOURED DINOSAURS

These were the nodosaurs and the ankylosaurs – medium-sized herbivores that walked on four short legs. Their bodies had bony plates embedded in the skin. Some had short body spines, others had tail clubs. The best known is *Ankylosaurus*.

HORNED AND BONE-HEADED DINOSAURS

Two other groups of dinosaurs with distinctive forms of body ornamentation were the ceratopsians (the horned dinosaurs) and the pachycephalosaurs (the bone-headed dinosaurs). Together, these two groups are known as marginocephalians, which means 'bordered heads' – a reference to their distinctive bony shields, skull shelves, and horns which grew from their heads. Some walked on all-fours (quadrupeds), others on two legs (bipeds). All were plant-eaters. The best known horned dinosaur is *Triceratops*. The best known bone-headed dinosaur is *Stegoceras*.

Torosaurus

Stegoceras

Some dinosaurs grew horns and bony shields, or frills, around their necks.

103

The stegosaurs lived on Earth for around 80 million years. They first appeared 170 million years ago, and a few members of the group survived until the mid-Cretaceous period, about 90 million years ago. Stegosaurs were at their most abundant 150 million years ago, at the end of the Jurassic period. They were widespread, and are known from Africa, Asia, Europe and North America.

SCELIDOSAURUS

Jurassic, 200 mya
Europe
4m (13ft) long

Although *Scelidosaurus* is not classified as a stegosaur, it is thought to be an ancestor of the group. It is not hard to see why, since its skin was studded with many small bony plates. Unlike the large, high-rise plates of stegosaurs, those on *Scelidosaurus* were small and low. Some plates were ridged, others were cone-shaped. *Scelidosaurus* seems to have been a slow-moving herbivore with a small head, whose tail was longer than that of a stegosaur.

DACENTRURUS

Jurassic, 155 mya
Europe
5m (16ft) long

Dacentrurus is one of the few plated dinosaurs discovered in Europe. It had pairs of spikes growing along its neck, body and tail, and was similar in appearance to the African stegosaur, *Kentrosaurus*.

Dacentrurus

Dacentrurus (this means 'Pointed Tail') was originally called *Omosaurus* ('Shoulder Lizard'), but this name had already been given to a species of extinct crocodile. When the mistake was realised, its name was changed.

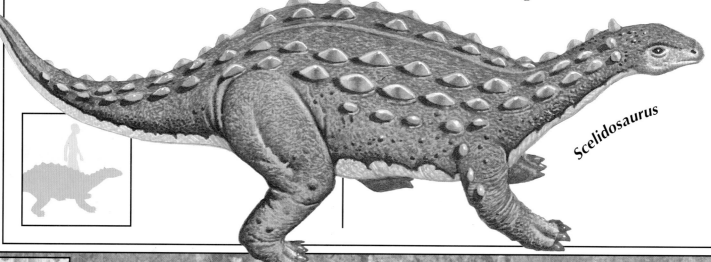

Scelidosaurus

TINY HEADS

All stegosaurs had small heads, about the same size as the predatory dromaeosaurs, such as Deinonychus. At the end of a stegosaur's head were beak-like horny sheaths – ideal for cropping low-growing vegetation. Its jaws held many small teeth which were designed for chewing and crushing plant material.

Stegosaur head

Dromaeosaur head

Kentrosaurus

KENTROSAURUS
Jurassic, 155 mya
Africa
5m (16ft) long
Two rows of bony plates were embedded into the skin of its back. There were fourteen plates in total, arranged in seven pairs, from its neck to half way down its body. Seven pairs of spines ran from its mid-section to the tip of its tail, and a spine protected each hip. Kentrosaurus had a small, narrow head inside which was a tiny brain – no bigger than a walnut. Its snout ended in a toothless beak and many small, weak teeth were packed inside its cheeks. Large nasal passages suggest it had a good sense of smell.

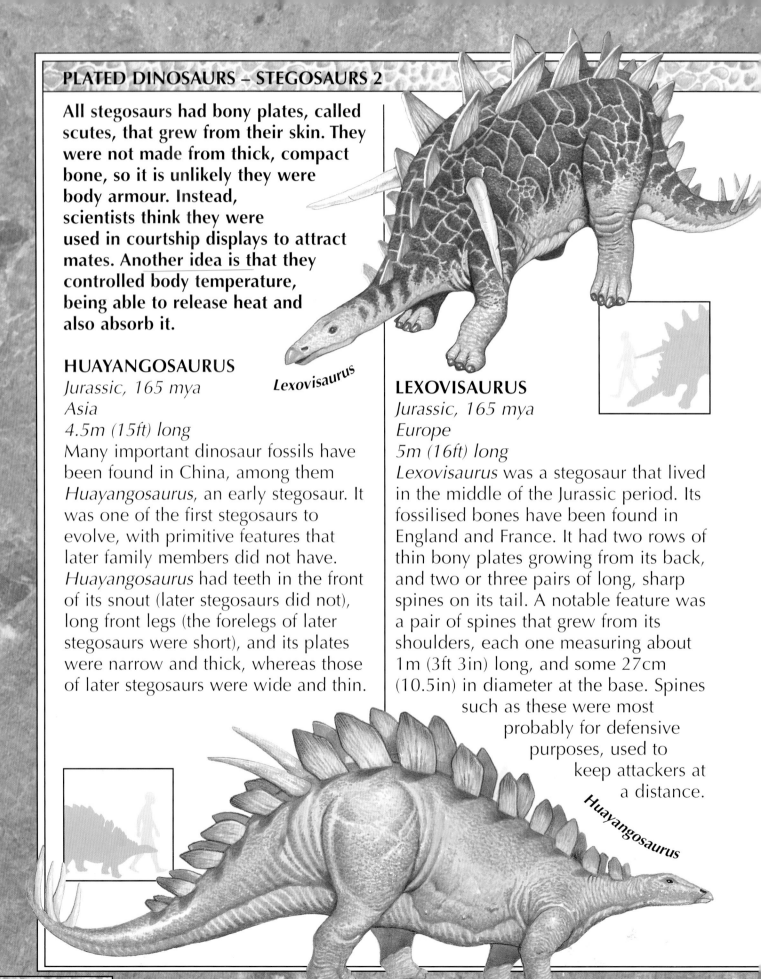

All stegosaurs had bony plates, called scutes, that grew from their skin. They were not made from thick, compact bone, so it is unlikely they were body armour. Instead, scientists think they were used in courtship displays to attract mates. Another idea is that they controlled body temperature, being able to release heat and also absorb it.

Lexovisaurus

HUAYANGOSAURUS

Jurassic, 165 mya
Asia
4.5m (15ft) long

Many important dinosaur fossils have been found in China, among them *Huayangosaurus*, an early stegosaur. It was one of the first stegosaurs to evolve, with primitive features that later family members did not have. *Huayangosaurus* had teeth in the front of its snout (later stegosaurs did not), long front legs (the forelegs of later stegosaurs were short), and its plates were narrow and thick, whereas those of later stegosaurs were wide and thin.

LEXOVISAURUS

Jurassic, 165 mya
Europe
5m (16ft) long

Lexovisaurus was a stegosaur that lived in the middle of the Jurassic period. Its fossilised bones have been found in England and France. It had two rows of thin bony plates growing from its back, and two or three pairs of long, sharp spines on its tail. A notable feature was a pair of spines that grew from its shoulders, each one measuring about 1m (3ft 3in) long, and some 27cm (10.5in) in diameter at the base. Spines such as these were most probably for defensive purposes, used to keep attackers at a distance.

Huayangosaurus

HIP AND SHOULDER SPINES

Several stegosaurs grew long, sharp spines from the sides of their bodies, either at the shoulders or the hips. Unlike their back plates which are not thought to have been used for self defence (they should not be thought of as 'armour'), body spines almost certainly were. Their low angle meant they would have pointed straight at a predator, who, in an attack, could easily have impaled itself on them.

TUOJIANGOSAURUS

Jurassic, 155 mya
Asia
7m (23ft) long

Tuojiangosaurus, a stegosaur from China, had fifteen pairs of narrow, pointed plates bristling from its neck, back and upper tail. The largest plates were ones that grew over its hips. At the end of its short tail were two pairs of long, sharp spines, a feature it had in common with Stegosaurus.

Like all stegosaurs Tuojiangosaurus was long and low, measuring around 2m (6ft 6in) tall at its hips. From the shape of its body it is clear that Tuojiangosaurus held its head low – the ideal position for an animal whose food grew at ground level. As a Jurassic dinosaur it probably ate cycads, horsetails, ferns and the soft parts of other plants.

Tuojiangosaurus

Stegosaurs were slow movers who walked on all-fours – most of the time. However, it is thought they could prop themselves up on their back legs, using their tails for support. They may have occasionally done this to reach plants that grew higher than they could normally reach. They were low-level feeders whose 'ordinary' browsing was limited to no higher than 1m (3ft 3in) from the ground.

CHIALINGOSAURUS

Jurassic, 165 mya

Asia

4m (13ft) long

Known from a number of partial skeletons discovered in the south of China, *Chialingosaurus* appears to have been a slender stegosaur whose neck and back plates were tall and spiky, not broad and thin. Plates of this type tended to occur on early stegosaurs, such as *Chialingosaurus*.

Chialingosaurus

ELEPHANT-LIKE LEGS

All stegosaurs had thick, elephant-like legs which were short and stiff. Their front feet had five short toes, while their back feet had four. Stegosaurs' heels were hoof-like, and they walked with straight legs, as elephants do. Even though they had wrists and ankles, there was very little movement in them.

Wuerhosaurus

Yingshanosaurus

'YINGSHANOSAURUS'
Jurassic, 145 mya
Asia
5m (16ft) long
Because *'Yingshanosaurus'*, a stegosaur from China, is still to be fully described by scientists, there is a chance its name might be changed to something else. Until then, it has been given this temporary name.

'Yingshanosaurus', had a pair of broad wing-like spines on its shoulders, which were flat, like the bony plates on its back, from which they may have evolved. Like the spines on other stegosaurs, they may have been to protect its flanks from attack.

WUERHOSAURUS
Cretaceous, 130 mya
Asia
8m (27ft) long
Instead of high plates on its back, *Wuerhosaurus*, from China, had plates that were long, low and slightly curved. Four bony spines might have grown at the end of its tail, but this is by no means certain since no complete fossils of this dinosaur have yet been found. *Wuerhosaurus* is one of the few stegosaurs to have lived in the Cretaceous period.

STEGOSAURUS

Stegosaurus is the best known plated dinosaur. It was the largest member of the stegosaur family.

Name: *Stegosaurus*
Lived: *140 mya*
Found: *North America*
Length: *9m (30ft)*
Diet: *Plants*
Habitat: *Open woodland, floodplains*

STEGOSAURUS PLATES

The plates on Stegosaurus may have been covered with skin, through which ran blood vessels. If so, when extra blood was pumped through the vessels the plates might have 'blushed' pink, sending out signals to other animals.

ROOF REPTILE

In 1877 a new, strange-looking dinosaur came to the attention of the world's scientists. It was given the name *Stegosaurus*, meaning 'Roof Reptile', because the bony plates found with its fossilised bones were thought to have covered its back, like the shell of a turtle. Only later was it realised that the plates had stood upright and had not 'roofed' its back as first thought. *Stegosaurus* was a long, low animal with a small head, and back legs twice as long as its front legs. Four long, horn-covered spines grew from the end of its thick, stiff tail.

STING IN THE TAIL

Stegosaurus was a slow-moving plant-eater that may have lived in small family groups. Its natural habitat seems to have been forests, and also the floodplains of rivers. It was vulnerable to attack from predators, such as *Allosaurus*. In an attack, *Stegosaurus* would have used its tail for self-defence. Standing still, and with its stiff legs pressed firmly to the ground, it would have twisted and flicked its tail through the air. If its attacker came too close, the tail spines would have pierced its body, causing deep wounds.

In a dispute over a female Stegosaurus, two males challenge each other. They make angry noises, flick their tails, and turn their bodies sideways to show their full size. Blood is pumped into their back plates, making them turn pink.

STEGOSAURUS PLATE PATTERN

Stegosaurus *had seventeen plates, of different sizes, along its neck, back and most of its tail. It is not known for certain how they were arranged. They may have been in one straight row, in a single staggered row, or as pairs in two rows.*

The first fully-armoured dinosaurs to appear were the nodosaurs, about 175 million years ago. Their name means 'node lizards', after the lumpy nodules of bone embedded in their skin. Although they resemble ankylosaurs, which appeared after them, the nodosaurs had slimmer and longer legs. The most obvious difference between the two groups is that nodosaurs did not have tail clubs.

MINMI
Cretaceous, 115 mya
Australia
3m (10ft) long
Minmi was the first armoured dinosaur found in the southern hemisphere. It was a small nodosaur whose skin was clad in different shaped bony plates. Even its belly was protected – most other armoured dinosaurs had no plates on their soft and vulnerable undersides. All this armour increased its weight, but far from being a slow-mover *Minmi* may have been able to move quite fast, since its longish legs suggest it could break into a trot.

Minmi

GASTONIA
Cretaceous, 125 mya
North America
2.5m (8ft) long
Gastonia was covered in many flat, bony spines which grew from its neck, along the sides of its body, and down to the tip of its tail. The longest spines, which were on its shoulders, stuck out for about 30cm (1ft). On its back were triangular-shaped bony plates. This was one of the most heavily armoured of all the nodosaurs, and was clearly built for self-defence. A predator would have found it hard to attack *Gastonia*, since it would have run the risk of harming itself in the process. Even though *Gastonia* did not have a tail club to swing at a predator, its tail spines were sharp enough to stab into a carnivore's flesh.

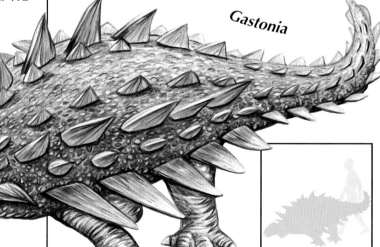

Gastonia

DINOSAUR BODY ARMOUR

The armour on nodosaurs and ankylosaurs was composed of bony plates, or scutes. They could be flat or raised into points. The largest scutes were on the neck and shoulders; smaller ones were on the back and tail. Spaces between scutes were filled with pea-sized bone pads.

Edmontonia

EDMONTONIA

Cretaceous, 70 mya
North America
7m (23ft) long

A large-sized nodosaur from Canada, *Edmontonia* is notable for the long spines that grew from its shoulders and sides. They faced forwards, and were probably used as anti-predator devices, defending *Edmontonia* from meat-eaters such as *Albertosaurus*. They may also have been used in contests of strength, where one *Edmontonia* locked spines with another, as stags do with their antlers, pushing hard until the weaker animal gave in.

GARGOYLEOSAURUS

Jurassic, 150 mya
North America
3m (10ft) long

Gargoyleosaurus had a triangular-shaped skull like an ankylosaur, but as it lacked a tail club its skeleton was more like that of a nodosaur. In other words, this armour-plated dinosaur had features common to both families, which suggests it was a mid-way stage between them. It is thought to be an ancestor of the ankylosaurs, which evolved after the nodosaurs.

Gargoyleosaurus

113

The first ankylosaurs appeared about 130 million years ago, in the early Cretaceous period. They survived to the end of the Age of Reptiles. Their name means 'fused lizards', which is a reference to the plates of bony armour joined, or fused, together over their bodies. Ankylosaurs were a widespread group of dinosaurs, whose fossils have been found on most continents (including Antarctica), but not South America. These armoured plant-eaters had bony clubs at the end of their tails.

SAICHANIA

Cretaceous, 80 mya
Asia
7m (23ft) long

An ankylosaur from China, *Saichania* lived in a hot, dry habitat that may have been almost a desert. Its head, body and tail were protected by numerous plates and spines of bone, giving it a tough, outer shell of body armour. A small bone club grew at the end of its tail. Like other members of its family, *Saichania* was unprotected on its belly.

Saichania

EUOPLOCEPHALUS

Cretaceous, 70 mya
North America
7m (23ft) long

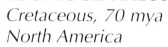

Euoplocephalus

Euoplocephalus lived in forests, where it may have been a herd-dweller. It was a heavily armoured dinosaur, clad in bony knobs and plates. Even its eyelids had a layer of bone over them. Bands of armour plating ran across its back, embedded into its leathery skin. Four horns guarded its neck, and spines ran down its back. If attacked, the bony club at the end of its tail was probably swung to warn a predator to keep away.

PINACOSAURUS

Cretaceous, 80 mya
Asia
5m (16ft) long

Discovered in China and Mongolia, *Pinacosaurus* lived in a hot, dry semi-desert habitat. It lived at the same time and in the same region as its close-relative *Saichania*, and the two may have competed for whatever food grew there, though it is not known what plants formed the basis of their diet. The skull of *Pinacosaurus* was only partially covered with bone plates, leaving some areas of exposed skin. Apart from this it looked much like all other ankylosaurs.

TALARURUS

Cretaceous, 85 mya
Asia
5m (16ft) long

Talarurus

Talarurus, from Mongolia, was squat and wide-chested, and its long tail ended in a heavy bone club. Its head and body were clad in bony plates and nodules that formed in the skin – they were not attached to its skeleton. *Talarurus* had four toes on its hind feet, whereas other ankylosaurs, such as *Euoplocephalus*, had three toes on their back feet.

Pinacosaurus

ARMOURED HEADS

Ankylosaurs had skulls which were almost triangular in shape. They had wide beaks which were suited to grazing on low-growing vegetation. Their teeth were tiny. Plates of bone covered their heads and short, pyramid-shaped horns grew from the back of their skulls.

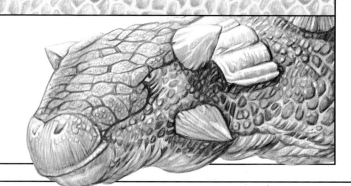

ANKYLOSAURUS

Ankylosaurus was one of the largest of the armoured dinosaurs. It appeared towards the end of the Age of Reptiles. Very few specimens of Ankylosaurus have ever been found, but despite its rarity it has become one of the best known of all dinosaurs, even though comparatively little is known about it.

Name: *Ankylosaurus*
Lived: *70 mya*
Found: *North America*
Length: *10m (33ft)*
Diet: *Plants*
Habitat: *Open woodland*

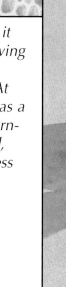

ALL ROUND PROTECTION

Ankylosaurus had a wide, barrel-shaped body, supported by four short legs. It was a squat animal, standing about 1m (3ft 3in) in height. It was twice as wide as it was tall. The whole of its top side was covered with thick oval plates of bony material embedded in its skin. They ran in bands across its back. Its head, face, and eyelids were sheathed in pads of protective armour, too. Rows of spines grew along its back, and horns poked from the rear of its head. Its tail ended in a wide, bony club made from plates of armour that were locked together.

ANKYLOSAURUS SKULL

The skull of Ankylosaurus *shows how it had pyramid-shaped bony spines growing at the back. Its jaws held many small chewing teeth. At the front was a wide, horn-covered, toothless beak.*

WARNING SIGN

Ankylosaurus may have spent most of its time feeding. If attacked it would have defended itself with its tail club. It might also have increased blood flow through its skin, in which case it could have 'blushed' pink, sending out a warning signal.

LOW FEEDER

Its short legs kept *Ankylosaurus* close to the ground, so it could only feed off plants that grew no more than 2m (6ft 6in) off the ground. It nipped and tugged at plants with its wide beak. It had a big tongue, which pushed food around inside its mouth before it swallowed.

Attacked by a predator, such as Tyrannosaurus, *an angry* Ankylosaurus *delivers a heavy blow by hammering it with its tail club.*

ANKYLOSAURUS TAIL CLUB

The bony club at the end of its tail was made from two or more plates of armour (scutes) fused together into a heavy mass. The lower part of the tail was stiff, and was reinforced with bony tendons to give it extra strength.

The ceratopsians were a widespread group of dinosaurs of the Cretaceous period. While some had horns on their heads, others did not. Some had frills of bone around their necks, which others lacked. They ranged from the size of a turkey to the size of an elephant. Despite the obvious differences, ceratopsians had one thing in common – a skull with a beak-like snout, like that of a parrot.

PSITTACOSAURUS

Cretaceous, 130 mya
Asia
2.5m (8ft) long

Psittacosaurus

Psittacosaurus, from China and Mongolia, was one of the first dinosaurs to develop a beak, which it used to slice through vegetation. It was a slender, two-legged plant-eater, and was an early member of the ceratopsian family of dinosaurs. *Psittacosaurus* had prominent cheek bones, which, over millions of years, may have evolved to become the horns of dinosaurs such as *Triceratops*.

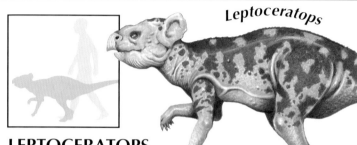

Leptoceratops

LEPTOCERATOPS

Cretaceous, 70 mya
Australia, North America
2m (6ft 6in) long

This slender animal, which may have been a fast-mover, was a primitive member of the ceratopsian family. It belongs to a small group of dinosaurs known as the protoceratopsians, meaning 'first horned faces', which is a bit misleading because it didn't have any horns on its face! However, *Leptoceratops* did have other key features, such as a bony neck frill, which is why it is grouped together with *Triceratops* and the other horn-faced dinosaurs.

PARROT BEAK

Psittacosaurus, meaning 'Parrot Lizard', was named after the distinctive shape of its skull, which has a tall, parrot-like appearance. Its bony beak was probably covered in a layer of rough horn. Behind its beak were many small chewing teeth, packed into the sides of its jaws. There were no teeth at the front of its mouth. It had large eyes and small nostrils.

PROTOCERATOPS

Cretaceous,
80 mya
Asia
2.5m (8ft) long

CHASMOSAURUS

Cretaceous, 75 mya
North America
5m (16ft) long

Protoceratops

Protoceratops is famous for being the first dinosaur found at a nesting site. Discovered in the Gobi Desert, Mongolia, its cylinder-shaped eggs were 20cm (8in) long and 17.5cm (7in) around the centre. They were laid in a spiral pattern in a shallow nest, which was a hole scooped into the desert sand. As the young grew they developed the distinctive bony frill of adults, which was designed to protect the soft skin around the neck.

Many fossils of *Chasmosaurus* have been found, making it one of the best studied of all the ceratopsian dinosaurs. It had one small horn on its nose and two longer upward-curving horns above its eyes. A large bony frill grew at the back of its head, and although it looked solid it was actually quite thin and fragile. In an attack, instead of using the frill as a shield to deflect blows, it may have been used to confuse or frighten the enemy, in an attempt to make *Chasmosaurus* appear bigger than it really was. This plant-eating, rhinoceros-like dinosaur weighed about 3.5 tonnes. It is thought to have been able to move quickly about on its four sturdy legs.

Chasmosaurus

119

Neck frills and horns are the most striking features of some ceratopsians. They are clues to how these dinosaurs behaved. It is thought the skin over the frills was coloured, perhaps to attract mates. From the position of the horns it seems that two animals could lock heads together, then push hard to decide who was the strongest.

Pachyrhinosaurus

Centrosaurus

STYRACOSAURUS

Cretaceous, 70 mya
North America
5m (16ft) long

Styracosaurus was one of the most heavily-horned of all the ceratopsians. Around its large neck frill grew six long horns, plus several shorter ones, and from its nose grew a horn that was 60cm (2ft) long. It is believed to have lived in large herds, and despite its 3-tonne weight and short legs it seems to have been able to run at speeds of up to 32 kph (20 mph).

CENTROSAURUS

Cretaceous, 75 mya
North America
6m (20ft) long

Centrosaurus lived among swampy forests, where it browsed on low-growing vegetation which it bit off with its powerful beak. Chewing teeth in the sides of its jaws broke its food into smaller pieces, and gastroliths (stones) rolling around in its stomach crushed plants and twiggy material to a juicy pulp for its digestive system to absorb. *Centrosaurus* was a herd animal, and it is thought vast numbers of them migrated long distances between feeding and breeding grounds.

Styracosaurus

PACHYRHINOSAURUS

Cretaceous, 70 mya
North America
6m (20ft) long

Pachyrhinosaurus was a large ceratopsian with a high neck frill, with small horns around its edge. It is unclear whether it had a horn on its nose, since no complete skulls have been found. It did have a large bony pad, or boss, of bone at the end of its snout, which some scientists think was in place of a horn. Others say it was the base for a horn, which may have broken off or been shed.

TOROSAURUS

Cretaceous, 70 mya
North America
7.5m (24ft 6in) long

Torosaurus had the largest horned head of all the ceratopsians, measuring 2.6m (8ft 6in) long. Its skull was the largest of any animal ever to have lived on land. It had one short horn on its snout, two long horns above its eyes, and a toothless horn-covered beak. Like other members of its family, *Torosaurus* had a short tail, and its back legs were longer than its front legs, giving it a stable posture. It may have lived in herds.

Torosaurus

SKIN-COVERED HOLES

Some neck frills had holes in them, making them lighter to carry. The frills were skin-covered, which, when flushed with blood, would have caused eye-spots to appear over the holes, to attract a mate or scare an enemy away.

Pachyrhinosaurus skull

Styracosaurus skull

TRICERATOPS

The best known horned dinosaur is *Triceratops*, whose name means 'Three-Horned Face'.

Name: *Triceratops*
Lived: *70 mya*
Found: *North America*
Length: *9m (30ft)*
Diet: *Plants*
Habitat: *Open woodland*

TRICERATOPS SKULL

Triceratops had a large, wavy-edged neck frill. It was made from solid bone, unlike the frills of some other ceratopsians which had holes in theirs. It had three horns. The two on its brow were up to 1m (3ft 3in) long; its nose horn was shorter.

Frill

Brow horn
Eye socket
Nose horn
Nostril

TOUGHENED FOR STRENGTH

Triceratops had a bulky body, a short tail, and stout legs with hoofed feet. It weighed around 10 tonnes. Its most distinctive features were its bony neck frill and its three sharp horns that grew on the front of its skull. The jaws of *Triceratops* ended in a large bony beak. There were no teeth in its beak, but many small chewing teeth were packed into the sides of its strong jaws.

PROTECTING THE WEAK

Triceratops was a group animal that probably lived in vast herds, hundreds, perhaps thousands, strong. For protection from predators, the young, weak, and old may have travelled in the centre of the herd, while stronger animals kept guard on the flanks.

VEGETARIAN DIET

Triceratops was a plant-eater. It ate low-growing vegetation which it bit through with its beak. Its chewing teeth cut the plant material into smaller pieces before being swallowed. Worn teeth were shed, and new ones grew in their place.

In an attack by carnivores, a family of Triceratops *protect their vulnerable young by moving them behind the adults of the group. The adults butt the attackers with their skin-piercing horns.*

CONTESTS OF STRENGTH

Triceratops skulls have been found that show signs of injuries, such as puncture holes and deep scratches.

Many of these wounds were probably caused by horn points when adults clashed heads together in disputes over mates or territory. The wounds healed.

The pachycephalosaurs, meaning 'thick-headed dinosaurs', are often called 'bone-heads', after their thick skulls. They appeared about 130 million years ago, and survived to the end of the Age of Reptiles. They ranged in size from small animals about 1m (3ft 3in) long, to ones five times as big. Bone-heads have been found in Asia, Europe and North America. None have yet been found in the southern hemisphere.

Prenocephale

Wannanosaurus

WANNANOSAURUS

Cretaceous, 85 mya
Asia
60cm (2ft) long

Wannanosaurus, from China, is one of the smallest dinosaurs known. It had a small, flat head with a thick bony skull, and many sharp teeth. It also had short arms with clawed fingers, a heavy tail, and strong hind legs with three-toed clawed feet. It was probably a fast runner that used its speed to escape from danger. *Wannanosaurus* may have been a herbivore, grazing on low-growing plants, and living in a herd.

PRENOCEPHALE

Cretaceous, 70 mya
Asia
2.5m (8ft) long

Discovered in Mongolia, *Prenocephale* had a high-domed head, giving the impression that there was a big brain inside its skull. However, like all other bone-headed dinosaurs, *Prenocephale* only had a small brain, protected beneath its bony dome. Short spikes and bony nodules ran around the skull shelf, or ridge, at the back of its head. Apart from these 'ornaments', the rest of its bone dome was very smooth. Its teeth were sharp, and were well suited to cropping the leaves and stems of low-growing plants and trees. It may have had small stones (gastroliths) in its stomach to crush its food into a digestible, mushy pulp.

HOMALOCEPHALE
Cretaceous, 80 mya
Asia
3m (10ft) long

Homalocephale

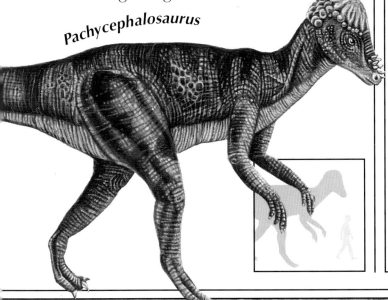

Many bone-heads had dome-shaped skulls, but not *Homalocephale*. This dinosaur had a flat skull. Bony nodules, short spikes, and ridges grew on the top and back of its head, and on its cheeks. It had large eyes, and possibly a good sense of smell. As it had no means of self-defence, *Homalocephale* may have detected an approaching predator by sight and smell, and then it would have used its long legs to run away from the oncoming danger.

Pachycephalosaurus

PACHYCEPHALOSAURUS
Cretaceous, 70 mya
North America
4.6m (15ft) long
Pachycephalosaurus was the largest of the bone-headed dinosaurs. Unfortunately, only its skull has been found, which makes it difficult to determine just how big this animal really was, and what it actually looked like. Its skull shows that it had bony nodules projecting from its snout, and also from the back of its head. Many tiny teeth were packed into its jaws. This was one of the last of the bone-heads, it died out with many other animal species at the end of the Age of Reptiles, 65 million years ago.

PACHYCEPHALOSAURUS SKULL

Pachycephalosaurus *had the largest skull of all the bone-headed dinosaurs. Not only was it really long, 60cm (2ft), but the bone that formed the dome was an incredible 25cm (10in) thick. Beneath this mass of protective bone was the brain cavity, inside which was a tiny brain.*

Dome of solid bone

Bony nodules

Brain cavity

Bony nodules

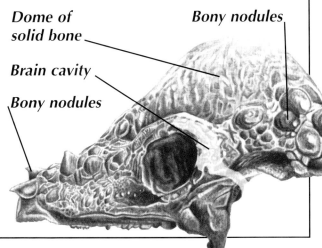

Animals evolve features for good reasons. In pachycephalosaurs, their thick skulls were developed to head-butt other bone-heads. It is thought they knocked heads together, or rammed them into each other's sides, pushing hard to decide who was the dominant animal in a group, who should have first choice of a mate, or who should have the best territory.

'MICROCEPHALE'

Cretaceous, 75 mya
North America
30cm (1ft) long (uncertain)
'Microcephale', discovered in Canada, is known from two small skull domes, each about 5cm (2in) across. It was clearly a tiny bone-head. As it is still to be fully described by scientists, there is a chance its name might be changed to something else. Until then, it has been given this temporary name, meaning 'Tiny Head'.

Stygimoloch

Microcephale

BUILT FOR SPEED

Pachycephalosaurs had long back legs, and short front legs. It is thought they moved about on their back legs only. They were fast runners, able to move at high speed over short distances to escape from predators, or to chase after small prey which they ate.

STYGIMOLOCH
Cretaceous, 70 mya
North America
3m (10ft) long

Stygimoloch is notable for being the only pachycephalosaur with spikes on its head, which measured from 10–15cm (4–6in) long. As well as the spikes, its head had many bumpy nodules. It is uncertain whether both males and females had head spikes, or if they were only a feature of one of them. *Stygimoloch* might not have engaged in head-butting contests, like other bone-heads. Instead, it might have taken part in displays, showing off its spikes to win its way.

Goyocephale

Pachycephalosaurs may have used their thick skulls as a means of self-defence. If attacked by a predator, a bone-head may have head-butted the enemy, knocking it off balance. This show of aggression would slow the predator down long enough for the bone-head to turn and run away from the danger.

GOYOCEPHALE
Cretaceous, 70 mya
Asia
2m (6ft 6in) long

A bone-head from Mongolia, *Goyocephale* had a flat skull rather than a rounded dome. This is one of the features used to distinguish different sub-groups of pachycephalosaurs – those from Asia had flat heads, those from North America had domed heads. *Goyocephale* is notable for its short canine teeth in its upper and lower jaws. When its mouth was closed, its lower canines slotted into notches in its upper jaws.

STEGOCERAS

Stegoceras and the other bone-heads are often thought of as head-bangers, but this might not be accurate. Animals that clash heads run the risk of harming themselves. Perhaps *Stegoceras* mainly used its head to butt into the sides of others. Head-banging might only have been used for specific purposes, for example to settle disputes over mates or territory.

Name: *Stegoceras*
Lived: *70 mya*
Found: *North America*
Length: *2m (6ft 6in)*
Diet: *Plants*
Habitat: *Forests*

In a dispute over territory, two adult Stegoceras *push and shove each other in a contest to decide which of them is the dominant animal in the herd. The loser may be forced to leave the group.*

LONG LEGS, LONG TAIL

Stegoceras was a medium-sized bone-headed dinosaur that moved about on two long legs. While the animal was young, the skull of *Stegoceras* was relatively flat, the high, bony dome only becoming a feature in its adult life. It had large eyes, and probably had a good sense of vision. Its short arms had five fingers on the hands, and its long back legs ended in four-toed feet. *Stegoceras* had a long tail, which was stiff and had little movement in it.

STEGOCERAS SKULL

An adult's head was about 20cm (8in) long, with a very thick, knobbly-looking front region. The thickest part of the skull, above the brain, was 6cm (2.5in) thick. On the back of its skull was a ridge (a skull shelf), which was covered with knobs and bumps.

Skull shelf

HEAD-BUTTERS

It is thought that *Stegoceras* lived in herds, moving through forests and along the margins of rivers and lakes. From time to time they engaged in head-butting behaviour. Head-butting by juveniles may have been playful, copying the real contests of adults.

RAZOR SHARP

Stegoceras was probably a plant-eater. Its jaws were packed with many small, sharp teeth, some of which had serrated cutting edges which would have been able to chop tough, woody vegetation into tiny pieces. It may also have taken the occasional insect, small lizard, or mammal.

HAND TO MOUTH FEEDING

The hands and fingers of Stegoceras *were suited to grasping at plants, perhaps pulling them towards its mouth for its teeth to bite through the leaves and stems. It may have used its finger claws to scratch up roots and other underground edibles.*

CHAPTER FIVE

DUCK-BILLS AND OTHER DINOSAURS

During the Jurassic and Cretaceous periods new forms of two- and four-legged plant-eaters evolved that walked on their toes – they were not flat-footed like many other herbivores, such as the sauropods. In 1881, American fossil-hunter Othniel Charles Marsh (1831–99) named them ornithopods, meaning 'bird-feet', in reference to their tip-toe style of walking. They were agile, capable of moving at speed, and ranged in size from small – less than 2m (6ft 6in) long, to large – about 20m (66ft) long. Ornithopods were the first plant-eating dinosaurs to have true chewing teeth, and also the first with cheek pouches. They were abundant and widespread, and their fossils have been found on every continent, including Antarctica. Many different groups, or families, of ornithopods have been identified.

'DIFFERENT TEETH' DINOSAURS

These were the heterodontosaurs, a family of dinosaurs characterised by having three different kinds of teeth (cutting, chewing, and stabbing). They appeared in the early Jurassic period, and were the first of the ornithopods.

Parksosaurus

Within the ornithopod group of dinosaurs were species that grew to vastly different sizes.

Iguanodon
10m (33ft) long

Hypsilophodon
2.4m (8ft) long

'HIGH RIDGE TEETH' DINOSAURS

These were the hypsilophodonts, characterised by high-ridged, chisel-shaped cheek teeth. A good example of a hypsilophodont is *Leaellynasaura*.

'IGUANA TEETH' DINOSAURS

These were the iguanodonts, noted for having many small, ridged cheek teeth, tightly packed together. The best known iguanodont is *Iguanodon*.

DUCK-BILLED DINOSAURS

These were the hadrosaurs, which means 'big lizards'. They are often called by the nickname 'duck-bills', because of the duck-like shape of their beaks. A well known hadrosaur is *Maiasaura*.

Edmontosaurus

Parasaurolophus

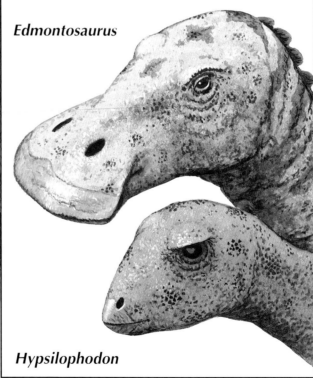

Edmontosaurus

Hypsilophodon

The snouts of ornithopods ended in horn-covered bony beaks, which were perfect for cropping vegetation.

Small groups of migrating ornithopods cross a Cretaceous landscape of 120 million years ago, moving from one feeding ground to the next.

The first ornithopods to evolve were the heterodontosaurs – the 'different teeth' dinosaurs. They appeared in the late Triassic or early Jurassic period, around 220 million years ago, and seem to have thrived in South Africa, though isolated finds have been made in Europe, South America, and possibly North America. All were small, two-legged plant-eaters, with bony beaks, and different types of specialised teeth.

Pisanosaurus

PISANOSAURUS
Triassic, 220 mya
South America
90cm (3ft) long (uncertain)
Some scientists think that *Pisanosaurus*, from Argentina, is the oldest known heterodontosaur. However, because all that has been found of this dinosaur is part of a skull, jaw, backbone, leg and foot – all pieces from a single individual – there are doubts as to whether it belongs to this family or not. *Pisanosaurus* had pointed teeth, but it does not appear to have had the tusk-like canine teeth found in other members of the group, such as the better-known *Heterodontosaurus*. Whatever group *Pisanosaurus* actually belongs to, one thing is certain – at 220 million years old it was one of the first dinosaurs on Earth. Its fossils clearly show that it was a small reptile, a feature common to all the early dinosaurs.

THREE DIFFERENT TYPES OF TEETH

Heterodontosaurus, *meaning 'Different-toothed Lizard', was named for its distinctive teeth. Behind its bony beak were chisel-shaped biting teeth. Then came tusk-like teeth (perhaps only in males), similar to the canines of a dog. Though they could have ripped through plants, their purpose is unclear. At the back of its mouth were many ridged cheek teeth, for chewing.*

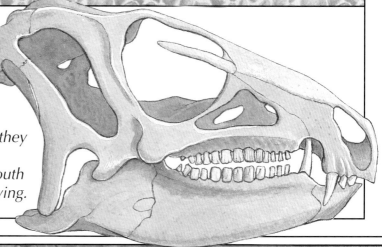

Abrictosaurus

ABRICTOSAURUS

Jurassic, 205 mya
South Africa
1.2m (4ft) long
Another of the early heterodontosaurs may have been *Abrictosaurus*. However, as with so many dinosaurs for which little fossil material has been found, its identification as a separate species is not entirely certain. The skull of this animal lacked any tusk-like teeth, and it may be that *Abrictosaurus* is none other than a female *Heterodontosaurus* – the difference being that females did not grow tusks, but males did. More fossils will need to be found to prove – or disprove – this theory.

HETERODONTOSAURUS

Jurassic, 205 mya
South Africa
1.2m (4ft) long
Heterodontosaurus had short arms, and long, slender legs and feet, showing that it was built for running. Its snout ended in a bony beak, and its jaws held three kinds of teeth – small, sharp teeth, then tusk-like teeth, behind which, at the back of its mouth, were chewing teeth. It is thought that only males grew the tusk-like teeth, which may have been used in courtship and mating displays. *Heterodontosaurus* grazed on low plants, nipping them off with its beak and front teeth.

Heterodontosaurus

Heterodontosaurs are usually thought of as herbivores, using their beaks to graze low-growing plants. However, they may actually have been omnivores, eating both plants and meat. They had strong arms, and their large hands had clawed fingers that appear well suited to digging. It could be that heterodontosaurs used their hands to dig not only for edible roots and tubers, but also for small burrow-living animals and insects.

LYCORHINUS
Jurassic, 200 mya
South Africa
1.2m (4ft) long
(uncertain)

All that has been found of *Lycorhinus* are its teeth, which show that it looked a little like *Heterodontosaurus*. It had large, slightly curved canine teeth in both its upper and lower jaws. They were sharp, and resembled small tusks. It was these distinctive teeth for which it was named – *Lycorhinus* means 'Wolf Snout'. The function of tusk-like teeth in plant-eaters such as *Lycorhinus* is unclear, since pointed teeth are more a feature of meat-eaters, which is why scientists believe they were used during courtship, or in fights, and not for biting into meat.

Lycorhinus

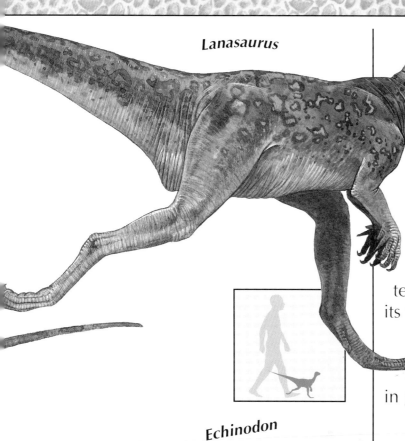

Lanasaurus

LANASAURUS

Jurassic, 200 mya
South Africa
1.2m (4ft) long (uncertain)
Another heterodontosaur from South Africa, also known only from its teeth, is *Lanasaurus*. It may turn out to be another specimen of *Lycorhinus*, but more bones will need to be found before this mystery can be cleared up. *Lanasaurus* had self-sharpening teeth. As its jaws opened and closed, its teeth ground against each other, keeping them sharp and chisel-like. As old, worn teeth fell out, new ones grew in their place in groups of three.

Echinodon

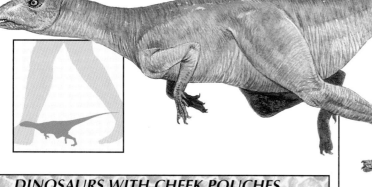

ECHINODON

Jurassic, 150 mya
Europe
60cm (2ft) long
Not all scientists think *Echinodon*, discovered in southern England, was a heterodontosaur. The presence of bony scales amongst its fossilised bones has led some scientists to place it in a separate family (the fabrosaurs) within the ornithopod group. However, its teeth seem to reveal another story. It had small canines – tusk-like pointed teeth – in both its upper and lower jaws, and these are a distinctive feature of heterodontosaurs. *Echinodon* was a small-sized plant-eater, and was one of the last members of its family.

DINOSAURS WITH CHEEK POUCHES

By studying the positions of teeth in their jaws, it is clear that heterodontosaurs had fleshy cheeks. This feature was common to all ornithopods – but the heterodontosaurs had it first. Because the surfaces of its cheek teeth slanted downward and outward, partially mashed-up food fell into its cheek pouches as it chewed. The animal's tongue constantly pushed food away from the cheeks, moving it back to its chewing teeth.

LESOTHOSAURUS

Lesothosaurus may, or may not, be an ornithopod. Its place in the group is uncertain. It has been put into a small family known as fabrosaurs.

Name: Lesothosaurus
Lived: 200 million years ago
Found: South Africa
Length: 1m (3ft 3in)
Diet: Plants
Habitat: Semi-deserts

SLEEPING THROUGH HOT WEATHER

Lesothosaurus *may have spent long periods in deep sleep, saving its energy. The evidence is from two skeletons found curled up together. Scientists think the animals had gone into a burrow, during a time of very hot weather, to aestivate (the summer equivalent of hibernation), but they had died in their sleep.*

SMALL BUT SWIFT

Lesothosaurus had long back legs, suggesting it was a fast runner. Its arms were short, with five fingers on each hand suitable for grabbing and seizing at things. It had a long pointed tail which was kept stiff by bony tendons, a flexible neck, and a small triangular head with large eyes. Its front teeth (incisors) were sharp and pointed, and it had many cheek teeth (for chewing) packed into the sides of its jaws.

LOW FEEDER

Lesothosaurus was a plant-eater. It lived in a hot habitat, where food may have been scarce at some times of the year. It ate low-growing plants, and maybe roots which it scratched up with its hands.

A group of Lesothosaurus *dinosaurs move across an early Jurassic semi-desert landscape, stopping to feed on the sparse vegetation that grows there, such as the tough leaves of cycads.*

LESOTHOSAURUS SKELETON

Bony beak

Grasping hands

Long feet

The skeleton of Lesothosaurus *reveals how, from the neck down, it looked like a small theropod (meat-eater), with long slender legs, and short arms with grasping hands. However, its skull tells a different story, since its bony beak and chewing teeth show how it was adapted to a life of eating plants, not biting meat.*

DOG-SIZED DINOSAUR

It is thought that *Lesothosaurus*, which was about the size of a dog, lived in groups that moved across hot, dry plains. Most of the time it was bipedal (moving on two legs), but it may have dropped to all-fours when feeding. If it sensed danger, a sudden burst of speed would have taken it to safety.

Hypsilophodonts – the 'high ridge teeth' dinosaurs – were a long-lived family of ornithopods. They were around for more than 100 million years, from 170 to 65 million years ago. Small to medium-sized animals, growing to a maximum of 4m (13ft) long, they were widespread, and have been found on most continents, including Antarctica and Australia.

HYPSILOPHODON

Cretaceous, 120 mya
Europe, North America
2.4m (8ft) long

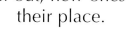

Hypsilophodon

OTHNIELIA

Jurassic, 150 mya
North America
1.4m (4ft 6in) long
Othnielia was a lightly-built animal with a small head, a bony beak, and self-sharpening cheek teeth. Like others of its family it had cheek pouches into which partially-chewed food slipped, before being pushed back on to its chewing teeth by its tongue. It had large eyes, sprinter's legs, clawed fingers and toes, and a stiff tail which helped it to keep its balance as it ran.

Hypsilophodon lived in herds. It was a fast-moving dinosaur that moved quickly about on its two long back legs. Each foot had four toes. It had a small skull, big eyes, a bony beak, and cheek pouches for holding partially-chewed food. Its jaws held about 30 chisel-like teeth. It was a herbivore, grazing on ground plants such as ferns and horsetails. Constant chewing eventually wore its teeth down, and as old ones fell out, new ones grew in their place.

Othnielia

FULGUROTHERIUM

Cretaceous, 130 mya
Australia
2m (6ft 6in) long
Little of *Fulgurotherium* has been found. At first it was thought to be a theropod (meat-eater). However, its jaw shows that it had the toothless beak and chisel-like cheek teeth of a plant-eating hypsilophodont. It may have been a migratory animal, moving north each year to escape cold winters, at a time when Australia was joined to Antarctica.

Thescelosaurus

BUILT FOR SPEED

Members of the hypsilophodont family were agile animals, built for speed. They are often compared with present-day sprinting animals such as gazelles, and may have been able to reach speeds of up to 37 kph (23 mph) over short distances. Being able to outrun a predator was their only means of self-defence.

THESCELOSAURUS

Cretaceous, 70 mya
North America
4m (13ft) long
Thescelosaurus was one of the last members of the hypsilophodont family, living right at the end of the Age of Reptiles. It was a plant-eater, and it lived in forests.

Incredibly, a fossilised heart from a *Thescelosaurus* (nicknamed 'Willo') has been found – the first from any dinosaur. It had four chambers, and was more like the heart of a bird or a mammal than a reptile. This is strong evidence that some dinosaurs, at least, had high metabolic rates, and were probably warm-blooded animals, allowing them to lead very active lives.

Hypsilophodonts are given this family name because of the distinctive shape of their chewing teeth, which have high (deep) ridges on their upper surfaces. When they chewed, their jaws came together, with the upper jaw sliding slightly outwards and moving in a circular pattern. This produced a grinding motion, breaking food down into smaller and smaller pieces against the ridged teeth. Animals that chew like this today include camels and cows.

AGILISAURUS

Jurassic, 165 mya
Asia
1m (3ft 3in) long
A small plant-eater from China, *Agilisaurus* puzzles scientists, who are undecided if it belongs in the hypsilophodont family or not.

It may be a member of a new family of dinosaurs. It had a short head, and its jaws held tall and closely packed leaf-like chewing teeth, with larger pointed teeth at the front. It had big eyes, a short neck, short arms, long legs, and a long tail.

A DIET OF PLANTS

There were no teeth at the front of a hypsilophodont's mouth. Instead, it had a bony beak which was used to slice through vegetation. Plant material was pushed into its cheek pouches by its strong tongue. Long chewing teeth, patterned with deep ridges, then began to grind away at its food, quickly reducing plants to a juicy pulp which was easy to swallow.

Agilisaurus

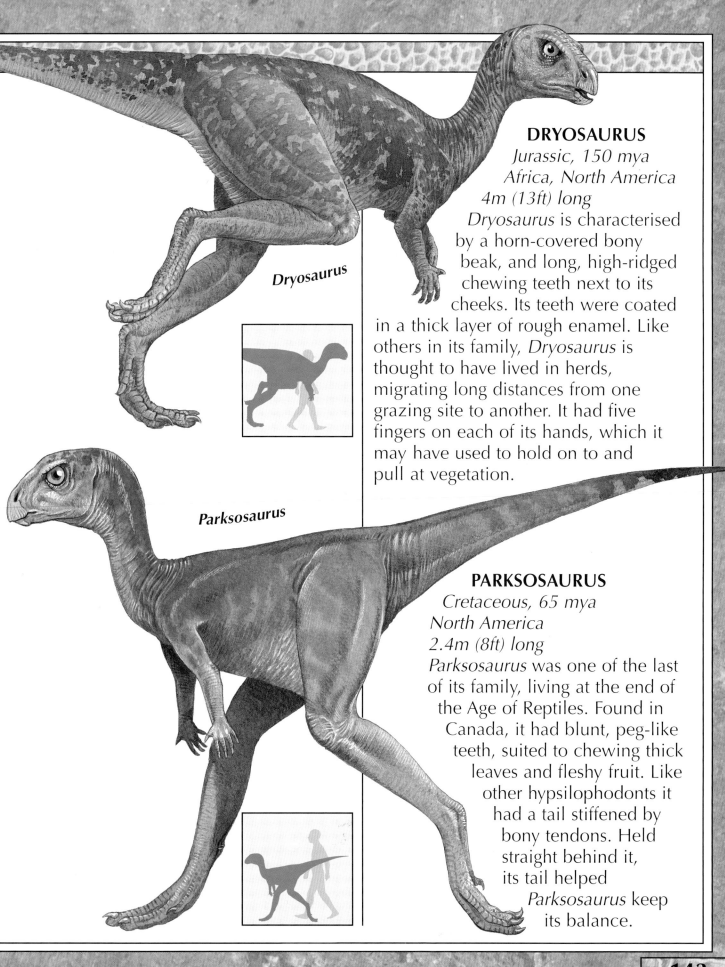

Dryosaurus

Parksosaurus

DRYOSAURUS

Jurassic, 150 mya
Africa, North America
4m (13ft) long
Dryosaurus is characterised by a horn-covered bony beak, and long, high-ridged chewing teeth next to its cheeks. Its teeth were coated in a thick layer of rough enamel. Like others in its family, *Dryosaurus* is thought to have lived in herds, migrating long distances from one grazing site to another. It had five fingers on each of its hands, which it may have used to hold on to and pull at vegetation.

PARKSOSAURUS

Cretaceous, 65 mya
North America
2.4m (8ft) long
Parksosaurus was one of the last of its family, living at the end of the Age of Reptiles. Found in Canada, it had blunt, peg-like teeth, suited to chewing thick leaves and fleshy fruit. Like other hypsilophodonts it had a tail stiffened by bony tendons. Held straight behind it, its tail helped *Parksosaurus* keep its balance.

LEAELLYNASAURA

LARGE EYES TO SEE IN THE DARK

Leaellynasaura lived near the South Pole, where there were about four months of total darkness every year. It is thought its large eyes, and optic nerve connecting them to its brain, were adapted to help it see in the dark.

When reptiles ruled the Earth, Australia was in a different position on the planet from where it is today. It was further south, and was joined to Antarctica. Animals that lived there survived in a cold, dark climate. One of them was *Leaellynasaura*, a small hypsilophodont.

Name: *Leaellynasaura*
Lived: *105 million years ago*
Found: *Australia*
Length: *1m (3ft 3in)*
Diet: *Plants*
Habitat: *Open woodland*

During the winter months Leaellynasaura *may have gone into a state of hibernation. If so, it would have slowed its heartbeat and breathing, and its body temperature would have fallen. This was to save energy. With the return of warm days it would have become active again.*

BUILT FOR SPEED

Leaellynasaura was little bigger than a turkey. This large-eyed, two-legged dinosaur had a toothless bony beak at the end of its snout, and high-ridged chewing teeth in its jaws. Its long legs suggest it was a fast mover, and it probably ran with its tail held stiff and straight behind it, counter-balancing its body and preventing it from falling.

ROOTS AND BERRIES

A plant-eater, *Leaellynasaura* nibbled at ground-level vegetation – leaves, stems, ferns, berries. It may also have scratched up edible roots and tubers.

WARM-BLOODED DINOSAUR?

Leaellynasaura may have been a group animal, living in herds in a forested environment. It may have been able to withstand extreme cold, which has led some scientists to think it could generate its own body heat, meaning that it was a warm-blooded animal. If this is so, *Leaellynasaura* could have been an active creature all year round, and may not have hibernated in winter.

In the near-constant twilight of Cretaceous Australia, a group of Leaellynasaura *dinosaurs gather to drink from a freshwater pool.*

Iguanodonts, which means 'iguana teeth', after the slight resemblance of their teeth to those of present-day iguanas, were the deer or cows of their day, eating vast amounts of plant material. They first appeared in the mid-Jurassic period, about 170 million years ago, and survived until the end of the Age of Reptiles, 65 million years ago. They were small to large-sized ornithopods, whose bones have been found on most continents.

OURANOSAURUS

Cretaceous, 110 mya
Africa
7m (23ft) long
Ouranosaurus was one of the larger members of its family, notable for its distinctive 'sail' of skin which grew along its backbone to a height of 50cm (1ft 7in). The function of the 'sail' is uncertain, but it may have been brightly coloured to scare predators away.

Muttaburrasaurus

MUTTABURRASAURUS

Cretaceous, 110 mya
Australia
7m (23ft) long
At first sight, *Muttaburrasaurus* looks like *Iguanodon*, which is the best known member of the family. However, there were

noticeable differences between the two iguanodonts. *Muttaburrasaurus* had a raised bony pad on its snout, whereas *Iguanodon* did not. Also, its cheek teeth were adapted for cutting through plants – *Iguanodon* had teeth that were designed for grinding its food into little pieces.

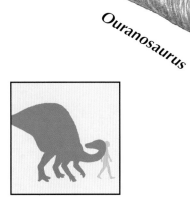

Ouranosaurus

HIGH AND LOW FEEDERS

Iguanodonts spent most of their time browsing on all-fours, using their beaks to nip at low-growing plants. They may also have stood on their back legs to reach plants higher up.

Camptosaurus

RHABDODON

Cretaceous, 75 mya
Europe
4.7m (15ft) long
Rhabdodon was a medium-sized iguanodont, with large rod-like teeth that had blunt chewing surfaces. Studies of its limb bones show that they have 'growth rings' inside them, like those seen in the bones of some modern reptiles. From such rings, which mark periods of rapid and slow growth in an animal, it has been calculated that it took *Rhabdodon* sixteen years to grow to its full adult size. The older it became, the less it grew.

CAMPTOSAURUS

Jurassic, 150 mya
Europe, North America
6m (20ft) long
Many *Camptosaurus* specimens have been found, and it is a well-known iguanodont. It was one of the first to evolve, living in conifer forests where it browsed on low-growing vegetation which it crushed between its chisel-like cheek teeth.

It had strong back legs, and it was probably a good runner. If *Camptosaurus* was attacked by a predator, such as *Allosaurus*, speed would have been its only means of self-defence. It may have used its curved finger claws to scratch on the ground for food.

Rhabdodon

During the 100 million years that iguanodonts lived on Earth, small, evolutionary changes happened to their bodies. In the first iguanodonts the bony tendons that stiffened their backs and tails were straight; in the last ones they were in a criss-cross pattern. The early iguanodonts had four toes; the last ones had three. The teeth of the last iguanodonts were packed ever closer together. By the time all these changes had taken place, iguanodonts had evolved into the final group of ornithopods – the duck-billed dinosaurs, or hadrosaurs.

Vectisaurus

VECTISAURUS
Cretaceous, 130 mya
Europe
4m (13ft) long

As more dinosaur fossils are discovered each year, and new information comes from them, fossils found in previous years are re-examined. Sometimes, dinosaurs that have been classified as belonging to separate species are then found to be the same as others. They should no longer be thought of as different from them. An example of this is with *Vectisaurus*, an iguanodont from southern England. It was named in 1879, and was then thought to be a new species. However, today's scientists believe it is none other than a young *Iguanodon*.

TENONTOSAURUS
Cretaceous, 115 mya
North America
7m (23ft) long

Tenontosaurus was a big plant-eater that resembled *Iguanodon*. Like its relative it had hoof-like hands and feet, and its tail was stiffened by tendons.

Tenontosaurus

The teeth of meat-eating *Deinonychus* have been found with the bones of *Tenontosaurus*, suggesting it may have been the victim of predator attacks. However, it is just as likely that *Deinonychus* scavenged meat from a *Tenontosaurus* that had already died.

PROBACTROSAURUS

Cretaceous, 100 mya
Asia
6m (20ft) long
Some of the features of *Probactrosaurus*, such as its long, flat-topped head, are like those found in the duck-billed dinosaurs (the hadrosaurs). This is to be expected, since the duck-bills evolved from the iguanodonts, and *Probactrosaurus*, from China, may be one of their early ancestors. This plant-eating dinosaur had a narrow snout, a long lower jaw, and flat cheek teeth for chewing. As its teeth wore down and fell out, new ones grew in their place.

Probactrosaurus

STIFF BACKS AND TAILS

Iguanodonts had stiff backbones and tails, which had very little movement in them.

The reason they were stiff is because bony tendons criss-crossed between each bone of the spine, locking them all tightly together.

IGUANODON

Iguanodon is one of the world's best known dinosaurs. One of its teeth was first found in 1822, at Cuckfield, a small town in Sussex, England. It came to the attention of local fossil collector Dr Gideon Mantell (1790–1852), who believed it was from an unknown prehistoric animal. While visiting the Royal College of Surgeons, London, Dr Mantell was shown the tooth from a present-day iguana, a reptile from South America. It was similar to the fossil tooth in his collection, but much smaller. In 1825, Dr Mantell named the ancient creature *Iguanodon*, meaning 'Iguana Tooth'. It was the second dinosaur ever named.

Name: Iguanodon
Lived: 130 million years ago
Found: Asia, Europe, North America
Length: 10m (33ft)
Diet: Plants
Habitat: Woodland

HORSE HEAD

Iguanodon was a big animal with a long stiff tail, whose horse-like head ended in a blunt, toothless beak which was covered in a layer of horn. Its jaws held many chewing teeth – 5cm (2in) long – packed tightly along its cheeks. It had three-toed feet with hooves, like today's cows and horses. Each hand had four fingers, and a spiked thumb.

TWO LEGS OR FOUR

Iguanodon could walk on its two hind legs and on all-fours, reaching a speed of up to 20 kph (12 mph). As it moved, it held its tail straight behind it, and kept its back level with the ground. It is thought *Iguanodon* lived in herds, in a woodland habitat of giant tree ferns, conifers and flowering magnolias.

SPIKED THUMB

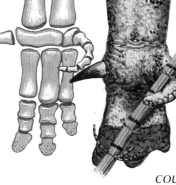

The hands of Iguanodon *had four clawed fingers and a big spiked thumb. Its fingers were jointed and could bend, particularly its little (fifth) finger which could be bent across its palm, helping it to hold on to things.*

GROUND TO A PULP

With its tough beak it cropped vegetation, browsing on leaves, stems, fruit and seeds. Its long, sharp chewing teeth moved in a circular pattern, grinding plants to a mushy pulp. Its tongue continually moved food around inside its mouth, into and out of its cheek pouches, until it was ready to be swallowed.

An Iguanodon *family drinks from a river, and browses amongst the early Cretaceous plants growing along its banks. After they move on, their footprints in the mud and piles of dung will be the only signs they were ever here.*

PUTTING THE THUMB SPIKE TO USE

Iguanodon *may have used its spiked thumb to defend itself from danger, using it like a dagger to stab an enemy. It might also have been used in disputes between rivals, where two* Iguanodon *reared up against each other until one backed away.*

Hadrosaurs, commonly known as 'duck-bills' after the duck-like shape of their beaks, were the last major group of dinosaurs to evolve. They grew out of iguanodonts and first appeared 100 million years ago. They were highly successful and colonised much of the planet. They died out at the end of the Age of Reptiles, 65 million years ago.

HADROSAURUS

Cretaceous, 75 mya
North America
9m (30ft) long
Hadrosaurus is famous for being the first nearly complete dinosaur skeleton found anywhere in the world. It was dug up in the USA in 1857, and named the following year. Its name simply means 'Big Lizard'.

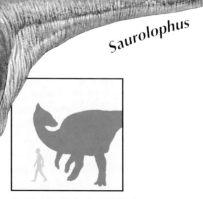

Saurolophus

SAUROLOPHUS

Cretaceous, 70 mya
Asia, North America
12m (40ft) long
Saurolophus had a long tail, short arms, and long back legs with three hoofed toes. A distinctive feature was a long bony spike on the back of its head, which extended along its snout to a hole near its nostrils. This hole may have been covered with a loose flap, or 'bag', of skin, which the dinosaur could blow into to produce honking noises, so that it could communicate with others.

Hadrosaurus

WIDE DUCK-LIKE MOUTHS

It's easy to see why early researchers dubbed hadrosaurs 'duck-bills'. The entire front half of a hadrosaur's mouth was toothless, and it flared outwards into a wide, flattish, semi-circular 'bill'. The upper 'bill' overlapped the lower jaw, and both parts were covered in a hard-wearing, thick layer of horn.

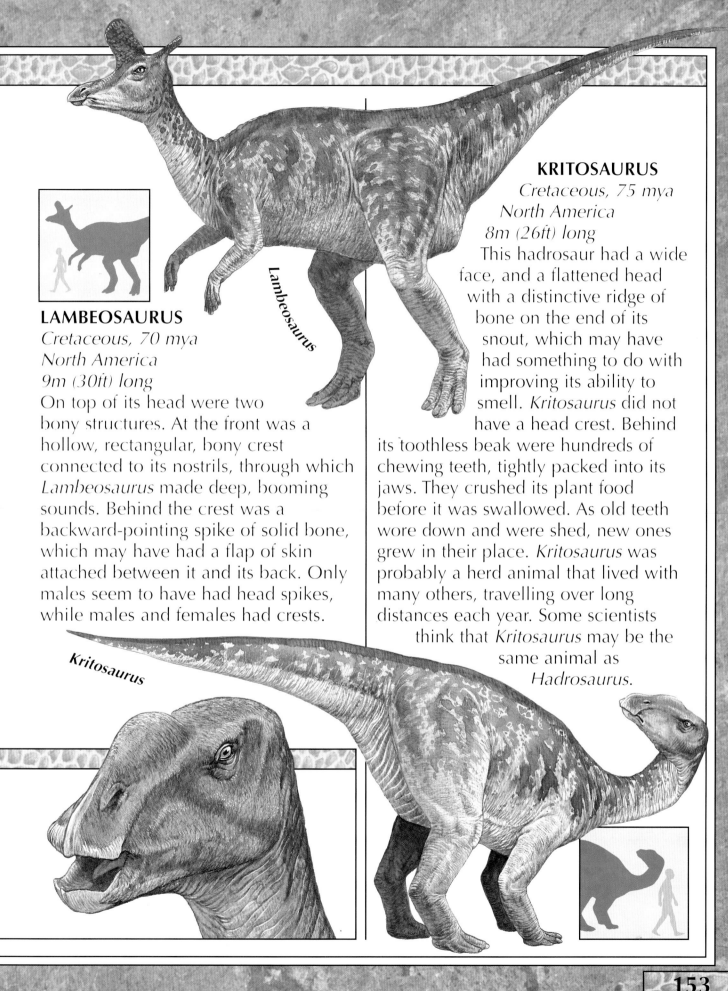

KRITOSAURUS

Cretaceous, 75 mya
North America
8m (26ft) long

This hadrosaur had a wide face, and a flattened head with a distinctive ridge of bone on the end of its snout, which may have had something to do with improving its ability to smell. *Kritosaurus* did not have a head crest. Behind its toothless beak were hundreds of chewing teeth, tightly packed into its jaws. They crushed its plant food before it was swallowed. As old teeth wore down and were shed, new ones grew in their place. *Kritosaurus* was probably a herd animal that lived with many others, travelling over long distances each year. Some scientists think that *Kritosaurus* may be the same animal as *Hadrosaurus*.

Lambeosaurus

LAMBEOSAURUS

Cretaceous, 70 mya
North America
9m (30ft) long

On top of its head were two bony structures. At the front was a hollow, rectangular, bony crest connected to its nostrils, through which *Lambeosaurus* made deep, booming sounds. Behind the crest was a backward-pointing spike of solid bone, which may have had a flap of skin attached between it and its back. Only males seem to have had head spikes, while males and females had crests.

Kritosaurus

Remarkable finds of hadrosaur fossils have helped scientists learn more about the duck-bills than any other group of dinosaurs. For example, the body of a 'mummified' *Edmontosaurus* has shown that duck-bills had thick, wrinkled skin covered in a 'pavement' of small, overlapping bony plates. Unfortunately, no fossils can reveal what colour hadrosaur skin was.

TSINTAOSAURUS
Cretaceous, 70 mya
Asia
10m (33ft) long
Tsintaosaurus, a large hadrosaur from China, had a long, bony spike-shaped head crest growing between its eyes. The spike, which was hollow, was up to 1m (3ft 3in) long, and pointed forwards. A flap, or 'bag', of skin may have stretched from the tip of the spike to the snout, which could have been inflated to produce a range of sounds.

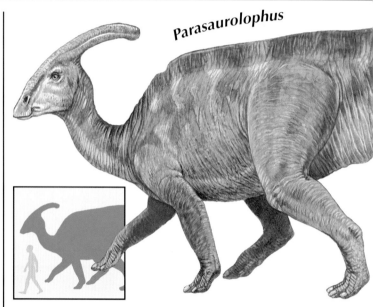
Parasaurolophus

PARASAUROLOPHUS
Cretaceous, 75 mya
North America
10m (33ft) long
Parasaurolophus was one of the most striking of the hadrosaurs. From its head grew a thin-walled bony crest, up to 1.8m (6ft) long. The crest was a hollow tube, inside which was a complicated series of nasal passages which passed down into the animal's throat. A deep-sounding trumpeting noise may have been made as *Parasaurolophus* blew air through its crest. When it leaned its head backwards, the tip of the crest rested in a notch on its back.

Tsintaosaurus

PROSAUROLOPHUS

Cretaceous, 75 mya
North America
15m (49ft) long

Prosaurolophus was one of the largest hadrosaurs. It had a wide snout and a bill that was smaller and shorter than the bills of other members of its family. On its head was a crest that ended in a spike. *Prosaurolophus* probably ate a mixture of tough vegetation (twigs, pine needles and seeds) and also softer parts of plants (leaves, stems and fruit). Standing on its back legs it could reach quite high up. It may be the ancestor of *Saurolophus*.

DENTAL BATTERIES

Hadrosaurs had up to 1,600 teeth packed tightly into their jaws, in what are known as 'dental batteries'. There were no spaces between any of the teeth, which were arranged in groups of three across the jaw. Each group formed a 'tooth family'. Juveniles had fewer teeth than adults, and all had new teeth lined up below the jaw to replace old ones as they fell out.

400 teeth per battery

EDMONTOSAURUS

Cretaceous, 65 mya
North America
13m (43ft) long

Edmontosaurus had a wide beak-like snout, long jaws with cheek pouches, and big eyes. As many as 1,000 tiny teeth were set into the back of its jaws. It lived in large herds and migrated thousands of miles each year. When grazing on low plants it moved on all-fours. In 1908, George Sternberg (1883–1969), an American fossil hunter, found a nearly complete *Edmontosaurus* with fossilised skin covering most of its body. This was the first dinosaur found with remains of flesh, and it is famous as 'the dinosaur mummy'.

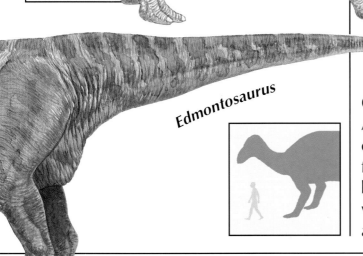

Prosaurolophus

Edmontosaurus

For many years it was thought that some hadrosaurs were aquatic animals that spent their lives in water, breathing through their hollow head crests like snorkels. This idea is no longer accepted. Instead, scientists believe that duck-billed dinosaurs lived on land, walking on their hind legs with their tails held stiff and straight behind.

BRACHYLOPHOSAURUS

Cretaceous, 80 mya
North America
9m (30ft) long

Like other hadrosaurs, *Brachylophosaurus* had a duck-like, toothless beak, and hundreds of small, replaceable chewing teeth at the back of its mouth. However, where it differed from many others was in its head crest, which was a low, flat, bony bump on the end of its snout. It was not hollow, but was formed from solid bone, so it could not have been used to make sounds. *Brachylophosaurus* may have gone nose-to-nose with another of its kind, pushing or butting an opponent in a contest to decide who was the strongest.

ANATOTITAN

Cretaceous, 65 mya
North America
12m (40ft) long

Anatotitan was a large, herd-living hadrosaur that lived in forests. It fed on a variety of plants including conifer needles, twigs, seeds and waterweed. At the front of its snout was a long, wide, toothless beak. Behind the beak were hundreds of strong chewing teeth, packed tightly into its jaws. Its teeth were lined up in dental batteries next to its cheek pouches, where food was temporarily held while the animal was eating. Its tongue scraped food out of the pouches and on to its teeth. *Anatotitan* had a long, pointed tail, three hoofed toes on its back feet, and its short arms ended in hands which had soft, mitten-like, fleshy palms.

Brachylophosaurus

Anatotitan

SHANTUNGOSAURUS
Shantungosaurus

SHANTUNGOSAURUS

Cretaceous, 75 mya
Asia
16m (52ft) long
A massive hadrosaur from China, *Shantungosaurus* is the longest and heaviest duck-billed dinosaur known, weighing around 7 tonnes. It was a flat-headed animal, without a head crest. Like all hadrosaurs its beak was toothless, but its jaws were packed with around 1,500 tiny chewing teeth. A large hole near its nostrils may have been covered by a loose flap, or 'bag', of skin, which could be inflated to make sounds.

CORYTHOSAURUS

Cretaceous, 80 mya
North America
9m (30ft) long
On top of the head of *Corythosaurus* was its most notable feature – a large semi-circular bony crest which resembled a flattened helmet. Only adult males seem to have grown fully developed head crests. The crests of females and juveniles were much smaller. *Corythosaurus* was a swamp-dweller that lived along the margins of forests. It lived in herds near water, and may have been able to swim, or at least wade through deep water, pushing floating debris out of its way with its wide, paddle-like hands.

HEAD CRESTS FOR SOUND AND SMELL

Baby hadrosaurs, such as Corythosaurus, *were born without head crests. As they grew into adults their skulls expanded up and to the back, to form the crest. It was hollow. Inside it were nasal passages, perhaps used for making sounds, and for improving the animal's sense of smell.*

Nasal passage

Corythosaurus

MAIASAURA

Maiasaura is the best-known duck-bill. Its life cycle from birth to death is understood, and is possible because a nesting site has been found, containing eggs and young. This hadrosaur seems to have been a loving parent, and its name, meaning 'Good Mother Lizard', was chosen for this reason.

Name: Maiasaura
Lived: 80 million years ago
Found: North America
Length: 9m (30ft)
Diet: Plants
Habitat: Forests

HORN-COVERED BEAK

Maiasaura had a broad snout with a horn-covered beak. It had cheek pouches, and its jaws were packed with teeth. There was a bony ridge on top of its head. Its arms were short, and its legs and tail were long.

SAFETY IN NUMBERS

Maiasaura lived in herds of as many as 10,000 animals. It was a plant-eater, and for an adult to keep its body in good shape it needed to eat 90 kg (200 lb) of vegetation every day. If attacked, the herd might have stampeded to safety.

MIGRATING IN VAST HERDS

With so many animals in the herd, there was a non-stop search for food. Herds may have migrated along well-known seasonal routes, travelling from feeding sites to nesting sites.

AT THE NEST SITE

Maiasaura did not sit on its nest. Instead, the nest was covered with plants. As they rotted, heat was made which kept the eggs warm. The eggs developed inside this 'incubator'. Hatchlings were about 30cm (1ft) long.

Food was brought to them by their parents. When they were 1.5m (5ft) long they were big enough to leave the nest. At the age of one year, a young *Maiasaura* was 2.5m (8ft) long – five times smaller than an adult. How long it stayed with its parents is a mystery.

With their nests built about one body-length apart from each other, adult Maiasaura tend to their eggs and young. Until the eggs have hatched, adults stay by their nests. Once the defenceless young have emerged, they are vulnerable to attack from predators.

MAIASAURA NEST

Maiasaura *made a nest about 2m (6ft 6in) across, scooped into the soil to form a hollow. Vegetation was placed inside to make a soft lining. Up to 25 oval eggs, each about the size of a grapefruit, were laid in circles. The eggs did not touch each other.*

CHAPTER SIX

PTEROSAURS

Dinosaurs never flew in the sky. None had wings. But another group of reptiles ruled the skies during the Dinosaur Age. These were the pterosaurs, 'wing-lizards'. (Although, like dinosaurs, they were not lizards.)

Pterosaurs appeared just after the earliest dinosaurs, in the Mid Triassic Period, more than 225 million years ago. They quickly evolved into a huge variety of shapes and sizes. But inside, they all had the same basic skeleton and body structure.

MANY AND VARIED

Pterosaurs had a wide range of foods and lifestyles. Most of their fossil remains are from pterosaurs which lived near water. Some were experts at scooping fish from rivers or lakes. Others skimmed over the sea, filtering tiny animals and plants from the surface. Others hunted over land, snatching insects in mid air or scavenging carrion on the ground.

WINGS OF SKIN

A pterosaur's front limbs or 'arms' had become wings. The main wing surface was a tough, elastic sheet known as the wing membrane or patagium. It was made of skin strengthened by stretchy fibres and very thin strips of muscle. The membrane was attached along each side of the body, from the shoulder to the back leg.

Phobetor

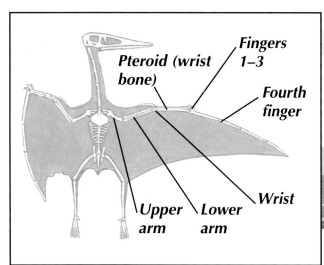

Pteroid (wrist bone)

Fingers 1–3

Fourth finger

Wrist

Upper arm

Lower arm

Pterosaur bones (like a bird's) were hollow and extremely thin-walled, to save weight.

LONG FINGERS

The wing membrane was stretched and held out by the bones of the arm and wrist, which were quite long, and the even longer bones of the hugely extended fourth finger.

SOAR OR DART?

Some pterosaurs were designed for long glides and effortless soaring. Their wings were long and slender, like the wings of the albatross today, to obtain maximum lift from the rising warm air of thermals, and the updraughts as winds blew against cliffs and hills. Other pterosaurs specialised in more agile, manoeuvrable flight. They had short, wide wings, and powerful flapping muscles to twist, turn and dart in the air, like hawks today. Detailed fossils show that a pterosaur's body was covered with a kind of fur, to keep its muscles warm for bursts of action. This means pterosaurs were probably warm-blooded.

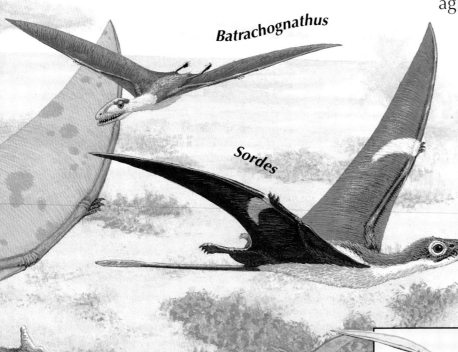

Batrachognathus

Sordes

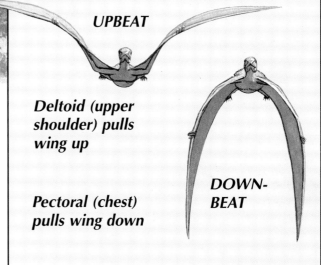

UPBEAT

Deltoid (upper shoulder) pulls wing up

Pectoral (chest) pulls wing down

DOWN-BEAT

Some pterosaurs had sharp teeth in their jaws, and long, trailing tails. Others had very short tails and toothless, bird-like beaks.

Large chest muscles pulled the wing down, thrusting the pterosaur up and forwards.

TRIASSIC PTEROSAURS

The Triassic Period was a time of rapid evolution for reptiles. Several new groups appeared – crocodiles, turtles, sea reptiles and pterosaurs, as well as dinosaurs. The earliest pterosaurs date back to about 230–225 million years ago. Yet even these first known kinds were already skilled fliers, with all the main pterosaur features, including fully formed wings. Even earlier pterosaurs, which showed features of their ancestors, probably existed. But for the present they are 'missing links', which are absent from our fossil collections.

PETEINOSAURUS
Late Triassic, 220 mya
Europe
60cm (2ft) wing span
Peteinosaurus is one of the earliest pterosaurs so far discovered. It had shorter wings than most later types, and a long tail with a vertical 'paddle' at the end, used as a rudder to steer in flight. Its tail bones were stiffened by bony rods.

Peteinosaurus lived on the shores of the ancient Tethys Sea, which today is the foothills of the Alps in northern Italy. It was small, about the size of a pigeon, and its thumb-sized head was mostly jaws, with two large front fangs. It probably swooped from a perch to grab insects such as dragonflies in mid air.

Peteinosaurus

WHERE DID PTEROSAURS COME FROM?

The origins of pterosaurs are still a mystery. Few suitable animals are known from fossil remains. Sharovipteryx shows the possible type of creature but it lived too late, in the Late Triassic, when pterosaurs were already around. It was a glider belonging to the thecodont reptile group – the same group which may have given rise to the dinosaurs. Its remains come from Kazakhstan in Asia. Only 25cm (10in) long, Sharovipteryx had flaps of skin between its long rear legs and tail, and perhaps smaller skin flaps between its short arms and chest.

PREONDACTYLUS

Late Triassic, 220 million years ago
Europe
45cm (18in) wing span

'Preone finger' was named from the Preone Valley in northern Italy, where its finger bones were discovered. It was another very early pterosaur, with short wings, long legs and a long, paddle-ended tail. Only blackbird-sized, it had narrow, pointed jaws with an array of sharp teeth of various sizes, suggesting it ate insects or fish. In one fossil find the bones of *Preondactylus* are packed into a lump. Perhaps this pterosaur crashed on the water and was eaten by large fish, which regurgitated or 'brought back' its hard remains as a pellet.

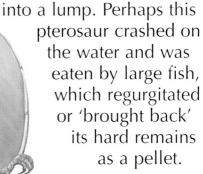

Preondactylus

PTEROSAURS AND BIRDS

Were pterosaurs birds? No – they evolved 75 million years earlier than birds, and from very different ancestors. A pterosaur's wings were quite unlike a bird's wings, being supported mainly by finger bones rather than arm bones. Also pterosaurs had no feathers, which all birds have, and they did have bones in the tail, which birds lack.

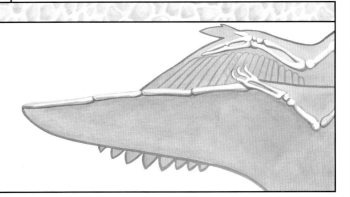

EUDIMORPHODON

Eudimorphodon lived in Late Triassic times, about 220 million years ago, in what is now northern Italy. Its name means 'true two-form tooth' because it had two kinds or shapes of teeth. There were sharp fangs at the front of its jaws, and smaller teeth, each with three or five cusps (points), at the back. No other pterosaur had many-cusped teeth. *Eudimorphodon's* other features – a long tail, but short neck, wings and legs – were all typical of its group, the rhamphorhynchs. This was the first main pterosaur group to appear, and is named after the later *Rhamphorhynchus* (see page 172).

FISH FOR SUPPER

The sharp teeth of *Eudimorphodon* suggest that it tried to catch slippery prey, probably fish. In fact, preserved fish scales have been found with the fossilised remains of this pterosaur, in the position where its stomach would have been in life.

Eudimorphodon probably lived in groups along the coast of the ancient Tethys Sea. It flew low over the water, swooping and turning to peer for shadowy fish just below the surface. Its fossil skull has large eye sockets, showing that *Eudimorphodon* probably had good sight. The long jaws could dart forwards or swish sideways to grasp prey, either from just above the surface or after diving below. The short neck was unlikely to reach far into the water from above, so diving was perhaps more likely.

DIVING FOR FISH

The 'diving theory' says that Eudimorphodon caught its fishy food by plunging like an arrow into the water. It scooped the prey into its mouth, as gannets do today. This method would need good eyesight to see under the surface, and very strong flight muscles so the pterosaur could flap hard to pull its body out of the water, and rise back into the air.

FINE FLIER

Eudimorphodon was certainly an active flier. Its breast bone was wide, with a raised ridge called a keel, to anchor the strong wing-flapping muscles. The three short fingers and claws halfway along each wing were also quite strong, perhaps for clinging to a cliff face or tree during rests between flights. The wing span was 1m (3ft 3in). *Eudimorphodon's* total length was about 70cm (2ft 4in), from the tip of its sharp, beak-like snout to the long tail with its diamond-shaped paddle.

Eudimorphodon had different shaped teeth when young. These 'baby teeth' were more suited to snapping at insects. Perhaps the youngsters stayed over the shore, until they were strong and skilled enough to risk diving into the sea.

EUDIMORPHODON SKULL

Three pairs of large openings in the skull reduced its weight. There were 58 teeth in the upper jaw and 56 in the lower.

Weight-saving openings

Eye socket

Nostril

Name: *Eudimorphodon*
Lived: *220 million years ago*
Found: *Europe*

Wingspan: *1m (3ft 3in)*
Diet: *Fish, insects*
Habitat: *Rivers, lakes*

From their beginnings in the Triassic Period, in what is now Europe, pterosaurs soon spread to other regions. During the Jurassic Period too, they began to increase in size. They also changed their body shapes, especially the head and tail, as the earlier rhamphorhynch group gave way to the later pterodactyl group, as shown on later pages.

DORYGNATHUS

Early Jurassic, 190 mya
Europe
1m (3ft 3in) wing span
Dorygnathus lived in what is now Germany. Its fossils are quite plentiful, for a pterosaur – their thin, fragile bones were so easily crushed after death, they rarely formed fossils.

Dorygnathus had extraordinary teeth. Near the front of both the upper and lower jaws, they were very long, curved and sharp. They pointed forwards and interlocked when the mouth was closed, to form a type of spiky grab which was perfect for impaling slippery fish at the water's surface. The smaller, finer teeth at the back of the jaws held the food firmly as *Dorygnathus* flew back to its roost for a feast. The jaws themselves formed sharp, toothless points at the very front. This feature gave the pterosaur its name, which means 'spear-jaw'.

Dorygnathus

PTEROSAUR HEADS ...

The earlier rhamphorhynchs like Rhamphorhynchus *itself had a relatively short head, held forwards on a stubby neck, and pointed jaws lined with sharp teeth. The later pterodactyls such as* Tropeognathus *had a head balanced at an angle on the long neck, a long beak with few or no teeth, and often a head-crest.*

SCAPHOGNATHUS

Late Jurassic, 150 million years ago
Europe
90cm (3ft) wing span

Scaphognathus had a short head with a fairly rounded, blunt snout, giving rise to its name of 'tub-jaw'. It had long, upright, sharp-pointed teeth – about 18 in the upper jaw and 10 in the lower jaw.

Scaphognathus

Scaphognathus was one of the first pterosaurs to be found in fossil form, in 1831. Some finds were of young, part-grown individuals. The way that their bones formed and hardened suggests that young pterosaurs grew very quickly to their adult size, and then stayed at this size. This is how birds develop today, but it is unlike most reptiles, which continue to grow slowly all through their lives (although at a decreasing rate). Fossils of *Scaphognathus* skulls show that pterosaurs had quite large brains for their body size, again more like birds than reptiles.

... AND TAILS

Rhamphorhynchs had a long, slender tail, with bony rods and tendons to prevent it bending except near the base. There was usually an upright paddle or vane of stiff skin at the end. Pterodactyls had a very short tail, usually just a few thin tail bones supporting small flaps of skin that joined to the legs.

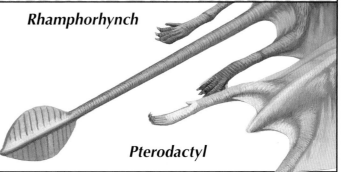

Rhamphorhynch

Pterodactyl

DIMORPHODON

One of the first of the Jurassic pterosaurs, *Dimorphodon* lived about 205 million years ago in what is today southern England. It had the big head, sharp biting teeth and long, stiff tail typical of the rhamphorhynch group. Its total length was 1m (3ft 3in), of which 20cm (8in) was head, and the wings were almost 1.5m (5ft) across.

NOT A HEAVY HEAD

The head of *Dimorphodon* seemed large and heavy, with its deep, narrow snout. But the skull inside consisted mainly of bony struts rather than large slabs, which reduced its weight greatly. *Dimorphodon*'s three fingers on each wing were strong and curved, with sharp claws, for climbing rocks or trees. Like many other pterosaurs, it probably made its home along coasts and shores.

ON WINGS OR FEET?

Dimorphodon was certainly a hunter, probably preying on a variety of victims such as fish, insects, lizards, worms and other small creatures. It had four pairs of large peg-like teeth at the front of both upper and lower jaws, and many smaller teeth behind. These two shapes of teeth led to its name, which means 'two-form tooth'. It is not known whether *Dimorphodon* caught food while on the wing, or by standing and walking on all-fours on the ground.

Dimorphodon's 'beak' was tall from top to bottom, but narrow from side to side. It may have been brightly coloured and used in visual displays, perhaps when courting a partner or claiming a patch of land as a territory, as in modern birds such as hornbills and puffins.

THE WALKING PTEROSAUR

Dimorphodon had very strong, well developed legs, unlike most other pterosaurs. It could stand with its legs under its body, to walk upright on them. Or it could lean forwards and use the fingers on its wings as front feet, to run fast on all-fours.

LEGS AND TOES

Studies of the hips, legs and feet of *Dimorphodon* show that it might have been able to walk like a modern bird, standing upright and balanced on its toes. This is also the way many dinosaurs moved. *Dimorphodon* had five toes on each foot, and all had claws except the fifth or 'little toe'. This was angled sideways or backwards and could have been used to improve balance when *Dimorphodon* was standing or running. Other pterosaurs had much weaker legs that splayed out to the sides, and could probably only shuffle with a sprawling gait.

A SMOOTH FLIER

The wide, backswept wings and trailing tail of *Dimorphodon* gave a naturally well-balanced shape, for gliding in a smooth, controlled and stable way.

Name: *Dimorphodon*
Lived: 205 million years ago
Found: Europe
Wingspan: 1.4m (4ft 6in)
Diet: Fish
Habitat: Coastal cliffs

Dimorphodon spreads its wings, grips with its toe claws, and springs into the air on its strong legs, to soar away on a clifftop breeze.

Rhamphorhynchus is a well-known pterosaur, with many fossils from sites such as the Oxford area of England, the Solnhofen region of Germany, and also Tanzania in Africa. It has given its name to the whole group of long-tailed pterosaurs, known as the Rhamphorhynchoids. Various types of *Rhamphorhynchus*, of different sizes, survived for more than 30 million years.

Rhamphorhynchus

RHAMPHORHYNCHUS

Late Jurassic, 150 mya
Europe, Africa
Up to 2m (6ft 6in) wing span
This pterosaur's name means 'beak-snout', and indeed it had a long, narrow, pointed beak with sharp teeth sticking out at angles from the sides – ideal for spearing and trapping wriggly, writhing fish. The head was about 20cm (8in) long, and the tail added another 1m (3ft 3in). *Rhamphorhynchus* probably caught fish by skimming its beak through the surface of the water. The beak would snap shut the instant a fish touched the very sensitive mouth.

TOUGH WING SKIN

A pterosaur's wings might look like weak, thin flaps of skin. But they had close-spaced fibres, actinofibrillae, which are beautifully preserved in some fossils of Rhamphorhynchus. These strengthened the wings and stopped tears spreading.

HOLLOW BONES

One of the pterosaur's main weight-saving features, for better flight, was its skeleton. Many of the bones were hollow tubes, with walls almost as thin as paper. But the space inside was not quite empty. It was criss-crossed by fine rods of bone. These struts made the bones extremely stiff and strong, despite their light weight.

FINE FLIERS

Some time ago, fossil experts thought that pterosaurs were poor fliers, little more than gliders with weak, floppy wings. But most experts now believe that, in general, pterosaurs were strong, capable fliers. The breast bone was large, with a keel (flange) for anchoring powerful chest muscles which flapped the wings. But, like modern birds, pterosaurs varied. Some were better fliers, with speed and agility, while others used gliding and soaring more.

Batrachognathus

Bone struts

BATRACHOGNATHUS

Late Jurassic, 150 mya
Asia (Kazakhstan)
50cm (20in) wing span
Only two specimens of this pterosaur are known, preserved in rocks that were once the bed of a lake. The name, 'frog jaw', describes the short head and wide mouth. The teeth were peg-like, suitable for catching insects – fossils of dragonflies, cicadas, beetles, wasps, caddisflies and mayflies are found in the same rocks. *Batrachognathus* must have been a very agile flier, with keen sight.

Although a member of the rhamphorhynch group, it may have had a stumpy tail, more like a pterosaur from the pterodactyl group.

THE PTERODACTYLS ARRIVE

The pterodactyls were the second main group of pterosaurs. Their fossils suddenly appear in Late Jurassic rocks as the first group, rhamphorhynchs, start to decline. Presumably the first group gave rise to the second, but this is not known for sure, because there is a gap in the fossil record. Only the pterodactyls survived into the next period, the Cretaceous.

GERMANODACTYLUS
Late Jurassic, 150 million years ago
Europe
1.35m (4ft 5in) wing span
'German finger' had the short tail and head crest typical of pterodactyls. The low, bony crest ran from the forehead halfway along the beak and was covered with horn. *Germanodactylus* may have roosted hanging upside down by its toes, like a bat.

Germanodactylus also showed another gradual change typical of the pterodactyl group – an even longer, narrower beak, with fewer or even no teeth. This may be because teeth are heavy and make flying more difficult. (Birds lack them.) *Germanodactylus* had some short, peg-like teeth, but the front of its beak was toothless, tapering to a horn-covered tip.

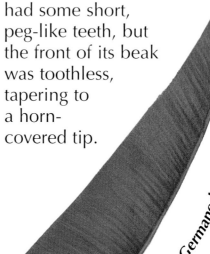

Germanodactylus

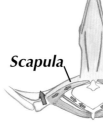

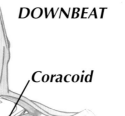

BRACED FOR FLIGHT

A pterosaur's chest, shoulder and arm bones were greatly adapted to stand the strains of flapping flight. The V-shaped coracoid (wishbone) braced the sternum (breast bone) against the scapula (shoulder blade), to withstand the pull of the main flight muscles.

DOWNBEAT

Coracoid

Breast bone

UPBEAT

Scapula

Upper arm

FURRY BODIES

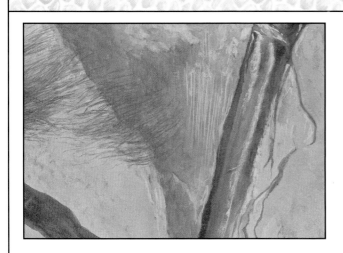

Several very detailed, finely preserved fossils show that a pterosaur's skin had tiny pits, like pin-pricks, from which short hairs grew. This fur would be dense or close-spaced on the head and body, but less or absent on the wings, toe webbings and tail. Pterosaurs probably had fur to keep their flight muscles and large brains warm and working more efficiently, as in birds and mammals today. But if pterosaurs were not cold-blooded, and not scaly – were they reptiles at all?

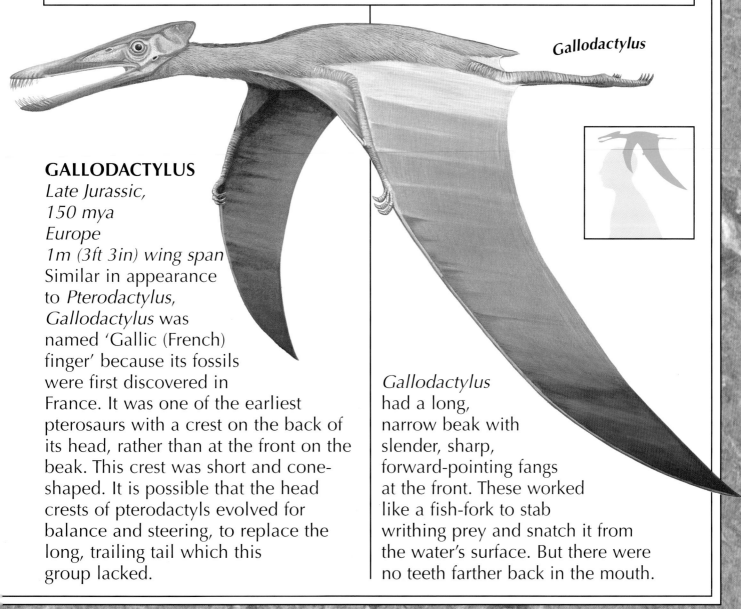

Gallodactylus

GALLODACTYLUS

Late Jurassic,
150 mya
Europe
1m (3ft 3in) wing span
Similar in appearance to *Pterodactylus*, *Gallodactylus* was named 'Gallic (French) finger' because its fossils were first discovered in France. It was one of the earliest pterosaurs with a crest on the back of its head, rather than at the front on the beak. This crest was short and cone-shaped. It is possible that the head crests of pterodactyls evolved for balance and steering, to replace the long, trailing tail which this group lacked.

Gallodactylus had a long, narrow beak with slender, sharp, forward-pointing fangs at the front. These worked like a fish-fork to stab writhing prey and snatch it from the water's surface. But there were no teeth farther back in the mouth.

UNUSUAL JURASSIC PTEROSAURS

At the end of the Jurassic Period, some 150–140 million years ago, both main groups of pterosaurs existed – but the long-tailed rhamphorhynchs were on the demise, as the short-tailed pterodactyls took over. Two of the most fascinating kinds are shown here. Their fossils give valuable clues to the lifestyles of these two groups.

SORDES

Late Jurassic, 150 million years ago
Asia (Kazakhstan)
60cm (2ft) wing span
The full name of this pterosaur, *Sordes pilosus*, means 'hairy devil'. The first fossils found, in the 1960s, were an almost complete skeleton with imprints of soft body parts – including a thick coat of long fur over the head and body, and thinner fur on the wings (but not the tail). *Sordes* was a smallish pterosaur of the rhamphorhynch group, with short, broad wings. It had an extra flap of wing membrane between the two back legs, attached as far down as the ankles, leaving the tail free to move beneath. Like other pterosaurs, on the ground *Sordes* probably folded its long fourth finger bones back. The elastic, stretchy wing membrane would shrink or contract into a narrow band.

TAKING OFF DOWNWARDS ...

From the design of their hips, legs and feet, most pterosaurs spent little time moving about on land. They probably rested on trees or rock faces, hanging by their curved finger or toe claws. To take off, they pushed with hands and feet, while letting go and twisting around, to flick themselves away from the surface. Then they opened their wings to halt their fall and begin the flight.

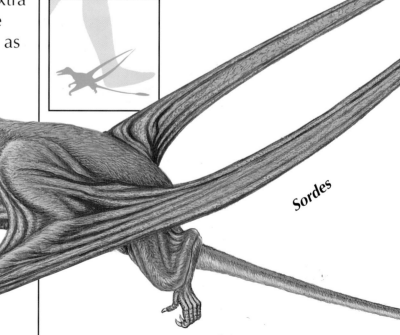

Sordes

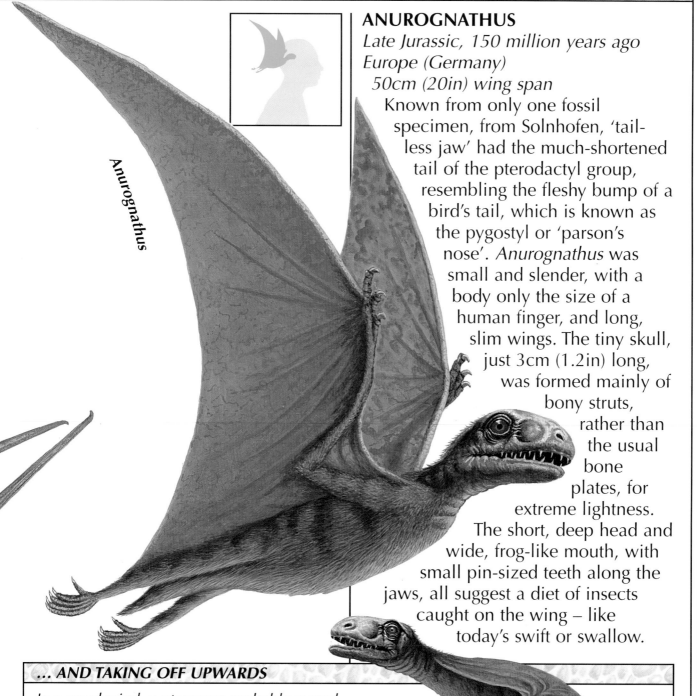

Anurognathus

ANUROGNATHUS
Late Jurassic, 150 million years ago
Europe (Germany)
50cm (20in) wing span
Known from only one fossil specimen, from Solnhofen, 'tail-less jaw' had the much-shortened tail of the pterodactyl group, resembling the fleshy bump of a bird's tail, which is known as the pygostyl or 'parson's nose'. *Anurognathus* was small and slender, with a body only the size of a human finger, and long, slim wings. The tiny skull, just 3cm (1.2in) long, was formed mainly of bony struts, rather than the usual bone plates, for extreme lightness. The short, deep head and wide, frog-like mouth, with small pin-sized teeth along the jaws, all suggest a diet of insects caught on the wing – like today's swift or swallow.

... AND TAKING OFF UPWARDS

In a good wind, a pterosaur probably reared up on its legs, opened its wings to face the wind, and jumped or hopped while flapping to lift itself away. Taking off in calm conditions or from water was more tricky. Some pterosaurs may have launched themselves back into the air from the crest of a wave, or pushed off using webbed feet.

PTERODACTYLUS

Pterosaurs are sometimes called 'pterodactyls', but this is the name for only one group of them – and in particular, for *Pterodactylus* itself. In fact there were several kinds of *Pterodactylus* living in different regions, from more than 160 to about 145 million years ago.

MANY SIZES

Different kinds of *Pterodactylus* varied in size from as small as a blackbird, with wings less than 30cm (12in) across, to giants with wing spans of more than 2.5m (8ft) – as huge as the vultures and condors of today. The fossils have been found in several parts of Europe, including Germany, France and England, and in Tanzania, Africa.

FUTURE FEATURES

Pterodactylus showed the future of pterosaur evolution. It had a very short tail, and a lengthened neck that joined to the base of the skull, rather than to the rear. The bones of the skull became even thinner and lighter, with larger weight-saving openings between them.

Some well-preserved fossils show that the main wing membranes attached to the upper leg and upper part of lower leg – but there was little or no 'tail' membrane between the back legs. However, there was a small, extra flap of wing at the front, between wrist and shoulder. This part is called the propatagium. It was supported by one of the wrist bones, the pteroid, which angled forwards and inwards.

BEAKS AND TEETH

Different Pterodactylus *species had slightly different beaks. Some had evenly-spaced teeth, smaller to the rear. Others had most teeth at the front, with a toothless region at the back.*

Name: *Pterodactylus*
Lived: *145 million years ago*
Found: *Europe*
Wingspan: *36–250cm (16–69in)*
Diet: *Fish, insects*
Habitat: *Rivers, lakes*

WINGS LARGE AND SMALL

The wings of *Pterodactylus*, 'wing-finger', were very long and narrow. This was partly due to the metacarpal (hand) bones, near the wing claws, which had become longer. One precious fossil is from a baby, probably just a few weeks old, with wings 18cm (7in) across, and a body less than 2cm (1in) long. Yet this tiny creature could already fly.

Pterosaur fingers and toes were poor for walking and running, but ideal at gripping and hanging from tree trunks, branches and rocky ledges. Maybe Pterodactylus *roosted in noisy colonies, and slept hanging upside down, wing membranes folded around the body, like a bat of today.*

FEEDING YOUNG?

Young Pterodactylus *could fly, but may have been too weak to catch food. Perhaps their parents brought meals. The adult could regurgitate or 'bring back' swallowed food. One* Pterodactylus *specimen shows a baggy throat pouch, which could have carried food back to the baby.*

The long-tailed (rhamphorhynch) pterosaurs did not survive into the Cretaceous. But the short-tailed pterodactyls evolved fast and spread to every continent. They still seemed to live mainly in coastal areas, with impressive teeth and beaks for catching fish, shellfish and similar food. Some even spread inland, as vulture-like scavengers.

ORNITHODESMUS

Early Cretaceous, 130 mya
Europe (England)
5m (16ft) wing span
One of the first really large pterosaurs, the fossil hip bone of 'bird-ribbon' was discovered long ago, in the 1880s. At first, it was thought to be part of a prehistoric bird. The beak of *Ornithodesmus* was wide and spoon-shaped, giving it the nickname of the

Ornithodesmus

'duck-billed' pterosaur. Both the upper and lower parts had short, sharp teeth, like tiny blades, which meshed together as the mouth closed. These were ideal for spiking and trapping fish. But the beak and teeth of *Ornithodesmus* were very different from the long, narrow, pointed types of other pterosaurs. So *Ornithodesmus* must have caught food by a very different method – although how is not known.

THE ADAPTABLE BEAK

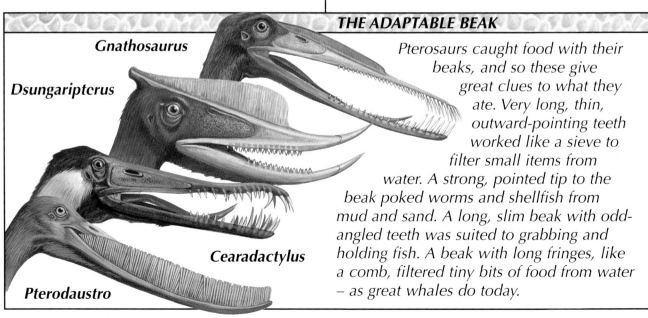

Gnathosaurus

Dsungaripterus

Cearadactylus

Pterodaustro

Pterosaurs caught food with their beaks, and so these give great clues to what they ate. Very long, thin, outward-pointing teeth worked like a sieve to filter small items from water. A strong, pointed tip to the beak poked worms and shellfish from mud and sand. A long, slim beak with odd-angled teeth was suited to grabbing and holding fish. A beak with long fringes, like a comb, filtered tiny bits of food from water – as great whales do today.

WHERE DID PTEROSAURS LIVE?

Fossils show that most pterosaurs lived near water, along seas, lakes, rivers and swamps. Fish was important food, and also some pterosaurs needed strong winds to take off and soar.

Some may have lived in other habitats, such as forests and deserts, but there is little fossil evidence to prove this.

Cearadactylus

CEARADACTYLUS

Early to Mid Cretaceous, 115 mya
South America (Brazil)
5m (16ft) wing span
'Ceará finger' is named from the region of north-east Brazil where its fossils were uncovered, in the mid 1980s. It had a big, powerful head nearly 60cm (2ft) long and lived 120–110 million years ago. The strong teeth, which stuck out at odd angles and were much longer at the front, look similar to those of the crocodile today called the gharial. This is an expert fish-catcher – *Cearadactylus* probably was, too'. It may have trawled the shallows of lakes for its catch. Then it flew to a rocky outcrop, where it held the meal in its finger-claws to eat. But only the skull of this pterosaur is known. The rest is clever guesswork.

Fish are not the only animals in the sea. There are shellfish, worms, jellyfish, shrimps, and the tiny drifting plants and creatures of the plankton. During the Cretaceous Period, pterosaurs became specialised for many of these food sources.

PTERODAUSTRO

Early Cretaceous, 140 mya
South America (Argentina, Chile)
1.3m (4ft 4in) wing span
Nicknamed the flamingo-pterosaur, this was one of the most unusual of the whole group. Its head was 23cm (9in) long and very narrow, with a beak that turned up at the end. The lower jaw had about 1,000 long, close-packed, springy bristles to sweep tiny bits of food from the water, which were mashed by tiny peg-like teeth on the upper jaw. Perhaps *Pterodaustro* stood in the shallows to filter-feed, waving its head from side to side like a flamingo. Or it flew over the surface, dragging its lower jaw in the water as a food-collecting basket.

Pterodaustro

PTEROSAUR NURSERIES

Pterosaurs probably laid eggs, as the dinosaurs did, and like most reptiles do today, as well as birds. A female pterosaur with babies inside would be very heavy and find it difficult to fly, feed and avoid predators. However no fossil eggs, which look as though they could have been laid by pterosaurs, have yet been found.

Many sea birds today make their nests in noisy groups or colonies, along coasts or on ocean islands. They find 'safety in numbers'. Pterosaurs were not birds, but they had very similar lifestyles. Perhaps they also nested in remote colonies, on cliffs, crags and faraway islands. Here they brought food to their tiny babies, safe from predators such as dinosaurs.

DSUNGARIPTERUS
*Late Jurassic to Early Cretaceous,
145 mya
Asia (China)
3m (10ft)
wing span*

Dsungaripterus

Named after the Chinese place where its fossils were found, 'Junggar-wing' may also have lived during Late Jurassic times in Africa. It was a sizeable pterosaur with a head and neck as large as a human arm. The beak's pointed, toothless, up-curved front resembled large tweezers. There were blunt, knob-shaped teeth further back. There was also a bony crest halfway along the upper beak, which ran between the high-set eyes, to stick out from the back of the head.

Dsungaripterus probably poked its pointed beak tip into sand, mud or crevices between rocks. It pulled out prey such as worms and shellfish, which it crushed with its knobbly teeth.

As the Cretaceous Period continued, pterosaurs began to spread farther across the world, and they also increased their range of sizes. Some became as small as today's sparrows, while others evolved into vast creatures, bigger than any bird that has ever lived.

ANHANGUERA

Early to Mid Cretaceous, 120 mya
South America
4m (13ft) wing span

'Old Devil' is the local name for the region of Brazil where these fossils were found. It is one of the best known Early to Mid Cretaceous pterosaurs, with a narrow skull 50cm (1ft 8in) long. The short, pointed teeth were along most of the beak, and longer at the front. Its very flexible neck allowed *Anhanguera* to grab prey from the water's surface. Its small, weak hips and legs would make walking difficult. Like many Cretaceous pterosaurs, *Anhanguera* had a bony crest – in this case, rounded like the edge of a plate, on the upper and lower front beak. Two sizes of crests have been found as fossils.

TOSS, GULP

Pterosaur jaws could open very wide, and the two halves of the lower jaw could move farther apart, sideways, to make a wider opening into the gular (throat) pouch and neck. The pterosaur probably tossed its catch to swallow it whole, head-first – there were no teeth for chewing.

These may be different kinds of *Anhanguera* – or males and females of the same type. In this case, the crests would be helpful when choosing a partner at breeding time (see next page).

Anhanguera

PTEROSAURS AND CLIMATE

During the Cretaceous Period, continents drifted apart, and climates became cooler, drier and more varied with the seasons. If pterosaurs were warm-blooded, they could cope with these changes well – provided they had plenty of food to 'burn' for body heat.

ORNITHOCHEIRUS

Early to Mid Cretaceous, 120 mya
Worldwide on most continents
Possibly up to 12m (40ft) wing span
No whole fossil specimens of 'bird-hand' Ornithocheirus are known – only single bones or fragments here and there. Even so, fossil experts have pieced together information for this great flier. It lived 125–110 million years ago and had a head and body some 3.5m (11ft) long – the beak and skull alone were 1.5m (5ft). Standing on four legs, head upstretched, Ornithocheirus would be 3m (10ft) tall! It is one of the few pterosaurs known in Cretaceous times from the group's original homeland, Europe. It probably soared over oceans, looking for fish and squid to snatch from the surface.

Ornithocheirus

PTEROSAUR HEYDAY

Pterosaurs, like birds and bats today, depended almost entirely on their wings. They needed to fly to hunt, and without food, they would starve. So a pterosaur must have taken great care to protect its huge but delicate wings, folding them out of the way while at rest, and avoiding any obstacles which might snag or tear them.

Like a mammal, a pterosaur would comb or groom the fur over its body, and the shorter hairs on the wings, to get rid of tangles, dirt and bits of seaweed. It probably used its teeth (if there were any), beak tip, and finger and toe claws. The hairs may have helped air to flow smoothly over the body and wings in flight.

FIRST PTEROSAUR FOSSIL

The first pterosaur fossil was discovered in 1784, in the Solnhofen limestone rock of Bavaria, Germany. It was thought to be an amphibious sea creature from an unknown group. In 1801, French animal and fossil expert Georges Cuvier decided it was a flying reptile. He gave its group a new name, Pterodactyle, 'wing-finger'.

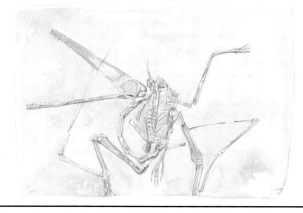

Tropeognathus

TROPEOGNATHUS
*Early Cretaceous, 120 mya
South America
6m (20ft) wing span*
Found in Brazil, this is one of the most unusual pterosaurs, named 'keel-jaw' for the ridge-like crests on its very narrow beak. The crest size may have distinguished females from males (see previous page). Also, or alternatively, the ridges helped to steady and stabilise the beak and prevent sudden sideways jerks, as *Tropeognathus* trailed it in the water, flying just above the surface to feed. The keel under a yacht works in the same way.

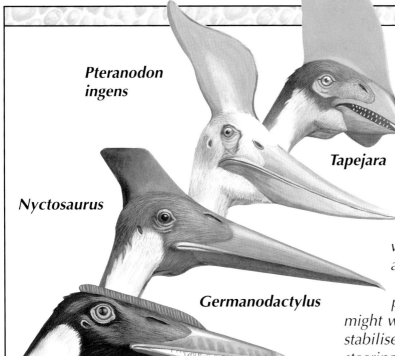

Why did Cretaceous pterosaurs, in particular, have such amazing head crests? There are several ideas for their use. Perhaps they were different sizes in males and females, or between closely related species, to help choose a breeding mate. They could even be brightly coloured for this purpose, like a hornbill's beak today. A long, back-pointing crest would balance the beak at the front, to reduce strain. A flatter, plate-like crest might work as a stabiliser and steering rudder in flight.

Pteranodon ingens

Tapejara

Nyctosaurus

Germanodactylus

PTERANODON

Late Cretaceous, 85 mya
Europe, North America, Asia
8m (26ft) wing span

Pteranodon

Pteranodon had one of the greatest wing spans of any pterosaur, but its body was short and almost tail-less. In fact, its overall proportions were similar to those of the albatross today. Yet, even though *Pteranodon* was more than twice the size of any living bird, it weighed less than 18kg (40lb). *Pteranodon* showed two Late Cretaceous trends in the group – no teeth at all, and a very large head crest. It probably lived near sea cliffs and launched itself into flight, to soar on the ocean winds and scoop up fish or squid in its long beak.

QUETZALCOATLUS

The Late Cretaceous Period, 70–65 million years ago, saw one of the most extraordinary animals of all time – the giant pterosaur *Quetzalcoatlus*. Fossils of this vast beast come from the border of Texas, USA and Mexico. Despite its size, *Quetzalcoatlus* was the last of its group. The same disaster that wiped out the dinosaurs also spelled the end for the pterosaurs. Nothing like them has lived since.

WERE PTEROSAURS NOISY?

In general lifestyle, pterosaurs were similar to certain sea birds. So were they noisy, squawking and calling like gulls and other modern birds? Fossils cannot tell us, yet. But pterosaurs could perhaps clack beaks and clap wings.

BIGGEST-EVER FLIER

Fossils from several kinds of *Quetzalcoatlus* have been found – or some could have been part-grown youngsters. However, nearly all the fossils are bits and fragments, so guessing the size of *Quetzalcoatlus* is difficult. Estimates of its wing span range from 11 to 15m (36 to 49ft), and its weight from 70 to 135kg (150 to 300lb). The head was bigger than a human body, at more than 2m (6ft 6in) in length, and so were the legs. The immense neck stretched out almost 3m (10ft).

Name: *Quetzalcoatlus*
Lived: *70 million years ago*
Found: *North America*
Wingspan: *11m (36ft)*
Diet: *Molluscs, crabs and carrion*
Habitat: *Inland rivers*

FUZZY FUR

The name *Quetzalcoatlus* means 'feathered serpent', after a god of the ancient Aztec people of Mexico. (Although, as far as we know, *Quetzalcoatlus* lacked feathers.) Unlike most other pterosaurs, the fossils of this great creature were found in rocks that did not form on the sea bed. It seems that *Quetzalcoatlus* lived inland, perhaps along rivers and lakes.

Quetzalcoatlus had a large brain and big eyes, suggesting very good sight for spotting food. Its body may have been covered with fuzzy fur or unusual hair-like versions of scales. Also, its main wing bones were not hollow tubes, as in other pterosaurs. They had a T-shape in cross-section, more like a bridge girder, to hold out the huge wings.

THE PTEROSAUR 'VULTURE'?

Quetzalcoatlus *may have soared in air currents, looking for dead and dying food – carrion – just like a vulture or condor today. As a dinosaur died below, it would land and poke its long, sharp-edged beak and neck into the body, to slice off flesh.*

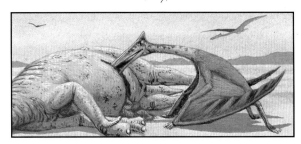

Another suggestion is that Quetzalcoatlus *searched for fish, shellfish and crabs along the flood plains, rivers and lakes. It could chop and slice these with the hard, thin, horny edges of its powerful beak.*

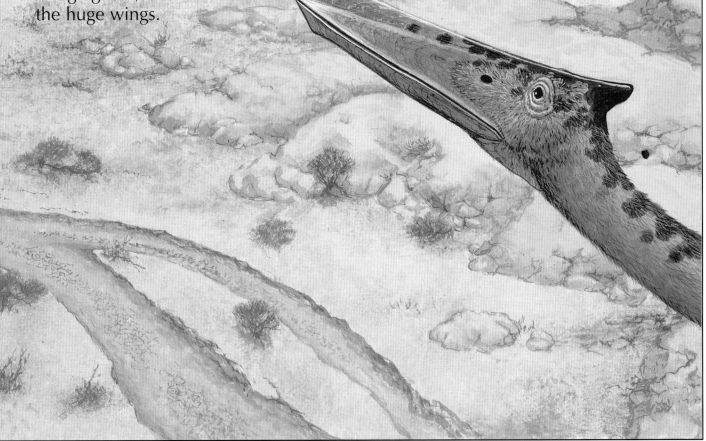

CHAPTER SEVEN

THE TEEMING SEAS

Most wild animals today, especially reptiles, can swim. Dinosaurs could probably swim, too, if they had to. Perhaps they splashed into a lake to escape from a predator, or crossed a river away from a forest fire. But no dinosaurs lived in water. Their legs and bodies were suited to moving on land. However, during the Age of Dinosaurs, the waters were busy with all kinds of life – including many types of reptiles.

TAKING OVER THE OCEANS

Reptiles truly ruled the world during the Mesozoic Era. Dinosaurs took over the land. Pterosaurs dominated the skies. Several groups of reptiles took control in the sea, including the nothosaurs, plesiosaurs, pliosaurs, ichthyosaurs and mosasaurs.

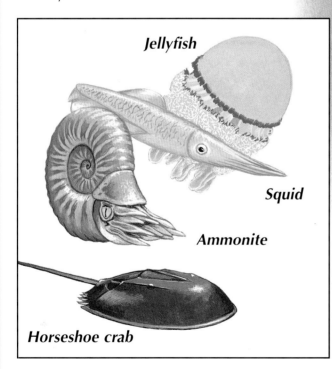

Jellyfish

Squid

Ammonite

Horseshoe crab

Apart from fish and reptiles, many other animals lived in the oceans. All those shown above survive today, apart from ammonites.

BENEATH THE WAVES

Sea-living reptiles had similar body features to their land-dwelling cousins such as dinosaurs. They had scaly skin, eyes, teeth, limbs and tails. Also, they had lungs and breathed air. They did not have gills, and could not breathe underwater like fish. So all of the sea reptiles had to come to the surface regularly, to take in air. Then they held their breath to dive beneath the waves.

Turtle

Ichthyosaur

Each main group of marine (sea-dwelling) reptiles had a distinct body shape. Only the turtles are left in modern times.

LEGS TO PADDLES

However, ocean reptiles had their own special features, which their land cousins lacked. Their body shapes were smooth and sleek, to slip easily at speed through the water. Their limbs had changed or evolved into flippers, for rowing or paddling, rather than for walking and running. Their teeth were suited to catching slippery fish or squid, or crushing hard-cased shellfish.

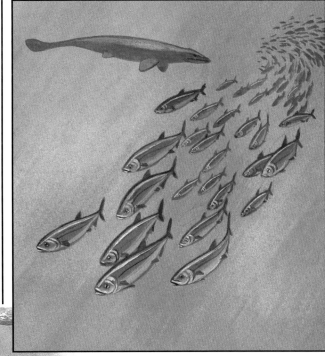

Fish had already been around for almost 300 million years when the first reptiles took to the sea.

Plesiosaur

Pliosaur

SEAFOOD

Why did some reptiles take to the sea, rather than stay on dry ground? The land was already being dominated by dinosaurs and other fierce predators. It was a tough life, finding food and avoiding danger. In the seas there were many kinds of foods – fish, shellfish, starfish, crabs, squid, even jellyfish and sea bed worms. The main large predators already in the oceans were sharks, which had been around since the Devonian Period, nearly 200 million years earlier. But the oceans were big enough for sea reptiles, too.

NOTHOSAURS

Nothosaurs were the first big reptiles to take to the sea. They began near the start of the Triassic Period, nearly 250 million years ago, but had all died out by the end of that period. They probably hunted fish in the shallow seas. Unlike some later reptiles, such as the ichthyosaurs, nothosaurs were not totally suited to life in water. They had webbed feet rather than true flippers. Perhaps they waddled out of the water to rest on the shore, as seals do today.

CERESIOSAURUS

Mid Triassic, 225 million years ago
Europe
4m (13ft) long
Compared to other nothosaurs, *Ceresiosaurus* had very long toes on its four feet. It probably swam by curving or undulating its long body and tail from side to side, and rowing with its front limbs. The back limbs may have helped to steer and slow down. Like all nothosaurs, *Ceresiosaurus* had many sharp teeth, for grabbing slippery prey like fish and squid, to be swallowed whole.

Ceresiosaurus

Lariosaurus

LARIOSAURUS

Mid Triassic, 225 mya
Europe
60cm (2ft) long
Lariosaurus was one of the smallest nothosaurs. Its fossils have been found in Spain, and show that its feet and toes were well suited to walking on land, rather than swimming. Also, its neck was not as long as other, later nothosaurs. So *Lariosaurus* may have spent more time paddling in the shallows or out on the shore, snatching small prey such as fish, shrimps, prawns and worms from rock pools, or feasting on reptile eggs. (There were no birds at the time.) In some coastal places today, monitor lizards follow the same lifestyle.

PART-TIME LAND-LOVERS

Nothosaurs may have spent part of their time on land, on the beaches and rocks.

Pistosaurus

NOTHOSAURUS

Early to Late Triassic, 225 mya
Asia, Europe and North Africa
3m (10ft) long

The name *Nothosaurus* means 'false lizard'. Nothosaurs were not lizards (or dinosaurs), even though some looked similar from the outside. *Nothosaurus* was one of the most widespread of the group, with fossil finds as far apart as the Netherlands and China. Its kind also survived for more than 25 million years. Some of its detailed fossils have the outline of the skin, showing that *Nothosaurus* had webbed feet which were equally suited to land or water. As in the rest of its group, the sharp upper and lower teeth fitted together like spiky bars, to trap prey.

PISTOSAURUS

Mid Triassic, 225 mya
Europe
3m (10ft) long

Pistosaurus was a nothosaur, but it had several features of another sea reptile group, the plesiosaurs – especially in its head bones. Its fossils also show that the backbone was quite stiff, rather than bendy. So *Pistosaurus* swam mainly with its limbs, rather than wriggling its body like a snake – again, like a plesiosaur. Indeed, some experts think that *Pistosaurus* or a very similar creature was the ancestor of the plesiosaurs. These appeared in the next period, the Jurassic, after nothosaurs had died out.

Nothosaurus

Their legs were partly suited to walking, and they could also squirm or 'hump' along like modern sea-lions. They probably came on land to bask and warm up in the sun, to rest, to catch food in rock pools, and possibly to breed by laying eggs.

PLESIOSAURS

During the Age of Dinosaurs, the two biggest groups of sea reptiles were the plesiosaurs, and the ichthyosaurs (shown on later pages). In turn, there were two main groups of plesiosaurs. One was the plesiosaurs themselves, which had small heads and long necks. The other was the pliosaurs, with big heads and short necks. Plesiosaur fossils first appear in early Jurassic rocks, about 200 million years ago.

PLESIOSAURUS
Early Jurassic, 200 mya
Europe
2.5m (8ft) long

Plesiosaurus

This was one of the first plesiosaurs. Yet it was no halfway 'link', partly evolved from another kind of reptile. It already had all of the main plesiosaur features – and these would hardly change for the next 130 million years. The name *Plesiosaurus* means 'ribbon reptile' from the many separate parts of the backbone, called vertebrae. These formed a long, flexible, ribbon-like strap inside the neck, body and tail.

There were several kinds of *Plesiosaurus*, over many millions of years. Their fossils are very numerous in southern England. They had quite slim bodies and their necks, although long, were quite short compared to the extraordinary necks of later kinds such as *Elasmosaurus*.

CRYPTOCLIDUS
Late Jurassic, 150 million years ago
Europe
4m (13ft) long
As the Jurassic Period continued, plesiosaurs grew larger and their necks became longer. Also, the number of bones increased in each digit (finger or toe) inside the flippers. A typical reptile had about three bones per digit. Some digits of *Cryptoclidus* had more than 10 bones! These extra bones meant there were many more, smaller joints in the flipper, rather than a few large 'knuckles'. This gave the flipper a smoother and more flexible curved surface, for better swimming.

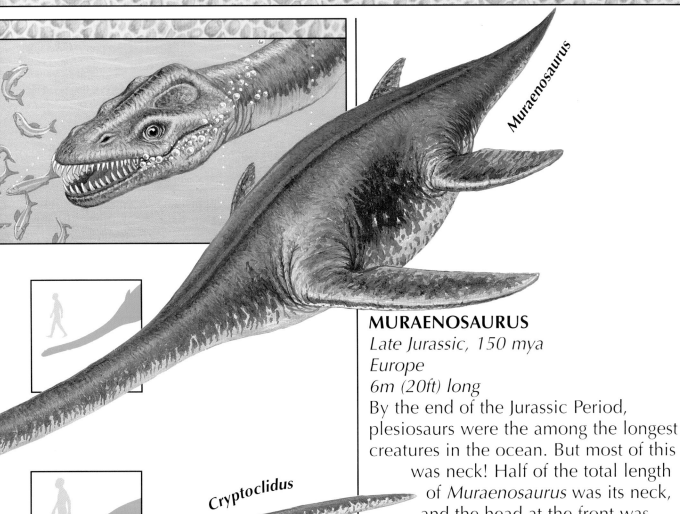

Muraenosaurus

Cryptoclidus

MURAENOSAURUS

Late Jurassic, 150 mya
Europe
6m (20ft) long

By the end of the Jurassic Period, plesiosaurs were the among the longest creatures in the ocean. But most of this was neck! Half of the total length of *Muraenosaurus* was its neck, and the head at the front was tiny. This plesiosaur probably darted its head to and fro on the bendy neck to 'pluck' small creatures from the water, almost like a bird pecks at food. Its body was much less flexible, so it swam using its flippers.

FLYING IN WATER

It was thought that plesiosaurs 'rowed' with their flippers, pulling each one forwards and then pushing it back. But they probably 'flapped', moving each flipper up and down. This is how birds fly through the air, and how penguins and turtles move through the water.

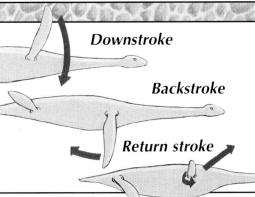

Downstroke

Backstroke

Return stroke

ELASMOSAURUS

The longest-necked plesiosaurs are called elasmosaurs, after the most famous member of the group, *Elasmosaurus*. It was described as 'a snake threaded through the body of a turtle'. More than half of its total length of 14m (46ft) was neck. The elasmosaurs were among the last of the plesiosaurs, living in the Late Cretaceous Period. Like the dinosaurs, the whole plesiosaur group was wiped out 65 million years ago.

MORE BONES

The great neck of *Elasmosaurus* was made possible by many extra bones, called caudal vertebrae, inside it. An average reptile has between five and ten of these vertebrae. An early plesiosaur had about 25. *Elasmosaurus* had more than 70! The extra caudal vertebrae made the neck very strong and flexible.

PLESIOSAUR SKULL

The skull of Elasmosaurus *was slim and low, hardly any wider than the neck. Its pointed snout gave a streamlined shape for fast movement through the water. The long teeth could not crush shellfish, but could trap them in the mouth, for swallowing.*

FAST PREDATOR

The teeth and jaws of *Elasmosaurus* show that it fed on small items like fish, squid and curly-shelled ammonites. It could dart its head about to grab these in a shoal, much faster than it could twist and turn its whole body to catch them.

EYES ON TOP

An older idea for the feeding method of *Elasmosaurus* is that it paddled at the surface, with its head held high out of the water on the long neck. After spotting a victim just under the surface, *Elasmosaurus* would strike downwards, almost like a snake.

However this method is unlikely. The eyes of *Elasmosaurus* were on top of its head. It would not be able to look down easily. However it could certainly look up, as it sneaked towards prey from below.

COULD THEY SURVIVE?

Fossils of *Elasmosaurus* have been found in Japan, East Asia and also in the Mid West of North America. Back in Cretaceous times, these rocks were part of the same large ocean bed. Some people believe plesiosaurs could still survive in deep, remote lakes, like the mythical 'Loch Ness monster' in Scotland.

A plesiosaur would have to stretch its very long neck straight ahead when swimming quickly. Otherwise the water would push it sideways with great force. Probably it moved slowly, snatching prey one by one. By paddling forwards with flippers on one side of the body, and backwards with the other side, the plesiosaur could spin around on the spot!

FOSSIL SKELETON

A plesiosaur's main body had the usual ribs curving down from the backbone – and an extra set, the belly ribs or gastralia, curving up from the chest. This made a strong 'box' to anchor the huge flipper-flapping muscles.

Also the shoulder and hip bones were wide and slab-like, to anchor the muscles even more firmly. The main arm and leg bones were short and broad. Most of the flippers were hand-and-finger or foot-and-toe bones.

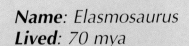

Name: *Elasmosaurus*
Lived: 70 mya
Found: Asia, North America
Length: 14m (46ft)
Diet: Fish

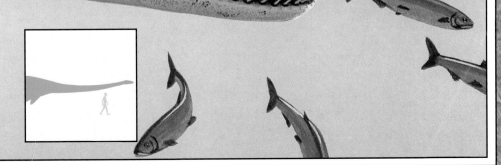

As plesiosaurs spread through Early Jurassic seas, they were quickly followed by their close cousins, the pliosaurs. With their short necks but huge heads, pliosaurs were suited to swimming faster and catching larger prey. By the Cretaceous Period, some pliosaurs were so huge they made meat-eating dinosaurs like *Tyrannosaurus* look puny!

HOLES IN THE HEAD

Like all reptiles, plesiosaurs and pliosaurs breathed air through nostrils. These were on the upper front of the head. The animal just had to poke this part above water to take a breath.

Macroplata

MACROPLATA

Early Jurassic, 200 mya
Europe
5m (16ft) long

This early pliosaur still had a long neck, like the plesiosaurs. But its head was relatively large and long, like a crocodile's, with rows of teeth for grabbing slimy meals. Also, its rear flippers were larger than the front ones, while in plesiosaurs, the front ones were bigger. So it seems that pliosaurs swam mainly with their back flippers. The tail was short and tapering, to allow water to slip easily off the rear of the creature. All plesiosaurs and pliosaurs had smooth, streamlined shapes to reduce water resistance.

Kronosaurus

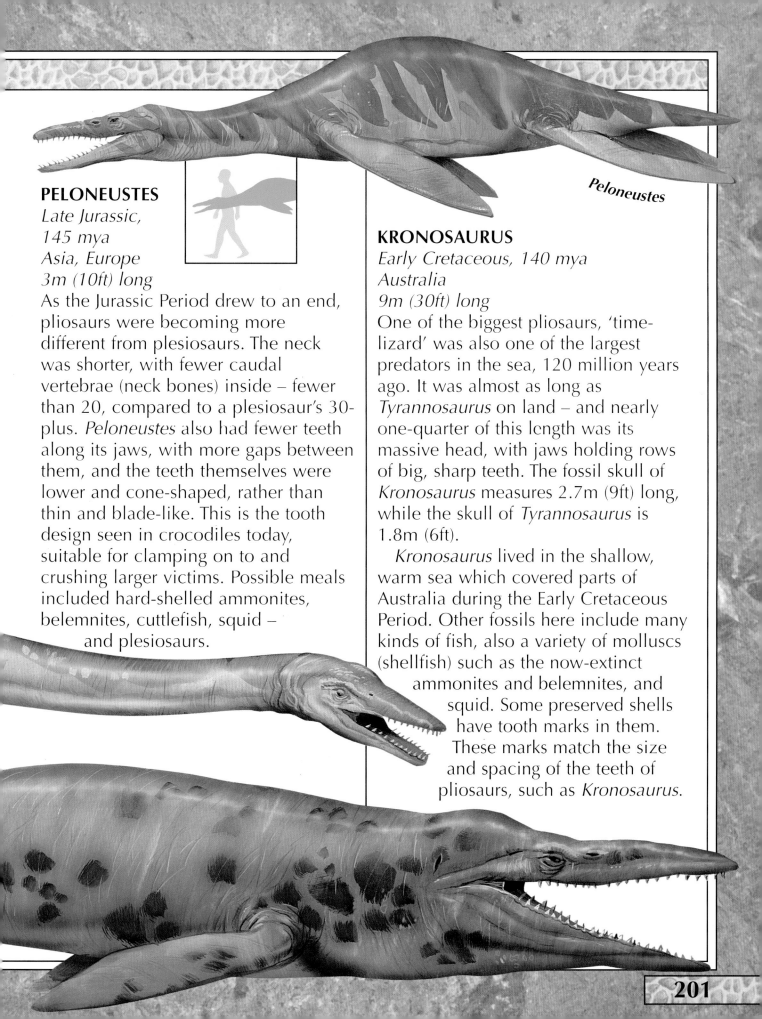

PELONEUSTES

Late Jurassic,
145 mya
Asia, Europe
3m (10ft) long

As the Jurassic Period drew to an end, pliosaurs were becoming more different from plesiosaurs. The neck was shorter, with fewer caudal vertebrae (neck bones) inside – fewer than 20, compared to a plesiosaur's 30-plus. *Peloneustes* also had fewer teeth along its jaws, with more gaps between them, and the teeth themselves were lower and cone-shaped, rather than thin and blade-like. This is the tooth design seen in crocodiles today, suitable for clamping on to and crushing larger victims. Possible meals included hard-shelled ammonites, belemnites, cuttlefish, squid – and plesiosaurs.

Peloneustes

KRONOSAURUS

Early Cretaceous, 140 mya
Australia
9m (30ft) long

One of the biggest pliosaurs, 'time-lizard' was also one of the largest predators in the sea, 120 million years ago. It was almost as long as *Tyrannosaurus* on land – and nearly one-quarter of this length was its massive head, with jaws holding rows of big, sharp teeth. The fossil skull of *Kronosaurus* measures 2.7m (9ft) long, while the skull of *Tyrannosaurus* is 1.8m (6ft).

   Kronosaurus lived in the shallow, warm sea which covered parts of Australia during the Early Cretaceous Period. Other fossils here include many kinds of fish, also a variety of molluscs (shellfish) such as the now-extinct ammonites and belemnites, and squid. Some preserved shells have tooth marks in them. These marks match the size and spacing of the teeth of pliosaurs, such as *Kronosaurus*.

LIOPLEURODON

The biggest meat-eater ever to live on our planet was not the sperm whale of today, which is about 20m (66ft) long and 50 tonnes in weight – bigger than any predatory dinosaur. The greatest meat-eater ever, as far as we know, was a pliosaur that roamed Late Jurassic seas – *Liopleurodon.*

MOST MASSIVE EVER?

Liopleurodon was truly enormous. Estimates of its length go up to 25m (82ft), which was as long as most of the giant sauropod dinosaurs such as *Apatosaurus* and *Mamenchisaurus*. Its weight could have been 75 tonnes, or perhaps even 150! This exceeds the weight of the biggest dinosaurs, such as *Brachiosaurus* and *Argentinosaurus*. *Liopleurodon* might have beaten its present-day rival for the most gigantic animal ever on Earth, the blue whale.

WATER SUPPORT

The amazing size of *Liopleurodon* was partly due to the fact that it lived in water. Compared to animals on land, water helps to support or buoy up a creature's weight, making it easier to move around. This is why today's biggest animals, the great whales, are found in the sea.

Fossils of *Liopleurodon* include fairly complete skeletons and many separate bones. They have been found in parts of Europe, mainly from France, Germany and England. Similar remains have been discovered in Chile, South America.

SKELETON, SKULL AND TEETH

A pliosaur's skull was up to one-quarter of its total body length. Liopleurodon's skull was a terrifying 5m (16ft) – longer than the whole bodies of many dinosaurs. The teeth were at the front of the jaws, like two curved rows of deadly daggers. The rear two flipper-limbs were larger than the front pair, which was the opposite of most plesiosaurs. A pliosaur probably pushed forwards by flapping the back pair, and used the front flippers for turning after prey, braking and surfacing for air.

Name: *Liopleurodon*
Lived: *150 mya*
Found: *Europe, South America*
Length: *25m (82ft)*
Diet: *Marine reptiles*

TOP PREDATOR

What did this colossal hunter eat? Anything it wanted! Most fish and shellfish were too small and would only make a light snack. The huge skull and teeth of *Liopleurodon* were suited to bigger meals, which included its sea-reptile cousins like ichthyosaurs, plesiosaurs and smaller types of pliosaurs.

Liopleurodon heaves its colossal bulk out of the water, trying to get its 30cm (12in) teeth into an ichthyosaur. Today, great whales such as the humpback, weighing 50-plus tonnes, can leap clear or 'breach' like this.

SHARK-LIKE SMELL

Liopleurodon had openings between the roof of its mouth and each nostril, to detect scents in the water flowing into the mouth. If the scent of prey was stronger in one nostril than the other, Liopleurodon would veer to that side and follow the trail – just like a shark.

During the Age of Dinosaurs, sea reptiles such as nothosaurs, pliosaurs and plesiosaurs had large, flipper-shaped limbs for swimming. But many of them could still probably waddle or wriggle about on land – perhaps to lay their eggs. Another group of ocean reptiles could never get about on land. They had to live their whole lives in the water. They grew a tail, like fish. They also had a back fin, like a fish. Indeed, from the outside, they looked almost identical to fish. But they were still reptiles. Their name means 'fish-lizard' – the ichthyosaurs.

SHONISAURUS

Late Triassic, 210 mya
North America
15m (49ft) long
A few fossils of 'halfway' ichthyosaurs show how they evolved stage by stage from land-living reptiles, during the Early Triassic Period. Only 30 million years later, they were huge. *Shonisaurus* had a greater length than the dinosaur *Tyrannosaurus*.

SKELETON SHOWS A REPTILE

Ichthyosaurs looked like either fish, or our sea-living mammals today, dolphins. But their fossil skeletons show that they were neither. Their flippers had arm-and-hand and leg-and-foot bones inside – a fish's fins do not. Also, unlike a fish, an ichthyosaur did not have gills to breathe underwater. And its tail was upright, with the end of the backbone bent down into it. A dolphin's tail is horizontal (side-to-side) and has no bones at all.

Shonisaurus

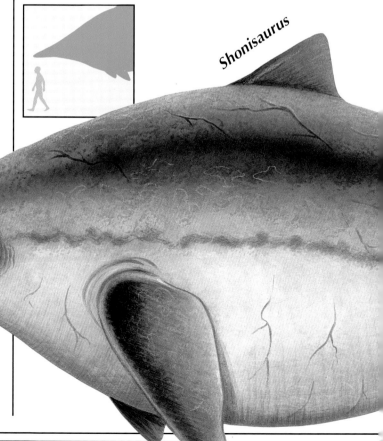

Its paddle-shaped limbs were much the same size, fairly narrow and long compared to its body. Later ichthyosaurs had shorter limbs, with the front two longer than the rear pair.

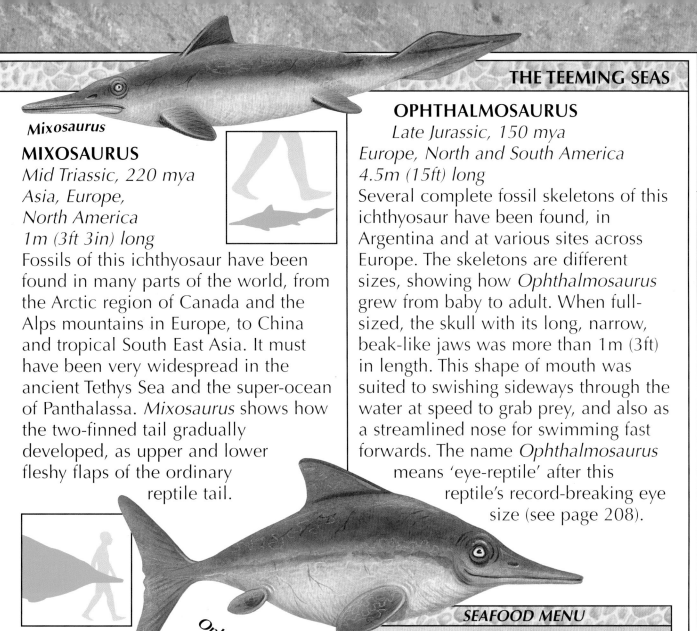

Mixosaurus

MIXOSAURUS

Mid Triassic, 220 mya
Asia, Europe,
North America
1m (3ft 3in) long

Fossils of this ichthyosaur have been found in many parts of the world, from the Arctic region of Canada and the Alps mountains in Europe, to China and tropical South East Asia. It must have been very widespread in the ancient Tethys Sea and the super-ocean of Panthalassa. *Mixosaurus* shows how the two-finned tail gradually developed, as upper and lower fleshy flaps of the ordinary reptile tail.

OPHTHALMOSAURUS

Late Jurassic, 150 mya
Europe, North and South America
4.5m (15ft) long

Several complete fossil skeletons of this ichthyosaur have been found, in Argentina and at various sites across Europe. The skeletons are different sizes, showing how *Ophthalmosaurus* grew from baby to adult. When full-sized, the skull with its long, narrow, beak-like jaws was more than 1m (3ft) in length. This shape of mouth was suited to swishing sideways through the water at speed to grab prey, and also as a streamlined nose for swimming fast forwards. The name *Ophthalmosaurus* means 'eye-reptile' after this reptile's record-breaking eye size (see page 208).

Ophthalmosaurus

SEAFOOD MENU

In some fossil skeletons of ichthyosaurs, there are strange, pointed lumps of stone where the animal's stomach would have been in life. These are preserved remains of the hard 'shells', called guards or pens, which animals like squid and belemnites had inside their bodies. Fish scales and fin-spines are also found.

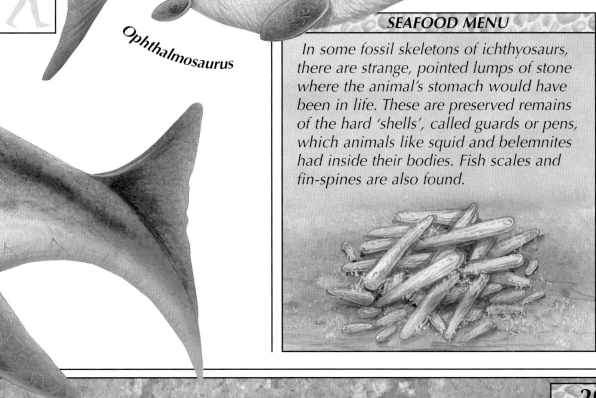

ICHTHYOSAUR MYSTERIES

Ichthyosaurs were similar in overall shape to modern dolphins and fish. So they probably lived similar lifestyles. By studying modern animals, and comparing them to the features of ichthyosaurs known from fossils, we can guess how the sea reptiles swam, dived and caught prey. But a mystery remains. Ichthyosaurs began with the dinosaurs, the Triassic Period. Yet they died out about 90 million years ago – long before the dinosaurs.

BIG AND SMALL

The largest ichthyosaurs, like Shonisaurus (see previous page), and Himalayasaurus, were more than 15m (49ft) long. This is twice the size of today's biggest reptile, the saltwater crocodile.
Fossils of Chaohusaurus from China show that it was just over 60cm (2ft) in length.

CYMBOSPONDYLUS

Mid Triassic, 220 mya
North America
10m (33ft) long
This early, large ichthyosaur lacked several general features of the group. It was shaped more like an eel with four paddles – it had not yet evolved the back fin and the two-part tail. Also its paddle-limbs were quite short and useful mainly for steering and slowing down. *Cymbospondylus* must have swum by wriggling its body from side to side, like an eel or its sea-dwelling reptile relative today, the sea-snake. However its jaws were long and narrow, with many sharp teeth – the sign of a fish-eater.

TEMNODONTOSAURUS

Early Jurassic, 200 mya
Europe
9m (30ft) long
By the start of the Jurassic Period ichthyosaurs had gained all of their main features and were slim, sleek, speedy swimmers. Swishing its big tail from side to side, *Temnodontosaurus* could surge through the water as fast as many fish today, perhaps more than 40 kph (25 mph).

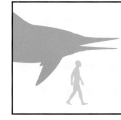

Shonisaurus

Chaohusaurus

Temnodontosaurus

EURHINOSAURUS
Early Jurassic, 200 million years ago
Europe
1.8m (6ft) long

One of the most unusual ichthyosaurs, *Eurhinosaurus* had an upper jaw much longer than the lower one. This upper snout was also flattened, like a sword blade, and had teeth which stuck out to the sides. The only modern fish with such a snout design is the sawfish. This uses its 'saw' to grub in the mud for worms and shellfish, and to defend itself.

Another suggestion is that *Eurhinosaurus* swished its toothy sword-nose from side to side, as it swam through a shoal of fish or squid, to slash and wound victims. Then it returned to swallow them.

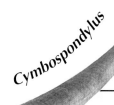

How long could an ichthyosaur hold its breath and stay under the water? Studies of swimming reptiles today, such as turtles, crocodiles and sea-snakes, and also whales, suggest that a long dive would have lasted 15–20 minutes.

Eurhinosaurus

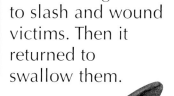

Cymbospondylus

ICHTHYOSAURUS

Few animals from the Age of Dinosaurs are better known than *Ichthyosaurus*. Hundreds of its fossil skeletons have been found, at many sites across North America and Europe. The rocks around these fossils date from the Early Jurassic Period to the Early Cretaceous, showing that various kinds of *Ichthyosaurus* survived for more than 60 million years – an amazing length of time for any single type of animal. Most of the remains show that *Ichthyosaurus* was about 1.8m (6ft) in length.

BIG EYES FOR HUNTING

Many fossils show that ichthyosaurs had huge eyes, rather like birds. So they probably hunted by sight rather than smell. Around the front of the bulging eyeball was a circle of bones, or sclerotic ring, for protection and support. The biggest eyes belonged to Ophthalmosaurus. They were 10cm (4in) across – the largest eyes of any animal with a backbone.

FINE FOSSILS

Because of the way fossils form, sea creatures are more likely to leave them, compared to land animals. Some of the best *Ichthyosaurus* fossils come from the area near Holzmaden, in southern Germany. The rocks have very fine particles or grains, so their fossils show great detail. Every bone of *Ichthyosaurus* is perfectly preserved. Some of the skeletons have all the bones articulated – arranged one next to the other, as though still joined, exactly as in life.

EVEN THE OUTLINE

Some *Ichthyosaurus* fossil bones have a thin, dark layer, like oil, in the rock around them. This is where the flesh rotted away, and it shows the whole body's outline. It is how we know that ichthyosaurs had a back fin and tail.

FOSSIL FOOD

Other fossils found with those of *Ichthyosaurus* show that its main food was fish. But it also ate squid, the long-bodied belemnites and the curly-shelled ammonites.

Ichthyosaurus seizes an ammonite, ready to crack its shell and gulp in the flesh.

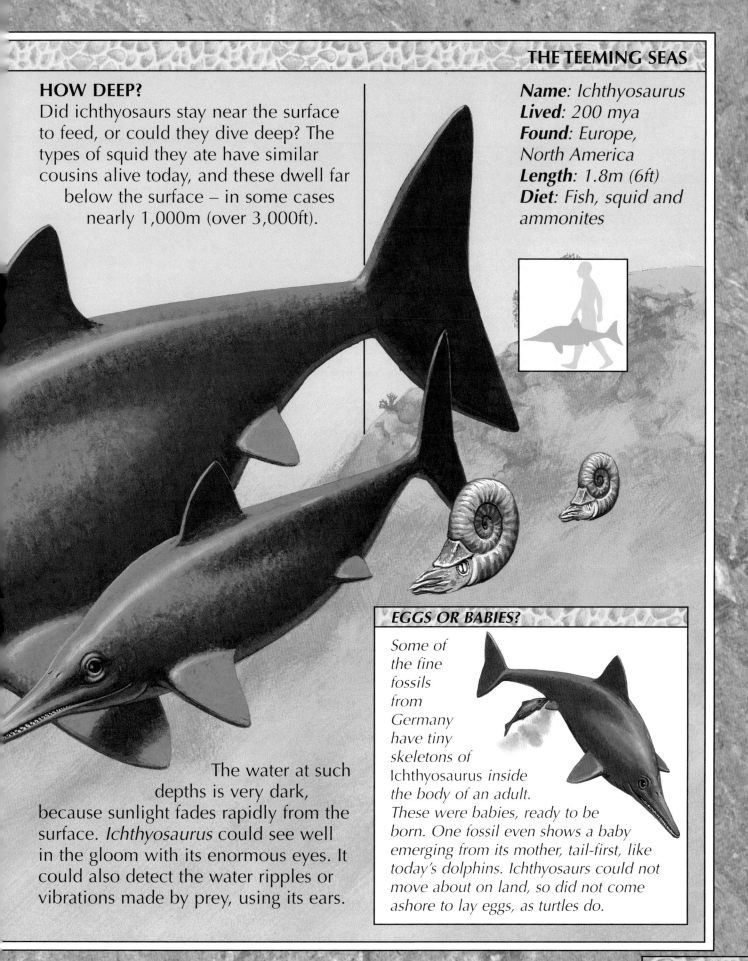

HOW DEEP?

Did ichthyosaurs stay near the surface to feed, or could they dive deep? The types of squid they ate have similar cousins alive today, and these dwell far below the surface – in some cases nearly 1,000m (over 3,000ft).

Name: *Ichthyosaurus*
Lived: *200 mya*
Found: *Europe, North America*
Length: *1.8m (6ft)*
Diet: *Fish, squid and ammonites*

The water at such depths is very dark, because sunlight fades rapidly from the surface. *Ichthyosaurus* could see well in the gloom with its enormous eyes. It could also detect the water ripples or vibrations made by prey, using its ears.

EGGS OR BABIES?

Some of the fine fossils from Germany have tiny skeletons of Ichthyosaurus *inside the body of an adult. These were babies, ready to be born. One fossil even shows a baby emerging from its mother, tail-first, like today's dolphins. Ichthyosaurs could not move about on land, so did not come ashore to lay eggs, as turtles do.*

MOSASAURS

Many reptiles from the Age of Dinosaurs have names ending in -*saur* which means 'lizard'. But most of them, including nothosaurs, plesiosaurs, ichthyosaurs and even dinosaurs, were not real lizards. However, mosasaurs were. Their closest relatives alive today are big, fierce lizards such as the Nile monitor and the Komodo dragon. But these are small and weak compared to the huge ocean-going mosasaurs of the Middle and Late Cretaceous Period. Sadly, they shared the fate of the dinosaurs, plesiosaurs and others, and died out 65 million years ago.

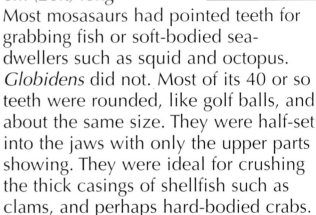

Tylosaurus

TYLOSAURUS

*Late Cretaceous,
70 mya
North America
9m (30ft) long*

The state of Kansas, USA is the 'world capital' for mosasaur remains. Shallow, warm seas, swarming with fish and shellfish, covered this part of North America in Late Cretaceous times. *Tylosaurus* had typical mosasaur features – four paddle-like limbs, a huge mouth with many sharp teeth, and a long tail with ridges or flaps along the top and bottom.

GLOBIDENS

*Late Cretaceous, 70 mya
North America
6m (20ft) long*

Most mosasaurs had pointed teeth for grabbing fish or soft-bodied sea-dwellers such as squid and octopus. *Globidens* did not. Most of its 40 or so teeth were rounded, like golf balls, and about the same size. They were half-set into the jaws with only the upper parts showing. They were ideal for crushing the thick casings of shellfish such as clams, and perhaps hard-bodied crabs. The teeth at the front of the mouth were longer and more finger-shaped, like pegs. *Globidens* may have used these to pull its shellfish meals out of sea bed mud or off rocks.

MOSASAUR MOTHER

Fossils show that mosasaurs – like ichthyosaurs, and sea-snakes today – gave birth to babies. They could not clamber on to land to lay eggs. And in the sea, reptile eggs would not survive salty water. Perhaps a mother mosasaur looked after her young, as some dinosaurs did.

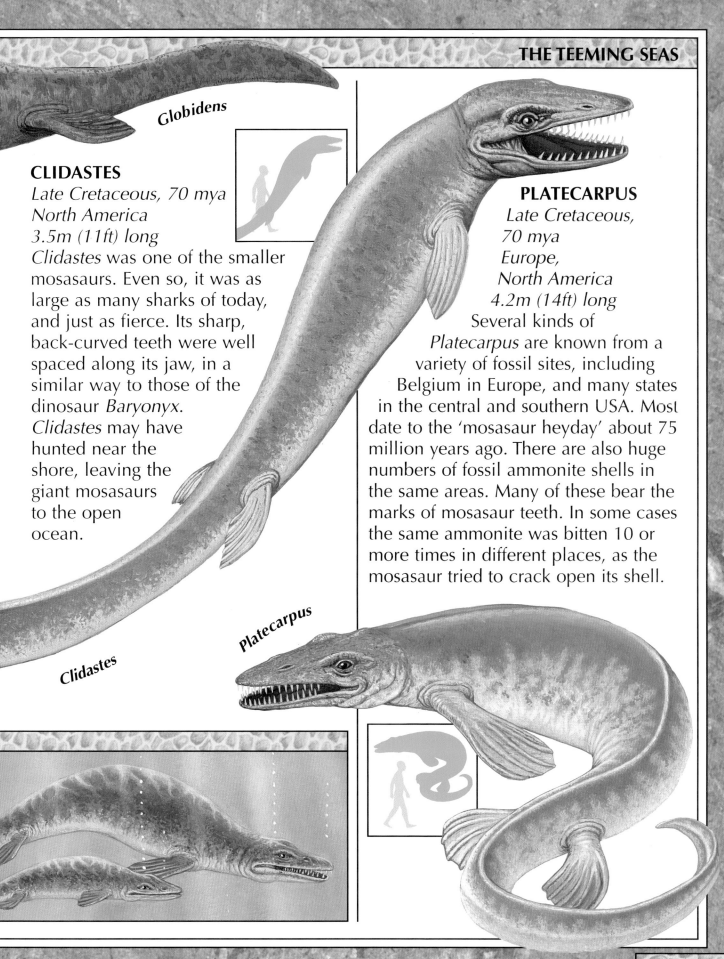

Globidens

CLIDASTES
Late Cretaceous, 70 mya
North America
3.5m (11ft) long
Clidastes was one of the smaller mosasaurs. Even so, it was as large as many sharks of today, and just as fierce. Its sharp, back-curved teeth were well spaced along its jaw, in a similar way to those of the dinosaur *Baryonyx*. *Clidastes* may have hunted near the shore, leaving the giant mosasaurs to the open ocean.

Clidastes

Platecarpus

PLATECARPUS
Late Cretaceous,
70 mya
Europe,
North America
4.2m (14ft) long
Several kinds of *Platecarpus* are known from a variety of fossil sites, including Belgium in Europe, and many states in the central and southern USA. Most date to the 'mosasaur heyday' about 75 million years ago. There are also huge numbers of fossil ammonite shells in the same areas. Many of these bear the marks of mosasaur teeth. In some cases the same ammonite was bitten 10 or more times in different places, as the mosasaur tried to crack open its shell.

MOSASAURUS

Mosasaurs are named after the first of their kind to be discovered and named, *Mosasaurus*, about 200 years ago. This 10m (33ft) hunter was more powerful than any predatory shark of today. Remains of several kinds of *Mosasaurus* have been discovered at numerous places across Europe and North America.

ORIGINS

The origins of the mosasaurs are a mystery. They began to take over the seas, along with the pliosaurs, in the Middle Cretaceous Period, as the ichthyosaurs faded. But mosasaurs did not evolve from these or any other sea reptiles. They probably began from Early Cretaceous times, as big meat-eating lizards which took to the sea, and their legs changed into paddle-like flippers.

DIED IN THE FLOOD?

Mosasaurs are named after a place rather than a body feature – 'Meuse lizards', after the Meuse region of the Netherlands. Huge fossil jaws and teeth were dug from a chalk mine here in the 1770s. In the early 1800s, world animal and fossil expert, Georges Cuvier, showed the fossils were from a massive water-lizard. He named the beast *Mosasaurus* and said that it had died out in a Great Flood, as described in the Bible. But the discovery of this and other long-extinct 'monsters' set some scientists thinking about the idea of evolution.

Name: *Mosasaurus*

Lived: *70 mya*

Found: *Europe, North America*

Length: *10m (33ft)*

Diet: *Fish, squid, turtles and ammonites*

SWIMMING TAIL

The flipper-legs of *Mosasaurus* were too small and weak for fast swimming. To power through the water, it must have swished its long, slim body and tail from side to side, like a giant snake. Ridges or keels along the upper and lower tail, like the long fins of a newt or eel, would help to give greater speed. Crocodiles lash their tails in the same way when swimming. The flippers were for steering and slowing down.

Fossils of the ancient bird Hesperornis are found with mosasaur remains in Kansas. In fact, this bird's long, toothed jaws were once thought to come from a mosasaur. As tall as a person, Hesperornis had tiny wings and could not fly. It paddled with its big webbed feet and dived for fish. It would make a tasty snack for a mosasaur!

Mosasaurus *locks its fangs on to the tough shell of another reptile, the sea turtle* Protostega, *while a shark lurks in the background. When mosasaurs died out at the Cretaceous Period's end, sharks would take over the seas.*

SKULL AND SKELETON

Several features of a mosasaur are similar to those of modern monitor lizards. One is the lower jaw, which had a joint in it, allowing the mosasaur to bend its mouth sideways.

The mosasaur's shoulder and limb bones are also more similar to lizards than to any other reptile group. In the rear body and tail, tall rods on the backbones probably held up long, fin-like flaps, to help with swimming.

Like the dinosaurs and many other reptile groups, turtles first appeared in the Triassic Period. The earliest turtles date back over 200 million years, just after the first dinosaurs. From the beginning, they had large, domed shells for protection. These first types probably lived on land, as tortoises. But some soon took to the water, and their feet changed into flippers.

Proganochelys

PROGANOCHELYS
Mid to Late Triassic,
220 mya
Europe
1m (3ft 3in) long
The whole turtle-and-tortoise group of reptiles is known as the chelonians. *Proganochelys* was one of its first members, from Late Triassic times, in what is now Germany. It was a land-dweller – a tortoise rather than a turtle. It already had a fully-formed shell about 60cm (2ft) long. The shell had two layers – curved slabs of bone, with plates of a horny substance over them. Like most early chelonians, *Proganochelys* could probably not pull its head and legs into its shell, and its jaws had teeth. Today's chelonians all lack teeth.

PROTOSTEGA
Late Cretaceous, 70 million years ago
North America
3m (10ft) long
The wide Cretaceous seas that once covered North America were a dangerous place, with mosasaurs and pliosaurs, sharks and sea-crocodiles. The turtle *Protostega* had a large shell over its main body. But this was not made of solid bone plates, as in many other chelonians. The bony layer of the shell was reduced to a ring-like border, a central girder above the backbone, and two rows of narrow struts between them. This made the shell less strong but much lighter, for a faster getaway. *Protostega* also had big flipper-like limbs for extra speed. Its powerful beak-shaped mouth had no teeth at all. It ate many sea animals, from soft jellyfish to hard-cased shellfish.

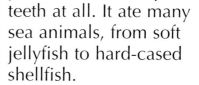

Protostega

EGGS ON BEACHES

Sea turtles today differ little from their cousins of over 100 million years ago. Fossils show that Mesozoic (dinosaur-age) turtles laid eggs in holes, dug into the sand on beaches. The mother turtle filled in the hole with sand, and the warmth of the Sun helped the eggs to hatch. Babies had to scuttle to the sea, avoiding predators such as lizards and other reptiles.

PLACOCHELYS

Late Triassic, 210 million years ago
Europe
90cm (3ft) long

Placochelys is an excellent example of what is called 'convergent evolution'. This is when two animals of different kinds evolve to look very similar, because they live the same lifestyles in the same places. On the outside, *Placochelys* was just like a turtle. But inside, as its fossil bones show, it was a member of a different reptile group – placodonts. These lived at about the same time as their cousins, the nothosaurs (see page 194). *Placochelys* had many more bones making up the inner layer of its shell, compared to turtles.

Placochelys

HENODUS

Late Triassic, 210 mya
Europe
1m (3ft 3in) long

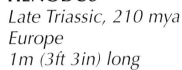

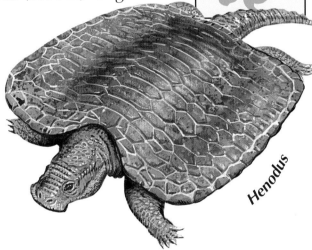

Henodus

Like *Placochelys* (left), *Henodus* was not a turtle, but a turtle-shaped placodont. This group lived only during the Triassic Period. The squared-off shell of *Henodus* protected it against predators of the time. These included the sharks, the crocodiles – who were just taking to the water after evolving on land – and a new group of sea-reptile predators, the ichthyosaurs. *Henodus* also had a squared-off head, and fed on shellfish with its hooked, toothless jaws.

The Late Cretaceous was a time of many giant animals, especially reptiles in the sea. The turtle group's greatest member, known from fossils found so far, was *Archelon*. Its remains come from North America, especially Kansas and South Dakota, USA. At 3.7m (12ft), it was the length of a family car – and almost the same width. *Archelon* was twice the size of the largest turtle and biggest chelonian today, the leatherback, which weighs more than half a tonne.

STEADY SWIMMER

Studies of today's sea turtles show that *Archelon* was not the swiftest swimmer in the ocean. But it could keep up a steady pace for hours, even days. Perhaps females migrated to favoured breeding beaches every year or two, and hauled their great bodies on to the shore, to lay their eggs in the warm sand.

HOLES IN THE SHELL

Archelon's 'shell' was not solid bone or plates of horn, but struts of bone covered by thick, rubbery skin. Long fingers and toes spread into the flippers.

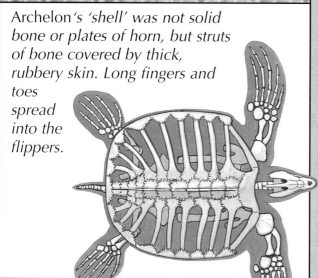

TOUGH ENEMY

The shell and flippers of *Archelon* were probably covered in thick, leathery skin, which was very difficult to bite through or grip. (The modern leatherback's skin is as tough as a car tyre!) Also *Archelon's* parrot-like beak would crush or snip off parts of an attacker. So it was far from defenceless.

The front flippers of *Archelon* were massive, each one as long as an adult person. They provided the swimming power. They did not row to and fro like oars. They flapped up and down to 'fly' through the water like the plesiosaurs, today's turtles, and sea birds such as penguins.

INVISIBLE MEAL

Like the leatherback, the main foods of *Archelon* were probably soft sea creatures like jellyfish, comb-jellies and sea-gooseberries. The stings of these simple animals would not affect the sharp-ridged, horn-covered jaws and tough mouth skin of the huge turtle.

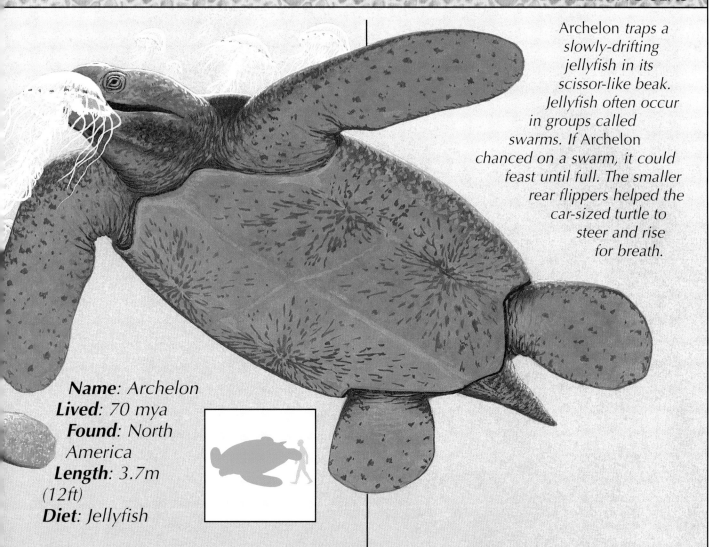

Archelon traps a slowly-drifting jellyfish in its scissor-like beak. Jellyfish often occur in groups called swarms. If Archelon chanced on a swarm, it could feast until full. The smaller rear flippers helped the car-sized turtle to steer and rise for breath.

Name: *Archelon*
Lived: *70 mya*
Found: *North America*
Length: *3.7m (12ft)*
Diet: *Jellyfish*

OFF TO SLEEP

Some modern sea turtles 'brumate' – they rest on the sea bed for hours, even days at a time. Their body processes slow down so much, that one deep intake of air can last for many hours. Brumation is similar to hibernation. It helps the turtle pass through spells of cold weather, or seasons when there is little food. Possibly *Archelon* rested on the shallow sea bed, rising to the surface only a couple of times each day for a few breaths of air, before sinking back to sleep in the mud.

SKULL

A turtle's skull has fewer bones than most other reptiles, and a more box-like design to protect the brain and eyes inside. The upper jaw of Archelon was longer than the lower, giving an 'overbite' as seen in birds such as macaws.

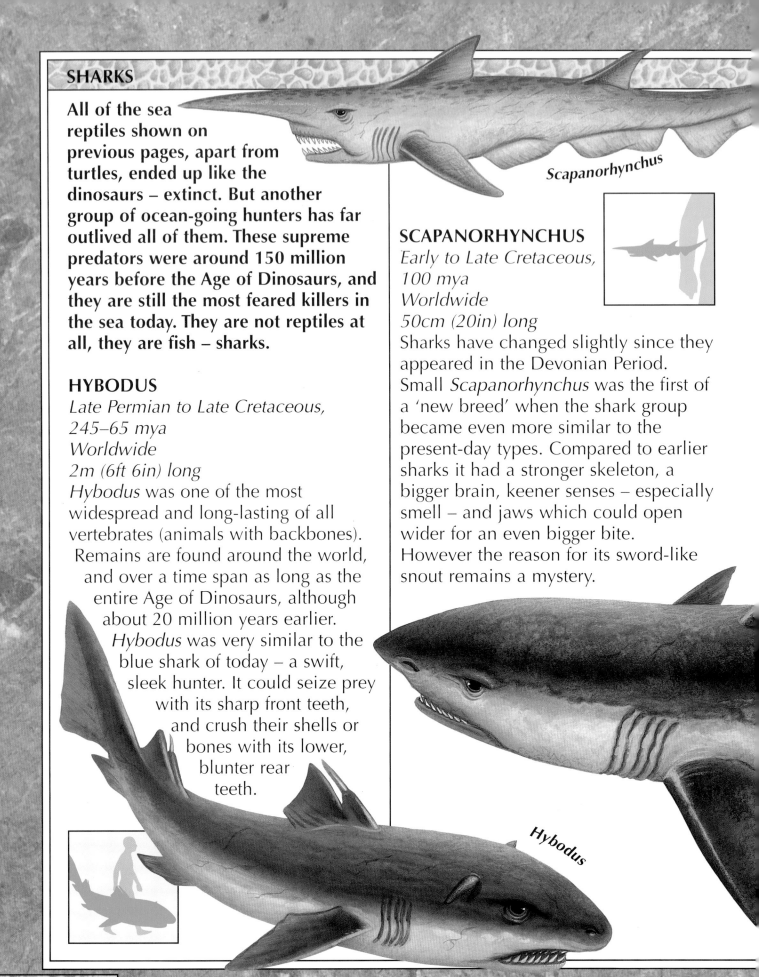

All of the sea reptiles shown on previous pages, apart from turtles, ended up like the dinosaurs – extinct. But another group of ocean-going hunters has far outlived all of them. These supreme predators were around 150 million years before the Age of Dinosaurs, and they are still the most feared killers in the sea today. They are not reptiles at all, they are fish – sharks.

HYBODUS

Late Permian to Late Cretaceous,
245–65 mya
Worldwide
2m (6ft 6in) long
Hybodus was one of the most widespread and long-lasting of all vertebrates (animals with backbones). Remains are found around the world, and over a time span as long as the entire Age of Dinosaurs, although about 20 million years earlier. *Hybodus* was very similar to the blue shark of today – a swift, sleek hunter. It could seize prey with its sharp front teeth, and crush their shells or bones with its lower, blunter rear teeth.

Scapanorhynchus

SCAPANORHYNCHUS

Early to Late Cretaceous,
100 mya
Worldwide
50cm (20in) long
Sharks have changed slightly since they appeared in the Devonian Period. Small *Scapanorhynchus* was the first of a 'new breed' when the shark group became even more similar to the present-day types. Compared to earlier sharks it had a stronger skeleton, a bigger brain, keener senses – especially smell – and jaws which could open wider for an even bigger bite. However the reason for its sword-like snout remains a mystery.

Hybodus

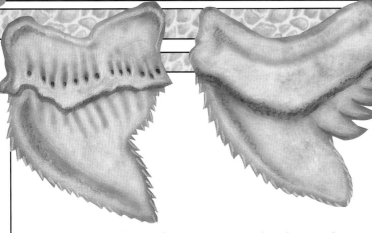

Fossil tooth of Squalicorax (an ancient shark)

Tooth of a modern-day Tiger Shark

TEETH

Sharks do not leave plentiful fossils – because they have no bones!

A shark's skeleton is mainly cartilage (gristle). But some parts of the skeleton, like the vertebrae (back-'bones'), are strengthened with bone minerals, and so leave good fossils. Scales are also preserved, as are teeth. These were thin, sharp and saw-edged, like triangular steak-knife blades.

CRETOXYRHINA

Late Cretaceous, 70 million years ago
North America
5.4m (18ft) long
Sharks such as *Cretoxyrhina* would have battled with reptiles – mosasaurs, pliosaurs and sea-crocodiles – for the position of top predator in Late Cretaceous seas.

Cretoxyrhina

This streamlined swimmer was the Great White shark of its time. It could chase prey at speed, and bite or tear off great lumps of flesh. But there were no sea mammals as victims – they had not yet evolved. So *Cretoxyrhina* probably preyed on fish and reptiles.

LIVING AND DEAD

Today, some sharks are active hunters, while others scavenge, or grub for shellfish in sea bed mud. The same lifestyles occurred in the Age of Dinosaurs. Scavengers such as Squalicorax would bite and then shake their heads from side to side, to 'saw' meat from the dead or dying bodies of fish, sea reptiles and dinosaurs washed out to sea.

CHAPTER EIGHT

THE WORLD OF THE DINOSAURS

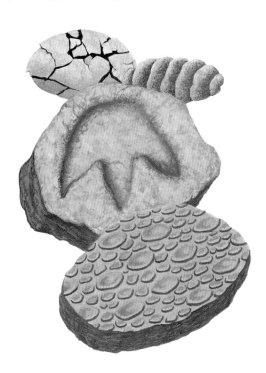

HISTORY OF THE EARTH

Dinosaurs were not the first animals on Earth. They were not even the first large animals. More than 150 million years before they appeared, creatures crawled from the sea on to the land. And for millions of years before that, animals of all kinds – from floppy jellyfish to massive sharks – swarmed in the seas. Going back even further, over 2,000 million years ago, tiny life-forms (like today's bacteria) thrived in the primeval oceans.

ERAS AND PERIODS

The whole history of Earth is split into lengths of time known as eras. The last three eras are shown on the right. The dinosaurs lived during the middle or Mesozoic Era. In turn, each era divides into smaller time spans called periods.

HOW TIME IS DIVIDED

Eras and periods are based on the way rocks have formed during past times, and also on the fossils they contain. Sudden changes between different colours and types of rocks, with new kinds of fossils, mark the boundaries.

CENOZOIC ERA (Recent life)	QUATERNARY PERIOD	**Holocene Epoch (0.01–Now)** *Most of recorded history*
		Pleistocene Epoch (2–0.01) *Early humans spread*
	TERTIARY PERIOD (65–2) *Rise of mammals and birds*	
MESOZOIC ERA (Middle life)	**CRETACEOUS PERIOD (144–65)** *Last of the dinosaurs*	
	JURASSIC PERIOD (206–144) *Dinosaurs reach their greatest size*	
	TRIASSIC PERIOD (250–206) *Many reptiles, first dinosaurs*	
PALEOZOIC ERA (Ancient life)	**PERMIAN PERIOD (286–250)** *Mammal-like reptiles*	
	CARBONIFEROUS PERIOD (360–286) *Many amphibians, first reptiles*	
	DEVONIAN PERIOD (408–360) *First amphibians walk on land*	
	SILURIAN PERIOD (438–408) *Plants spread from water to land*	

* All numbers are millions of years ago

EARLY EARTH

Our planet formed about 4,600 million years ago. At first it was hostile to life. Giant storms poured endless rain and sparked colossal lightning bolts. Volcanoes exploded and red-hot, runny rocks oozed over the surface. Gradually, conditions became cooler and more settled. By 3,000 million years ago, microscopic living things drifted in the oceans. The evolution of life had begun, and gathered pace.

MOVING CONTINENTS

Over millions of years, Earth's land-masses or continents have drifted slowly around the globe. In the Triassic Period, when the dinosaurs began (1), continents were joined as one vast land-mass known as Pangaea.

During the Jurassic Period this began to split (2). By the Cretaceous Period (3), the map of Earth was becoming like the one we know today (4). These changes had great effects on which dinosaurs lived in different areas.

1   2   3   4

The first dinosaur fossils occur in rocks dating back to the Middle Triassic Period, about 230 million years ago. The world was very different then. The climate was warmer and less moist. Vast areas of land were dry scrub and desert, with tough, shrubby plants, and fewer trees than today.

The central regions of the vast Triassic supercontinent were far from the sea. Great deserts developed, where the thin soil was blown over bare, rocky uplands.

PLANT LIFE

The main trees of the Triassic were needle-leaved conifers, ginkgoes and cycads. (Only one type of ginkgo survives now – the maidenhair tree, with its fan-shaped leaves.) Cycads look similar to squat palm trees, with a straight trunk and an umbrella of long fronds. On the ground in damper places were carpets of ferns, horsetails and mosses.

TRIASSIC TRENDS

There were several trends in evolution during the Triassic. The earliest dinosaurs, such as smallish Eoraptor and larger Herrerasaurus, were meat-eaters. Plant-eating prosauropods appeared, with their small heads, long necks and barrel bodies.

The prosauropods quickly increased in size, to one tonne or more, and were able to reach three or four metres above the ground. The first pterosaurs flapped across the skies.

The Triassic world did not have climate zones as we know them today. There was no ice at the poles. In fact, Pangaea drifted towards the North Pole, while the South Pole was open ocean. Temperatures varied from mild to hot; rain was sparse.

TRIASSIC MAP

All continents were grouped as one great land-mass, Pangaea, surrounded by a single massive ocean, Panthalassa. However the Tethys Sea was beginning to divide Pangaea into two.

Panthalassa

PANGAEA

Tethys Sea

In the valleys, small rivers flowed during the rainy season. But their beds were dry much of the year.

TRIASSIC ANIMALS

Apart from the first dinosaurs, many kinds of reptiles flourished in the Triassic. They included the pig-sized, herbivorous rhynchosaurs and fierce, dog-like cynodonts. Early crocodiles scuttled over the land, and turtles swam in lakes and seas. The first mammals, tiny and shrew-like, also evolved.

THE JURASSIC PERIOD

As the Triassic gave way to the Jurassic, around 200 million years ago, climates began to change. Global temperatures started to cool, although it was still warm by today's standards. Rainfall increased, bringing damp lushness to many regions that were previously parched. Dinosaurs grew to their greatest size.

The break-up of the continents meant that more regions were nearer the sea, where moist winds could bring rain to the land. With this extra rainfall, and less extreme heat, forests spread from valleys to cloak large areas of uplands.

PLANT LIFE

As the Jurassic Period progressed, plant life spread to cover former desert regions. The main trees were conifers related to modern redwoods, pines and Chilean pines ('monkey-puzzles'), also cycads and tall tree-ferns. Lower vegetation included liverworts and mosses, and especially clubmosses, ferns and horsetails.

JURASSIC TRENDS

With so much plant growth, in the form of leaves and fronds high in trees, and greenery carpeting the ground, herbivorous dinosaurs had plentiful food. The biggest of all dinosaurs, the immense sauropods, reached their greatest size by the Late Jurassic, craning their heads many metres to browse.

They thundered away, pursued by some of the largest predatory dinosaurs, such as Allosaurus. Stegosaurs were another common group. In the air, pterosaurs were also evolving greater size.

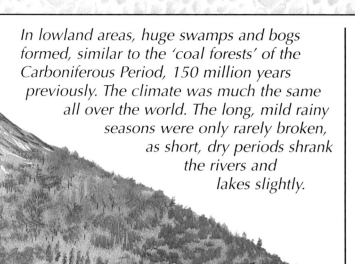

In lowland areas, huge swamps and bogs formed, similar to the 'coal forests' of the Carboniferous Period, 150 million years previously. The climate was much the same all over the world. The long, mild rainy seasons were only rarely broken, as short, dry periods shrank the rivers and lakes slightly.

JURASSIC MAP

Pangaea was breaking up into two main land-masses. Gondwana in the south consisted of today's South America, Africa, Australia, India and Antarctica. The other modern continents were situated in Laurasia.

LAURASIA

Tethys Sea

GONDWANA

Plentiful rivers and lakes encouraged fish, which some dinosaurs relied on for food.

JURASSIC ANIMALS

At the start of the Jurassic, mammal-like reptiles were abundant on land. But dinosaurs soon took over. Smaller reptiles included lizards and little dinosaurs such as Compsognathus. Many other creatures flourished, as they did before and after the dinosaurs – insects, worms, snails and spiders. The first birds also appeared.

THE CRETACEOUS PERIOD

The Cretaceous, at 80 million years, was the longest period of the Mesozoic Era. It saw the beginning of the climate zones we have today, being colder near the Poles and warmer towards the Equator, where tropical forests began to form.

The Cretaceous was one of the most active times of mountain-building on Earth. Lava and fumes poured from volcanoes. Drifting continents threw up massive rumples and wrinkles in the planet's outer rocky layer, the crust.

PLANT LIFE

A great change in vegetation occurred from the Middle Cretaceous. Flowering plants appeared – the forerunners of the herbs, flowers and broadleaved trees that dominate today's world. The first of the trees were types of magnolias, maples, oaks and walnuts. They invaded areas formerly covered by conifers.

CRETACEOUS TRENDS

Cretaceous dinosaurs became much more varied, as they evolved in isolated groups on the separating continents. Ornithopods like Iguanodon were followed by the duck-billed hadrosaurs. Armoured ankylosaurs and, later, horned ceratopsians such as Triceratops also appeared.

Other Late Cretaceous groups included ostrich-dinosaurs and the dome-headed pachycephalosaurs. Meat-eaters were dominated by the huge tyrannosaurs. Despite this great diversity, the end was near.

Seasons became more distinct during the Cretaceous. Wet and dry periods alternated in the tropics. Although it was generally warm, rainfall was less than during the Jurassic, so forests became thinner. Summers and winters began to occur farther north and south.

CRETACEOUS MAP

The two land-masses of Laurasia and Gondwana broke into the continents we know today. The Atlantic Ocean widened as the Americas drifted away from Europe and Africa.

North America
Europe
Asia
South America
Africa
India
Antarctica
Australia

Shallow seas covered much of what is now dry land, allowing fish and shellfish to thrive.

CRETACEOUS ANIMALS

In addition to the increasing variety of dinosaurs, other reptiles also flourished – crocodiles, turtles, lizards and the first snakes. Birds became more varied too, but had to share the skies with the largest winged animals ever, the giant pterosaurs like Quetzalcoatlus. Mammals were still generally small and hardly noticeable.

DINOSAUR SKELETONS

Most dinosaur fossils are bones. In rare cases a whole skeleton is found articulated – the fossil bones are in position next to each other, as in life. A typical dinosaur skeleton was broadly similar to the skeletons of other reptiles, like crocodiles, and other four-legged animals, from amphibians to mammals. However, dinosaurs had their distinctive and unique bone features, especially in the jaws, skull, hips and legs. Hip bones are especially important, dividing them into two groups – ornithischians and saurischians (see page 234).

HIP BONES

The hip 'bone' (pelvis) is made of three pairs of individual bones. In saurischians the pubis bones point forwards and down. In ornithischians they slope back.

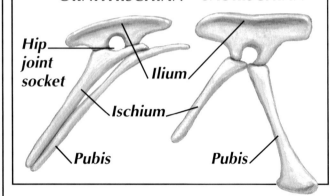

ORNITHISCHIAN   SAURISCHIAN

Hip joint socket — Ilium — Ischium — Pubis

DINOSAUR POSTURE

Stegoceras was an ornithischian or 'bird-hipped' dinosaur. Like all dinosaurs, its legs projected straight down beneath the body. Other reptiles had legs which extended sideways and then angled down at the knee.

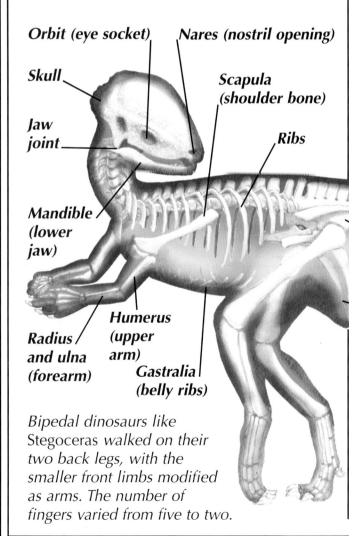

Orbit (eye socket)   Nares (nostril opening)

Skull

Jaw joint

Scapula (shoulder bone)

Ribs

Mandible (lower jaw)

Humerus (upper arm)

Radius and ulna (forearm)

Gastralia (belly ribs)

Bipedal dinosaurs like Stegoceras walked on their two back legs, with the smaller front limbs modified as arms. The number of fingers varied from five to two.

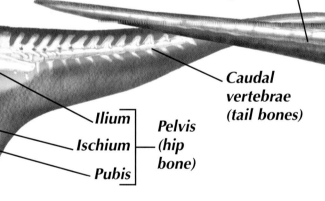

Stiffening tendons

Caudal vertebrae (tail bones)

Ilium

Ischium

Pubis

Pelvis (hip bone)

STEGOCERAS SKELETON

This bone-head or helmet-head dinosaur is known from a partial skeleton and many skull remains. The pattern of the main bones of the skull, spinal column and limbs follows the standard layout for all four-limbed animals (including ourselves). As in most dinosaurs, missing parts are 'filled in' from a collection of finds or from similar dinosaur types.

INSIDE FOSSIL BONE

In some very well-preserved fossil bones, the detailed internal structure can be seen. This gives clues to whether a dinosaur was warm- or cold-blooded. Dinosaurs like raptors had an inner bone structure which resembled the bone of mammals today, which are warm-blooded, rather than today's reptiles, which are cold-blooded.

JOINT TYPES

Deinonychus *was, like all meat-eating dinosaurs, a saurischian or 'lizard-hipped' type. The detailed shape of the bone ends, where they met in their joint, reveals if the joint was flexible or stiff. Reinforcing bony tendons along the tail show it was very rigid.*

Sacral vertebrae (hip backbones)

Knee joint

Tibia and fibula (shin)

Femur (thigh)

DEINONYCHUS SKELETON

Several almost complete fossil skeletons of this dromaeosaur or 'raptor' were discovered in the 1960s, making it a well-known type. Holes or 'windows' known as fenestrae in slabs of bone, such as the skull, were filled by skin and muscle in life, to help save weight.

TENDONS

Tendons are the tough, rope-like ends of a muscle, where it tapers and is anchored on to a bone. Being soft tissues, tendons usually decay before fossilisation. But in some heavily used areas, they become stiffened and ossified – hardened with deposits of bone. This makes them more likely to fossilise, and also shows that the nearby joints were rigid rather than flexible. Ossified tendons along the rear two-thirds of the tail of *Deinonychus* signify that this part could only be bent at its base.

The size of the brain cavity in the skull gives a general idea of a dinosaur's 'intelligence'. The brain case or cranium of Deinonychus was relatively large, especially compared to the plant-eaters.

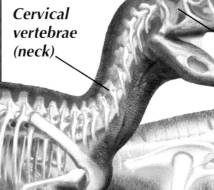

Cervical vertebrae (neck)

Brain case

Ankle joint

Metatarsals (foot)

Sickle claw on second toe

Phalanx (toe bone)

DINOSAUR MUSCLES AND ORGANS

Fossils of dinosaur bones, teeth and other hard parts are rare enough. Preserved remains of a dinosaur's soft parts are even more scarce. There are some specimens of skin, and, rarely, a dark oily film in a layer of rock might show the outline of an internal part, such as the stomach. But most reconstructions of dinosaur muscles, guts and other fleshy organs are made by intelligent guesswork, using living animals as 'models' – especially the dinosaurs' closest surviving relatives, the crocodiles and birds. Marks on fossil bones help to show where muscles were anchored, and holes reveal where nerves passed though.

BRAINS

In rare cases, a dinosaur's skull is so well preserved that it has a cavity inside where the brain was positioned in life. The detailed shape of the cavity can be seen by using it as a mould to make an internal cast, or endocast, from rubbery material. This represents the shape of the brain.

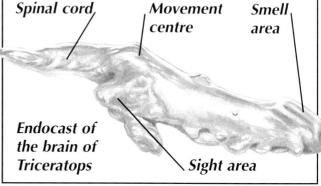

Spinal cord, Movement centre, Smell area

Endocast of the brain of Triceratops

Sight area

The layout of the internal organs is very similar in all living reptiles, including crocodiles, lizards and turtles. This is used as the basic pattern for a dinosaur's insides.

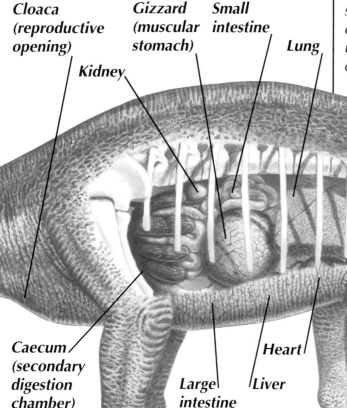

Cloaca (reproductive opening)

Kidney

Gizzard (muscular stomach)

Small intestine

Lung

Caecum (secondary digestion chamber)

Large intestine

Liver

Heart

DIGESTIVE SYSTEM

In the plant-eating sauropods, food was simply plucked and swallowed. Its physical breakdown was carried out in the huge gizzard, which was the size of a small car.

MUSCLE SCARS

Muscle scars are not injuries which heal, but normal surface features of a bone, where a muscle attached. Where they show up on fossil dinosaur bones, they are in similar positions to those on the bones of living reptiles.

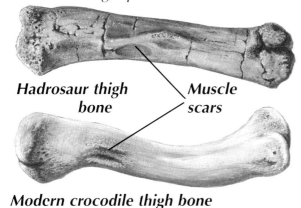

Hadrosaur thigh bone

Muscle scars

Modern crocodile thigh bone

NAMING THE MUSCLES

Many muscles are named after their overall shape, such as the deltoid ('triangular'), or the bones where they are anchored, such as the femoro-tibial (thigh-shin).

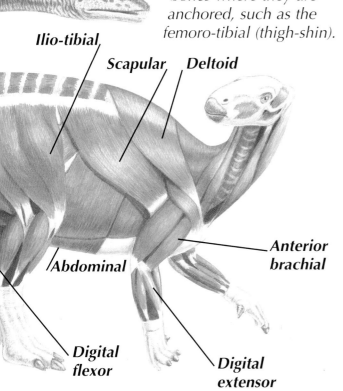

Ilio-tibial

Scapular   **Deltoid**

Abdominal

Anterior brachial

Digital flexor

Digital extensor

CLUES TO MUSCLES

Most bones of living animals have knob-like projections, ridges, flanges and roughened patches called 'scars' on them, where the muscles attach, to pull the bones and the skeleton, and so move the whole animal. These features, including the muscle scars, sometimes show up on fossil bones. This gives information about which muscles were well-developed in the living dinosaur, and which movements it could make with ease and power. Some fossil bones have signs of healed breaks or fractures, where the dinosaur was injured but managed to survive, as the bone mended itself.

WHAT DINOSAUR NAMES MEAN

Many dinosaurs are named from their most distinctive bodily features.

acro – top	odon(t) – tooth
allo – strange	ophthalmo – eye
alti – high	ornitho – bird
brachio – arm	pachy – thick
brachy – short	physis – body
cera – horned	plateo – flat
cheirus – hand	pod, pus, pes – foot
coelo – hollow	poly – many
compso – pretty	ptero – winged
corytho – helmet	quadri – four
derm – skin	raptor – thief
di – two	rhino – nose
diplo – double	salto – jumping
echino – spiny	saurus – lizard,
elaphro – light	reptile
hetero – different	stego – roofed
hypsi – high	thero – beast
lepto – slender	tops – head, face
lopho – ridge, crest	tri – three
mega – huge	tyranno – tyrant
micro – small	veloci – fast

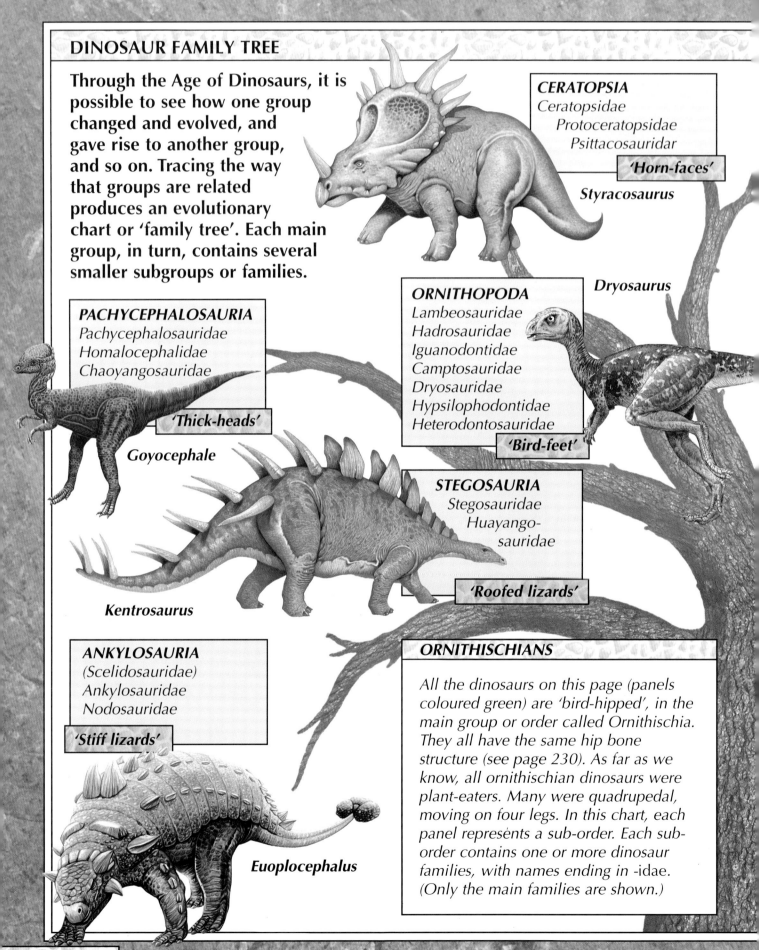

DINOSAUR FAMILY TREE

Through the Age of Dinosaurs, it is possible to see how one group changed and evolved, and gave rise to another group, and so on. Tracing the way that groups are related produces an evolutionary chart or 'family tree'. Each main group, in turn, contains several smaller subgroups or families.

CERATOPSIA
Ceratopsidae
Protoceratopsidae
Psittacosauridar

'Horn-faces'

Styracosaurus

Dryosaurus

PACHYCEPHALOSAURIA
Pachycephalosauridae
Homalocephalidae
Chaoyangosauridae

'Thick-heads'

Goyocephale

ORNITHOPODA
Lambeosauridae
Hadrosauridae
Iguanodontidae
Camptosauridae
Dryosauridae
Hypsilophodontidae
Heterodontosauridae

'Bird-feet'

STEGOSAURIA
Stegosauridae
Huayango-
sauridae

'Roofed lizards'

Kentrosaurus

ANKYLOSAURIA
(Scelidosauridae)
Ankylosauridae
Nodosauridae

'Stiff lizards'

Euoplocephalus

ORNITHISCHIANS

All the dinosaurs on this page (panels coloured green) are 'bird-hipped', in the main group or order called Ornithischia. They all have the same hip bone structure (see page 230). As far as we know, all ornithischian dinosaurs were plant-eaters. Many were quadrupedal, moving on four legs. In this chart, each panel represents a sub-order. Each sub-order contains one or more dinosaur families, with names ending in -idae. (Only the main families are shown.)

OVIRAPTOROSAURIA
Caenagnathidae
Oviraptoridae
Elmisauridae
Ingeniidae

'Egg-thief lizards'

Oviraptor

MANIRAPTORIA
Therizinosauridae
Troodontidae
Dromaeosauridae

'Wristy thieves'

Therizinosaurus

AVES
Archaeopterygidae

'Birds'

Archaeopteryx

ORNITHOMIMOSAURIA
Deinocheiridae
Garudimimidae
Ornithomimidae

'Bird-mimic lizards'

Compsognathus

COELUROSAURIA
Compsognathidae
Avimimidae
Coeluridae

'Hollow lizards'

Ornithomimus

Neovenator

CARNOSAURIA
Allosauridae
Itemiridae
Dryptosauridae
Aublysodontidae
Baronychidae
Spinosauridae
Torvosauridae
Tyrannosauridae

'Flesh-eating lizards'

Supersaurus

SAURISCHIANS

There were two distinct kinds of
'lizard-hipped' dinosaurs in the
order Saurischia (panels coloured
pink). One group was the theropods or
'beast-feet' – meat-eaters that walked
mainly on their larger rear legs. All
carnivorous dinosaurs belonged to this
group, which is divided into several sub-
orders (above). The other saurischian
groups were the massive plant-eating
sauropods and their earlier, smaller
cousins, the prosauropods (right).

SAUROPODA
Barapasauridae
Brachiosauridae
Camarasauridae
Titanosauridae
Cetiosauridae
Diplodocidae
Vulcanodontidae

PROSAUROPODA
Plateosauridae
Anchisauridae

'Lizard feet'

HOW FOSSILS ARE FORMED

Fossils are the remains of long-dead living things, which have been trapped in the rocks and turned to stone. So a dinosaur 'bone' is not bone at all – it is solid rock. Most dinosaurs and other living things did not form fossils. And most of the fossils which once formed, were then gradually destroyed by natural rock processes. So fossils are rare and valuable finds.

WHAT FORMED FOSSILS?

Not only dinosaurs, but many living things left fossils – insects and other animals, plants, even microbes. The hardest parts last longest and have the best chance of being preserved – bones, teeth, horns, claws, shells, bark, wood, seeds and cones. Water creatures like ammonite shellfish are more likely to be covered by mud and turned into fossils, compared to land animals.

BONE TO STONE

Fossilisation depends on a series of very unusual chances. A living thing, such as a dinosaur, must not be totally eaten by scavengers or rotted away. Then its remains are covered by sediments – small particles such as mud, silt or sand. These particles are squashed and cemented by minerals into solid rock, trapping the remains.

Heterodontosaurus skull

Ammonite

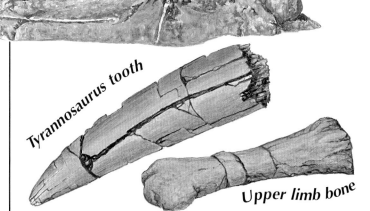

Tyrannosaurus tooth

Upper limb bone

CAST AND MOULD FOSSILS

In a mould fossil, a body part is buried by sediments, which form rock around it. Then the part gradually breaks down or dissolves to leave a hole, which has the original shape as a 'mirror image' in the surrounding rock. In a cast fossil, this hole is slowly filled in by minerals and water. They form new rock in the mould, in the shape of the original part.

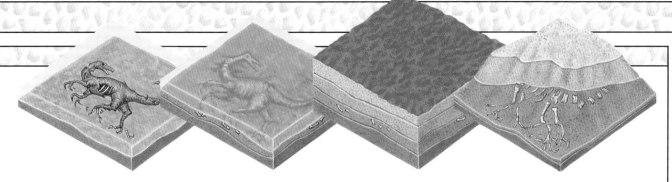

A dead dinosaur is washed into a river.

Over the years the bones are covered with layers of silt which becomes rock.

The bones are chemically changed into stone – fossils.

The rock is gradualy worn away to reveal the fossilised bones.

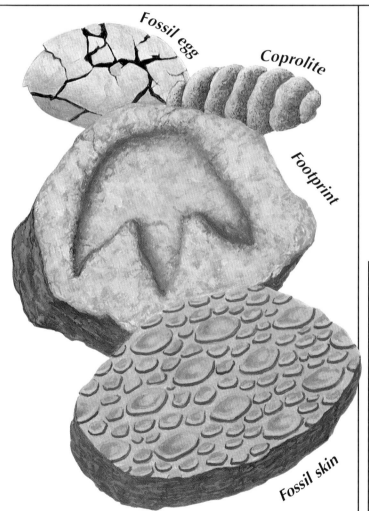

Fossil egg

Coprolite

Footprint

Fossil skin

TRUE FOSSILS

Fossils of actual body parts or even whole bodies are true or true-form fossils. Dinosaur skin is one of the scarcest true fossils. Even more rarely, a dinosaur was preserved as its body slowly dried out, in desert conditions, rather than rotting. This is mummification.

TRACE FOSSILS

Preserved remains of the signs or traces of an animal, rather than its actual parts, are known as trace fossils. They include egg shells, nests, burrows, footprints, claw marks, furrow-like tail-drags, stomach-stones (gastroliths) and even droppings – coprolites. A coprolite is no longer squishy and smelly, but has turned to stone. It can be broken apart to reveal its contents, such as pieces of bone or hard plant seeds, to show what the dinosaur ate.

PERFECTLY PRESERVED

Amber is a golden-yellow substance often used to make jewellery. It was once the sticky resin of a prehistoric tree such as a pine. This oozed from the tree's bark, to protect against damage by sap-eaters or disease. The thick resin trapped small animals such as flies, bees, mites, even frogs or mice. Then it slowly fossilised, preserving every detail of the animal.

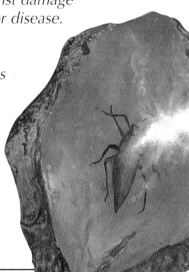

THE HISTORY OF DINOSAUR-HUNTING

Since our own history began, people have found huge fossil teeth and bones, and wondered about the beasts which left them. Some 1,700 years ago Chang Qu wrote of 'dragon bones' found in Wucheng, China. They were almost certainly dinosaur remains. In the 1800s in Europe, nature-collecting became the latest fashionable hobby, and fossils were included in displays. At the time, most people believed that fossils were from creatures drowned in the Great Flood, as described in the Bible. But some scientists wanted a more factual explanation.

NAMING THE DINOSAURS

In the 1820s, a family doctor and keen fossil-hunter in southern England, Gideon Mantell, found teeth and bones which he thought were from a giant extinct lizard. In 1825, he named the creature *Iguanodon*. The year before, another rock and fossil expert, William Buckland, had described the jaw bone and teeth of another huge reptile, which he called *Megalosaurus*.

In 1833, Mantell studied the part-skeleton of another big, long-gone reptile, *Hylaeosaurus*. By 1841, nature expert Richard Owen realized that these animals were not lizards. They represented a different group of reptiles from an earlier age, which had no survivors. In 1842, he invented the group's name, which we know so well today – Dinosauria, 'terrible lizards'.

ANNING AND OWEN

To supply fossil displays, people made a living by collecting the specimens. From the 1820s, Mary Anning gathered remains from Jurassic rocks of England's south coast. She found many beautiful fossils, especially of sea reptiles.

Richard Owen was an eminent animal expert. His skill was the study of similarities between different animal groups, called comparative anatomy. He became head of London's Natural History Museum.

MARSH AND COPE

North America's dinosaur finds were given an early boost by two collectors, Othniel Charles Marsh (left) and Edward Drinker Cope (right). From 1877, they were bitter rivals for 20 years, each racing to find and name the most dinosaurs. Their feuds led to the discovery of more than 130 kinds of dinosaurs, mainly in the rocky 'Badlands' of the US Midwest.

FAR AND WIDE

Huge, fierce and mysterious, dinosaurs quickly caught the public imagination. Fossil-hunting spread to Europe, then in the 1860s to North America, by the 1900s to Africa, and in the 1920s to China. From the 1970s, South America and Australia yielded amazing finds.

In the days of the American Wild West, Marsh and Cope waged their battles. Their teams spied on each other's digs, sabotaged supplies, raided camps, smashed finds and even planted fake fossils to mislead the other.

DIGGING FOR DINOSAURS

The chances of a dinosaur ending up as a fossil are too small to imagine – and the chances of someone finding this fossil are just as tiny. In some regions, rocks from the Mesozoic Era – the age of dinosaurs – are exposed at the surface. They are bare of soil or plants, and continually broken and worn away by wind, sun, rain and ice (or mining and quarrying machines). These are the places to dig.

THE FINDS CONTINUE...

Exciting new discoveries of dinosaur fossils continue to be made around the world – bigger, longer, fiercer, earlier. US fossil expert Paul Sereno has suggested major new ways of grouping the dinosaurs, and discovered early kinds such as Eoraptor and Herrerasaurus.

SEARCHING FOR SITES

An odd-shaped pebble on a beach, or a piece of a bone or tooth sticking out of a cliff, are clues to the presence of fossils. Experts visit the new site to assess the age of the remains, and whether it is worth setting up a proper excavation or 'dig'.

Many fossil sites are in very remote, rocky 'badland' regions. Conditions are harsh – baking sun by day, freezing winds at night, and few comforts in the makeshift camp. Excavation is a long, tiring process, needing great care and patience – and it may yield nothing.

TOOLS AND TECHNIQUES

The tools for digging up fossils may begin with explosives or a huge mechanical excavator, to lift away tonnes of soil and debris. This is the 'overburden' which covers the fossil-bearing rocks. Next, large pick-axes, shovels, hammers and chisels get rid of smaller rock lumps. As the fossil comes to light, hand tools such as awls and trowels are used with increasing care, so as not to crack or scratch the specimen. Even smaller hand tools like ice-picks, dental picks and brushes carry out the most delicate stages.

IMPORTANT FOSSIL SITES WORLDWIDE

Dinosaur fossils have now been found on every continent, even Antarctica. Many locations have been made into protected parks and even World Heritage Sites.

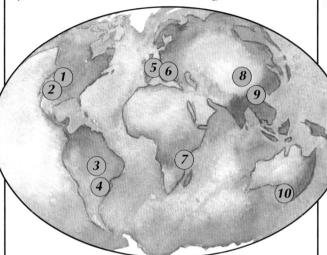

1 Dinosaur Provincial Park, Alberta, Canada
2 Dinosaur National Monument, Utah and Colorado, USA
3 Cerro Rajada, Argentina
4 Chubut Province, Argentina
5 Isle of Wight, England
6 Solnhofen, Bavaria, Germany
7 Tendaguru, Tanzania
8 Gobi Desert, Mongolia and China
9 Lufeng Province, China
10 Dinosaur Cove, Melbourne, Australia

At each stage, workers make notes, diagrams, measurements, lists, maps, sketches and photos. Every bit of rock is labelled for later study, back in the laboratory. Fragile specimens are wrapped in wet plaster-coated bandages, which harden to support and protect them.

DISPLAYING DINOSAURS

Dinosaur fossils are on display in museums and exhibitions around the world. They are usually the best, most complete specimens, of the most exciting and famous dinosaurs. Even more spectacular are life-like, life-sized models, which suddenly move and roar to scare onlookers. Much hard work lies behind these reconstructions.

CLEANING

Cleaning is known as preparation and conservation. The surrounding rock, called matrix, is removed – often under a microscope – to reveal tiny marks such as scratches or bites on the fossils. This is done with tiny drills, burrs, scrapers and picks, similar to those used by dentists. Some rocks can be soaked in chemicals such as acids, to expose the fossil.

Computer-controlled animatronic dinosaurs wow the crowds at the latest displays. The basic skeleton is known from fossils, but the skin and outer appearance are guesswork.

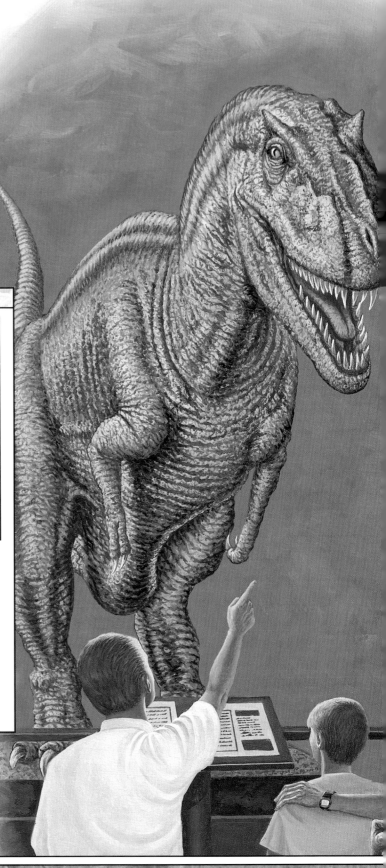

BACK IN THE LAB

After the dig, out in the wild, fossils are brought back to the workroom or laboratory for the slow, painstaking work of cleaning. All of the fossils are revealed, not just the dinosaurs'. This shows which other animals lived at the time, such as birds and insects, and which of these might be a carnivorous dinosaur's prey. It also reveals the plants of the landscape, and which of these were food for herbivorous dinosaurs. A picture is built up of the living world at the time – the science of palaeo-ecology.

COPIED BITS

Most dinosaur skeletons are far from complete. So other finds, from similar types of dinosaurs, are used to 'fill in' missing parts. The cleaned fossils are used as a basis for life-like models to put on show. The fossils themselves are often copied in materials such as fibre-glass, which is lighter and stronger than rock.

MOUNTING

In a living dinosaur, bones provided the body's strong framework – but without muscles, they flopped into a heap. When rebuilding a dinosaur, a metal or plastic frame known as an armature is used to support the skeleton. Skill is needed to obtain the correct posture.

READY TO DISPLAY

Did a dinosaur stand upright, or lean forward, or usually crouch down? Could it bend its neck and tail, and if so, by how much? These types of questions are important when trying to put the dinosaur into a life-like position. Even when a reconstruction is finished, new research may lead to fresh facts – and rebuilding starts again.

SEEING INSIDE ROCKS AND FOSSILS

Medical scanners reveal the insides of the body, and penetrating radar sees into solid ground to reveal what is inside. These high-tech methods of making images (pictures) are also used on fossils. They can show if rock has a well-preserved, detailed fossil inside, and if so, whether it is worth weeks or months of cleaning. Some fossils are made of rock that falls to pieces so easily, imaging is the only way to know what is within. CT and MR scanners even 'see' fossil baby dinosaurs still inside their eggs.

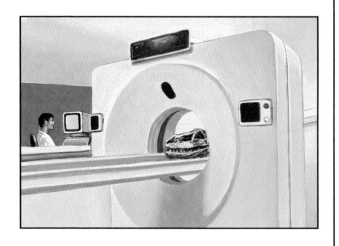

There have been several mass extinctions on Earth. These are times when many kinds of living things disappear. About 65 million years ago, there was a mass extinction which involved the dinosaurs – and every one of them died out.

NOT ONLY DINOSAURS

Not only the dinosaurs disappeared in this great disaster. So did certain other reptiles, including pterosaurs in the air, and mosasaurs and plesiosaurs in the seas. Many kinds of shellfish also died out, and numerous plants, too.

HOW LONG?

Mass extinctions usually happen quite suddenly – in less than a million years. The end-of-Cretaceous extinction, which involved the dinosaurs, may have taken 100,000 years – or perhaps it was over in just one hour.

Before it happened, from about 70 million years ago, in some regions the dinosaurs already seemed to be on the decline. Fossils show that they were becoming less numerous and less varied. But it is difficult to know if this was true all around the world, from the rare and patchy fossil record.

THE ASTEROID IMPACT

In the asteroid theory, a giant piece of rock was whizzing through space – and Earth got in the way. There are many such pieces of rock, called asteroids and meteorites. The asteroid of 65 million years ago could have been 10 kilometres across, and travelling at 60 kilometres per second. It slammed into Earth, threw up massive clouds of dust, vapour and water, and set off tidal waves and earthquakes.

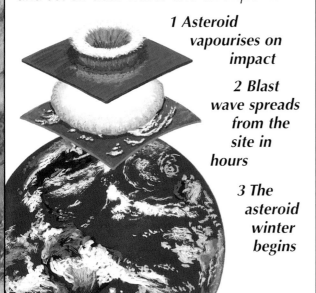

1 Asteroid vapourises on impact

2 Blast wave spreads from the site in hours

3 The asteroid winter begins

THE ASTEROID IDEA

One of the most popular ideas about the death of the dinosaurs is that, by chance, a giant block of rock from space smashed into Earth. The impact sent huge clouds of dust and debris into the air, to spread on the wind. The skies darkened for days, perhaps years, cutting out the Sun's light and warmth. In the cold gloom of this 'asteroid winter', plants withered and died. With no food to eat, plant-eating animals starved – and the meat-eaters followed, as their food also disappeared. (More ideas are on the next page.)

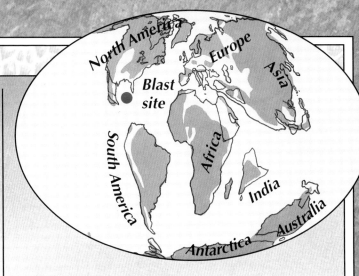

A vast bowl-like crater called Chicxulub, under the sea bed mud off the coast of Mexico, may be the asteroid's impact site.

The impact's giant, unstoppable 'blast wave' raced overland, destroying all in its path.

IN SUPPORT OF THE ASTEROID

Several pieces of scientific evidence support the asteroid theory. A huge crater dating back to about the same time has been found near Mexico (above). Also a thin layer occurs in rocks formed at the end of the Cretaceous ('Kreta') Period, as the Tertiary Period begins. Known as the K-T boundary layer, it contains unusually large amounts of the metal iridium. This is very rare on Earth – but less rare in asteroids.

INVISIBLE RAYS FROM DEEP SPACE

As a huge star reaches the end of its life, it may explode in a cosmic fireball called a supernova. The blast sends out rays and radiation at the speed of light. Perhaps a supernova fairly nearby in space occurred 65 million years ago. Dangerous radiation bathed the Earth, killing animals which could not hide – larger beasts on land, and creatures near the ocean surface. This idea fits with the kinds of animals that disappeared in the mass extinction.

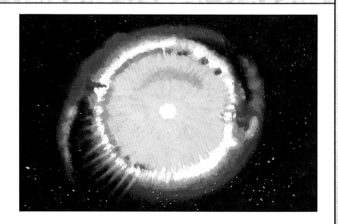

A herd of Triceratops treks across the land, searching in vain for warmth. Climate change has brought global cooling. But warm-blooded mammals and birds could survive.

Apart from the asteroid idea (see previous page), there at least 20 other theories on why the dinosaurs died out. Some are very unlikely – for example, aliens arrived on Earth and hunted them all to death!

DISEASES

Another possibility is that some living things were struck down by a new and deadly disease. This affected only certain reptile groups, including dinosaurs. But it left other reptiles to survive, such as crocodiles, turtles, snakes and lizards.

THE PROBLEM OF SURVIVORS

The disease theory does not explain why shellfish in the sea, or certain plants, were also wiped out in the mass extinction. This is a general problem. Many theories cannot give reasons why only some groups died, yet others lived. It seems that all land animals larger than a sheep of today perished – which included dinosaurs – as well as most ocean-surface life.

CHOKED TO DEATH

Another mass extinction theory involves widespread, long-lasting volcanic eruptions. They poured poisonous, choking fumes into the air and darkened the skies with dust. There is some evidence for this idea. The Deccan Traps are a vast area of volcanic rocks in what is now southern India. Parts of these uplands date back to the end of the Cretaceous Period. The eruptions could have been set off by rock movements and drifting continents (or by the impact of an asteroid!).

CLIMATE CHANGE

Another theory involves the slowly drifting continents (see page 223). This altered sea currents and wind patterns, set off earthquakes and volcanoes, and triggered a rapid change in global climate – and the dinosaurs froze.

THE FINAL STRAW

Yet more theories include increasing numbers of small mammals, which ate all the dinosaur eggs, or a big change in the types of plants, which herbivorous dinosaurs could no longer digest. However, it is possible that there was no single reason for the death of the dinosaurs. Perhaps climate change and volcanic eruptions began their demise, and an asteroid impact was the 'final straw'.

AFTER THE DINOSAURS

After 65 million years ago, there are no dinosaur fossils in any rocks, anywhere in the world. But there are fossils of another animal group, the mammals. They soon dominated the Tertiary Period (65–2 million years ago), just as the dinosaurs had done for 160 million years previously.

AN EARLY START

Mammals did not suddenly appear after dinosaurs died out. They had been around since dinosaurs began, in the Mid Triassic Period, some 220 million years ago. But through the Age of Dinosaurs they were rare, small and shrew-like, none bigger than a pet cat.

TAKING OVER

From about 60 million years ago, mammals began to spread across the land. They changed or evolved rapidly into many different shapes and sizes. By 50 million years ago some had taken to the air, as the first bats. Others went into the sea, as the early whales. On land, mammal evolution produced fierce predators, bulky plant-eaters like rhinos and elephants, and swift-running browsers such as deer and camels. About 25 million years ago, a new group of plants evolved – grasses. Various types of mammals developed to graze on them, including horses, while monkeys stayed in the trees.

THE LAST TAKEOVER

The Age of Mammals, during the Tertiary, gave way to the Age of Humans. The human group began to evolve some four million years ago, in Africa. A type of ape, Australopithecus, *began to walk upright on two legs. Later another type,* Homo habilis, *could manipulate tools and weapons with its hands, and use its large brain to think about survival. Several kinds of humans have come and gone. Only we,* Homo sapiens, *survive.*

Coryphodon

Phenacodus

Hyracotherium

Crocodile

NOT ALL SURVIVED

Not all of the mammal groups which evolved during this time have survived. Creodonts were fearsome flesh-eaters, similar to dogs, cats and hyenas. They began 60 million years ago, but all had gone by 7 million years ago, replaced by our modern carnivores. Indeed, evolution continues today – but sadly, extinctions are now of our making.

The Tertiary Period saw many strange mammals come and go, from huge multi-horned rhinos to small, early horses. Various reptiles also lived on, and still thrive today.

DINOSAURS ALL AROUND?

Like mammals, birds were small and rare during the Age of Dinosaurs. But they quickly spread and became more varied in the Tertiary Period. Many experts now believe birds evolved from dinosaurs, more than 150 million years ago. If so, can birds be regarded as members of the dinosaur group, with feathers instead of scales? That means 'dinosaurs' flap through our skies and twitter in the trees!

Hyaenodon

Uintatherium

Smilodectes

Metacheiromys

GLOSSARY

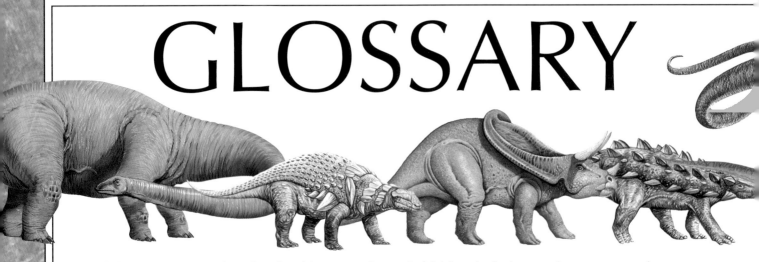

Amphibian An animal with a backbone and four legs that lays its eggs in water, such as a frog. In the larval (young) stage it lives in water. In the adult stage it lives on land and in water.

Anapsid A reptile whose skull does not have an opening behind the eye, such as a turtle.

Ankylosaur An armoured dinosaur covered with bony plates, knobs and spines.

Biped An animal that stands, walks, or runs on its two hind legs.

Carnivore An animal that eats meat.

Ceratopsian A large plant-eating dinosaur with pointed horns and a bony frill growing from the back of its skull.

Cheek teeth Teeth used for chewing behind the front teeth or beak, especially by plant-eaters.

Cold-blooded A popular term to refer to an animal that receives most, or all, of its body heat from external sources, usually the Sun.

Conifer A tree or shrub that produces seed cones, such as fir and pine.

Coprolite Fossilised animal droppings.

Cycad A non-flowering plant with a thick trunk, no branches, and palm-like leaves. Related to today's conifers.

Dental battery A large number of interlocking teeth that form a shearing and grinding surface.

Diapsid A reptile whose skull has two openings on either side, such as a lizard.

Dinosaur A reptile with an upright posture, not a sprawling lizard-like one.

Embryo The early stages in the development of a plant or an animal.

Evolution The process by which a plant or animal changes through time.

Extinction The disappearance of a species of animals or plants.

Family A group of animals or plants which are related to each other.

Fern A non-flowering plant with finely divided leaves called fronds.

Fossil Any evidence of past life. Dinosaur fossils are bones and teeth, footprints, coprolites, gastroliths, eggs, and skin impressions.

Gastrolith Stone found in the stomachs of some plant-eating dinosaurs to help them break down and digest vegetation.

Ginkgo A tree that looks like a conifer but which sheds its leaves in autumn. The only living species of ginkgo is the Maidenhair tree.

Gondwanaland The southern super-continent made up of Africa, Australia, Antarctica, South America, and India.

Hadrosaur A large plant-eating dinosaur with a wide, flat beak. Also called a duck-billed dinosaur.

Herbivore An animal that only eats plants.

Horsetail A plant with an upright stem and tiny leaves. Related to ferns.

Ichthyosaur A dolphin-like reptile that lived in the sea.

Iguanadont A plant-eating dinosaur with hoof-like nails on their hind feet and spikes on their hands instead of thumbs.

Invertebrate An animal without a backbone.

Laurasia The northern super-continent made up of North America, Europe, and Asia.

Mammal A warm-blooded animal covered with hair and which feeds its young with milk.

Omnivore An animal that eats both meat and plants.

Order A group of animals or plants that belong to related families. There are two orders of dinosaurs – Ornithischia and Saurischia.

Ornithischia One of the two orders of dinosaurs. Bird-hipped plant-eating dinosaurs such as the ankylosaurs, ceratopsians, and stegosaurs.

Ornithomimid A fast-running, meat-eating dinosaur with a long neck and slender legs. Similar in appearance to a present-day ostrich.

Ornithopod A two-legged plant-eater, some of which had crests on their heads.

Pachycephalosaur A two-legged plant-eater with a thick skull.

Pangaea The single land mass or super-continent of the Permian Period. It broke up during the Triassic Period. It means 'All Earth'.

Plesiosaur A long-necked reptile that lived in the sea.

Predator An animal that kills other animals (prey) for food.

Prey The animal that is killed by a predator.

Quadruped An animal that stands, walks, or runs on all four limbs.

Reptile A cold-blooded animal with scales and a backbone that lays its eggs on land.

Saurischia One of the two orders of dinosaurs. Lizard-hipped dinosaurs that include all theropods and sauropods.

Sauropod Bulky, long-necked, long-tailed plant-eaters that walked on all four feet.

Scute A bony plate set into the skin of a dinosaur.

Serrated Notched along an edge, such as the teeth of theropods.

Stegosaur A large plant-eating dinosaur with rows of triangular bony plates on its back and spines on its tail.

Synapsid A mammal-like reptile whose skull has one opening on either side.

Thecodont A big, heavy reptile that crawled on all four legs. Thecodonts were probably the ancestors of dinosaurs.

Theropod A two-legged meat-eating dinosaur, such as *Allosaurus* and *Tyrannosaurus*.

Vertebra A bone of the spine. Vertebrae is the plural.

Vertebrate An animal with a backbone.

Warm-blooded A popular term for an animal which can control its own body temperature, such as a mammal or a bird.

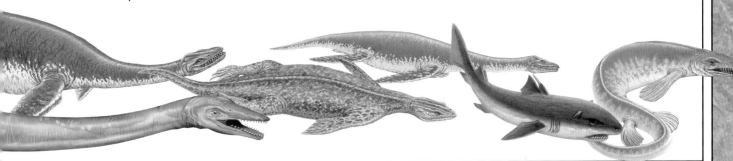

INDEX

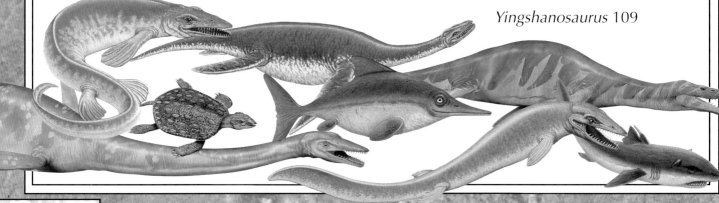